MW00721392

Social Security, the Economy and Development

Social Security, the Economy and Development

Edited by

James Midgley

and

Kwong-leung Tang

Contents

v

List of Tables and Figures

Tables

Figures

Acknowledgements

The relationship between social security, the economy and economic development has been hotly contested and debated especially over the past two decades when criticisms of government social welfare intervention gained momentum and resulted in palpable changes to established social policy approaches. However, these debates have often been reduced to simplistic rhetorical claims and, as this book hopes to show, the issue is far more complicated than many believe. By examining the arguments and the experiences of a number of countries in different parts of the world, the book seeks to offer a more nuanced analysis of the way social security programmes and policies affect economic development and how, in turn, economic development affects social security.

The book would not have been possible without the enthusiastic participation of the authors of the country case studies that offer such interesting and insightful accounts on the relationship between social security, the economy and economic development. We are grateful to them for their willingness to work with us on this book. We are also grateful to Amanda Hamilton at Palgrave for her support and encouragement which has been invaluable. We wish also to thank Alec Dubber who gave willing assistance at the production stage and to Vidhya Shankari for her meticulous copy editing. This has truly been a team effort for which we are grateful.

JAMES MIDGLEY AND
KWONG-LEUNG TANG

List of Contributors

Silvia Borzutzky is Teaching Professor of Political Science and International Relations and Director of the Political Science Undergraduate Program at Carnegie Mellon University. She is the author of *Vital Connections: Politics, Social Security and Inequality in Chile* (Notre Dame University Press, 2002) and co-editor of *After Pinochet: The Chilean Road to Capitalism and Democracy* (University Press of Florida, 2006). She has also published more than thirty articles dealing with Chilean politics, social security and health policies, as well as Latin American politics and international relations.

Espen Dahl is Professor and head of the interdisciplinary research programme Care, Health and Welfare at Oslo University College, Oslo, Norway. His research interests are health and welfare policies in comparative perspective, active labour market policies, research on social assistance dynamics and social exclusion, and health inequality research. He has published extensively on these topics.

Martin Evans is Senior Research Fellow in the Social Disadvantage Research Centre and Centre for Analysis of South African Social Policy at the University of Oxford. He has published widely on United Kingdom and international social security, social assistance and welfare-to-work programmes. He is currently a UK Economic and Social Research Council Research Fellow, grant RES-000-27-0180 and acknowledges its support in his work on child poverty for this book. His recent work includes model lifetime analysis of British social security, research on Vietnamese social security for United Nations Development Programme in Hanoi and analysis of British child poverty programmes.

Joon Yong Jo recently completed his doctoral degree at the School of Social Welfare University of California, Berkeley. His doctoral research focused on the impact of Korea's welfare-to-work programme on poverty alleviation and social investment. He specializes in social development issues.

James Lee is Associate Professor and Associate Head of the Department of Public and Social Administration, City University of Hong Kong, China. He is a founder of the Asian Pacific Network of Housing Research. He specializes on comparative housing policy research in East Asia as well as housing reform in China. His recent publications include, *The Crisis of Welfare in East Asia* (edited with K. W. Chan: Rowan & Littlefield, 2007; *Housing and Social Change: East West Perspectives* (edited with Ray Forrest, London: Routledge, 2003) and *Housing, Home Ownership and Social Change in Hong Kong* (Ashgate, 1999).

Thomas Lorentzen is a senior researcher at the International Research Institute of Stavanger and researcher at Research Group for Inclusive Welfare Policies, Oslo University College. He works with longitudinal studies on social security and social assistance benefits and has written several articles about Norwegian social assistance dynamics and activation policy.

James Midgley is Harry and Riva Specht Professor of Public Social Services at the School of Social Welfare University of California, Berkeley. He has published widely on social development and international social welfare. His most recent books include *Social Policy for Development* (edited with Anthony Hall, Sage Publications, 2004); *International Encylopedia of Social Policy* (edited with Tony Fitzpatrick, Huk-ju Kwon, Nick Manning and Gail Pascall, Routledge, 2006) and *International Perspectives on Welfare to Work Policy* (edited with Richard Hoefer, Haworth Press, 2006).

Raymond Ngan Man-hung is Associate Professor at the Department of Applied Social Studies, City University of Hong Kong. His research interests are in social security, reforms in old-age pension and long-term care. His publications have appeared in international journals and in edited collections. In 1997, he was awarded the Outstanding Research Award in Gerontology, and in 2004 he was honoured by the Hong Kong Association of Gerontology with the Outstanding Paper Presentation Award presented at the 12th Annual Congress of Gerontology.

Leila Patel is the Director of the Centre for Social Development in Africa and Professor of Social Development Studies at the University of Johannesburg. She was previously the Director General of Social Welfare in South Africa and Deputy Vice Chancellor and Vice-Principal of the University of the Witwatersrand, Johannesburg. She played a leading role in the development of South Africa's welfare policy after apartheid. Her research interests are social welfare, social security, social development and civic engagement. She is editor of the *Social Worker Researcher Practitioner*, and her most recent book is *Social Welfare and Social Development in South Africa* (Oxford University Press, 2005).

Kwong-leung Tang is Chair and Professor of Social Work at the Department of Social Work, the Chinese University of Hong Kong. His academic interests include East Asian social welfare, social development, law and social policy, and human rights. He is the author of *Colonial State and Social Policy: Social Welfare Development in Hong Kong 1842–1997* (University Press of America, 1998) and *Social Welfare Development in East Asia* (Macmillan & St. Martin's Press, 2000) and co-editor of the two-volume set entitled *National Perspectives on Globalization and Regional Perspectives on Globalization* (Palgrave, 2007).

Jean Triegaardt is a policy analyst with the Development Bank of Southern Africa. Her research interests are social security, poverty, unemployment and social welfare policy. She obtained a senior researcher Fulbright award and spent her sabbatical conducting research at the School of Social Welfare, University of California, Berkeley in 2003. During the period 2001–2005, she was the chair of the Association of Social African Social Work Education Institutions (ASASWEI). She co-authored chapters in the book *Social Welfare and Social Development in South Africa* (Oxford University Press, 2005).

S. Vasoo is Associate Professorial Fellow at the Department of Social Work and Psychology, National University of Singapore. He previously served as Head of the department. He also served as a Member of Parliament of Singapore from 1984–2001 and in various capacities in both governmental and non-governmental organizations in Singapore. He is advisor to the Central Singapore Community Development Council, Ang Mo Kio Family Service Centre, Beyond Social Services, Movement of the Intellectually Disabled (MINDS) and Downs Syndrome Association. His recent publication includes *Challenges of Social Care in Asia* (co edited with N. T. Tan, Marshall Cavendish, 2005).

Wouter van Ginneken is a former staff member of the International Labour Office. He has published extensively on employment, income distribution, technology and social security – in both developed, transition and developing countries. His latest book is *Social Security for the Excluded Majority* (ILO, 1999). He is presently Chairperson of the Editorial Board of the *International Social Security Review* and just edited – with Roddy McKinnon (ISSA) – a special double issue of the journal on *Extending Social Security to All* (vol. 2–3, 2007).

Introduction

James Midgley and Kwong-leung Tang

This book hopes to contribute to an ongoing debate about the relationship between social security and economic development. Although the expansion of social security in the early decades of the twentieth century was widely endorsed by politicians, academics and the public at large, a small group of critics predicted that extensive government involvement in income protection would have dire consequences. One of these predictions focused on social security's effects on economic development. Critics claimed that social security would have negative fiscal consequences, harm work incentives and distort labour markets. Although comprised of a motley collection of anti-government traditionalists, libertarians and free-marketeers, social security's critics have been led by neoliberal economists, chiefly from the United States. Since then, they have articulated a persuasive set of arguments against social security programmes.

Criticisms of social security gathered momentum in the 1980s when the steady rates of economic expansion experienced by many Western countries in years following the Second World War slowed and unemployment and inflation increased dramatically. Although these changes were in fact caused by different economic, political and social factors, opponents of social security seized the opportunity to blame the economic ills of the time on social security and other welfare programmes. They were supported by powerful ideological and commercial interests, and their claim that social security impedes economic progress has been aggressively publicized. Today, the contention that social security harms economic growth has been quite widely accepted. Proposal for the replacement of statutory forms of social security with commercially managed retirement accounts have also gained increasing support. Social security's supporters have clearly been placed on the defensive.

1

However, despite the almost hegemonic popularity of neoliberalism in economic and political circles, the campaign against social security has not achieved its objectives. While there has been a noticeable receptivity to marketization in many parts of the world, and the actual replacement of social insurance with commercial provisions in countries such as Chile, many countries have resisted privatization and many have retained their statutory social security schemes. Conventional social security programmes have proved to be resilient despite the best efforts of commercial interests and the policy recommendations of neoliberals. Although it is recognized that social security schemes are faced with various challenges, governments in many parts of the world are satisfied that social security is an effective policy instrument for both poverty prevention and poverty alleviation. Similarly, although the privatization campaign has been waged with great intensity and mobilized massive political and monetary support in the United States, the nation's venerable, popular and highly effective retirement social insurance programme remains intact. Although Republicans had a comfortable majority in Congress when President Bush's privatization proposals were deliberated in 2005, key members of his own party refused to endorse these proposals, largely in response to constituent pressure. In some countries, such as China and Korea, new programmes based on collective participation and risk pooling have been introduced. In others, there is growing recognition that effective income protection requires proactive state intervention which transcends an exclusive reliance on the market and incorporates different forms of income protection. Indeed, many governments have actively fostered a pluralistic approach in which statutory social security programmes of different kinds are effectively harmonized with familial, community and market provision.

It is also clear that the supporters of social security have become more organized and that the case for statutory income protection has been more effectively presented in recent years. The International Labour Organization and the International Social Security Association have stoutly resisted the privatization agenda and tirelessly challenged market-liberal academics, the World Bank and other advocates of commercially managed retirement accounts. Complex statistical data and quantitative analyses have been used to refute the claims of social security's detractors, and more sophisticated interpretations that question claims about the deleterious effects of social security have appeared. Another development is a growing body of theoretical and empirical information about the positive economic effects of social security. This approach transcends the defensive posture of many previous attempts to refute the neoliberal critique in that it asserts the beneficial economic consequences of government income-protection schemes. Of course, claims of this kind are not new. Since the Great Depression of the 1930s, when unemployment reached unprecedented levels, social security's role in labour force stabilization, stimulating demand and supporting anti-cyclical economic policies has been recognized. The idea that social security is a complementary adjunct to the economy has since been augmented by the argument that social security is an investment that generates positive rates of return and contributes to economic growth and development. This argument was originally formulated with reference to social policy in the developing countries of the Global South, but it has since been generalized and is now more frequently used to legitimate statutory intervention in the Western countries. In these countries, social policy scholarship has long been committed to a perspective that emphasizes a non-economic, humanitarian rationale for social security.

These developments suggest that it may be opportune to re-examine the relationship between social security, the economy and development in the light of more recent scholarly inquiry and the experiences of different countries. This book seeks to meet this challenge by discussing different points of view about social security's economic development effects and reporting on trends in various parts of the world. It is not committed to critiquing the neoliberal position but to give fair consideration to different points of view. Indeed, Chapter 2 seeks to offer a balanced review of different normative interpretations of the relationship between social security and economic development. However, this does not mean that the book's authors and editors do not have a position of their own. On the contrary, it will soon become clear that they have a long-standing academic and professional commitment to the field of social policy, which has historically professed a belief in the desirability of judicious collective responsibility for social welfare. However, they are not unmindful of the criticisms that have been made of government welfare programmes or of the limitations of statism. It is hoped that the arguments presented in the book will be fair minded and that the controversial and complex issue of social security's relationship with economic development will be objectively assessed.

Although, questions about the relationship between social security and economic development have been raised previously, much of the debate has been esoteric and the frequent use of mathematical notation to formulate the arguments has inhibited an easy comprehension of the issues. By seeking to avoid technical terminologies, the book hopes to inform non-professionals interested in the relationship between social security's effects on economic progress. In addition, it is hoped that the country case studies will concretize and clarify the issues. The countries included in the book range in population size, cultural characteristics, political organization and level of economic development. Although purists may complain that it is undesirable to compare such different societies, their very diversity is helpful in analysing the issues and appreciating their complexities. Their experiences also offer helpful policy lessons. While caution is obviously needed when making generalizations on the basis of these case studies, their findings can inform and elucidate the debate.

The case studies are preceded by two chapters that deal first with the definition, history and features of social security and second with arguments concerning the relationship between social security, the economy and development. These chapters point out that the issues have often been oversimplified. They show, for example, that debates on the relationship between social security and economic development have often been based on an analysis of one type of income maintenance provision and then generalized to all forms of social security. Obviously, arguments about social security and economic development raise different concerns and elicit different responses when linked to social insurance, social assistance and other types of social security schemes. The complexities of the concept of economic development will also be considered. The tendency to equate development with national income growth oversimplifies a great number of interlinked processes that transcend the importance accorded to growth in the literature.

Defining key terms

But first, brief reference should be made to the key terms in the title of this book; namely, social security, the economy and development. These terms have not been defined in ways that are universally accepted, and the lack of standardization and precision has inevitably clouded the issues. Although the book will not attempt to offer precise definitions of these terms, it is helpful to review their meanings and clarify the way they have been used. Chapter 1 hopes to achieve this goal by discussing the definition, history and features of social security in more detail.

With regard to social security, the literature reveals that the term is used loosely to cover a wide range of statutory income protection and health care programmes. However, there are significant differences in the way the term is employed in different parts of the world. As is well known, it is used in the United States to refer specifically to the federal government's old age retirement insurance programme. On the other hand, in Britain and many other English-speaking countries, it connotes a variety of income-protection schemes including social insurance as well as social assistance, employer mandates and demogrant social allowances. However, in United States, social assistance is not regarded as a part of the social security system but as a separate federal programme known as welfare. Unlike Britain, the term is used in many continental European and Latin American countries to include the provision of medical services to those covered by social insurance funds. In some Latin American countries, the term also includes a variety of social and recreational services. In addition, some writers use the term to include tax incentives and subsidies, occupational benefits, housing allowances and other social programmes. Since these differences are reflected in the way scholars in different parts of the world use the term, the task of making international comparisons is obviously complicated.

Despite these differences, the international social security literature focuses on statutory income-protection programmes. As shown in Chapter 1, this usage reflects the official meaning of the term enshrined in the International Labour Organization's conventions which have been signed by the organization's member states. These conventions emphasize the statutory nature of social security, which obligates governments to provide income protection. The role of social security in maintaining income in the event of the involuntary loss of earnings is also stressed. Because of these conventions, social security's objectives are widely accepted as meeting contingencies that reduce, interrupt or terminate income. Major contingencies include sickness, work injury, long-term disability, unemployment, maternity and death. Social security's income-protection role is revealed in the widespread use of the term 'income maintenance' as a synonym for social security. Other terms that are widely used include 'income protection' and 'income security'.

In addition to protecting or maintaining income when specified contingencies arise, social security programmes are also used to supplement or support income. Child benefit is one of the most common forms of income support. Many Western nations pay regular cash benefits to mothers with children in order to help them meet the costs of child rearing. In addition, low-paid workers may receive income supplements through the social security system or increasingly through the fiscal system. Income maintenance and support are widely recognized as the two major forms of income protection provided through social security today.

Income maintenance and support are provided through a variety of mechanisms based on different legislative and funding approaches. These approaches are usually classified into five different types of schemes known respectively as social insurance, social assistance, employer mandates, demogrant social allowances and provident funds – this latter category includes commercial savings accounts based on the provident fund approach. Although benefits provided through the fiscal system are not always recognized as a form of social security, some scholars regard tax credits as well as innovative forms of social security such as matched savings accounts as comprising social security. These different types of social security will be described in more detail in Chapter 1.

It should be stressed that no particular social security mechanism is used exclusively to respond to a particular contingency. For example, the contingency of retirement has been met through all five approaches. Provident funds are widely used in many developing countries to fund retirement pensions, while in most European countries social insurance is preferred. In South Africa and India, social assistance is used. In addition to creating a commercially managed provident fund, the government of Hong Kong also uses the social allowance approach to provide pensions and, until recently, the government of China used the employer mandate approach to require its state-owned enterprises to meet the income needs of retired workers. This approach has since been replaced by a mixture of social insurance and statutorily mandated savings accounts. Governments may also use the fiscal system to pay tax credits to elderly people or to encourage commercial firms to create their own occupational retirement schemes.

The economy, growth and development

The term economic development is generally used today to connote economic growth and the improvements in incomes and standards of living that are believed to accompany economic growth. Previously, the term was associated with the developing countries of the Global South or Third World, as they were known, but it is now more widely employed. Initially, the term's association with the developing countries reflected the post-Second World War view that the Western industrial countries had achieved an end state of economic and social progress and that the role of the economic policy was to manage and correct the disequilibriating tendencies of the market rather than to promote continuous economic growth. Because of the tendency in many Western countries to experience recession and unemployment, equilibrium management was given priority and, as many economic historians have pointed out, growth was largely ignored or otherwise taken as given (Arndt, 1987; Rostow, 1990). On the other hand, faced with the challenges of subsistence poverty and the privations of agrarian life, the developing countries were believed to have a special need to stimulate growth and promote economic and social transformation. By the 1950s, a special field of economics known as development economics had emerged to investigate the nature and dynamics of economic growth and to offer policy prescriptions, which the governments of the developing countries could adopt to bring about significant improvements in the standards of living of their people.

The problems facing the global economy in the 1970s created pressures to end the bifurcation of equilibrium management for the Western countries and economic growth for the developing nations. The low growth rates, falling productivity, persistent unemployment and a condition known as stagflation in the West persuaded many Western governments that much more attention needed to be paid to economic growth. Although the renewed interest in growth did not, at first, foster an integration of development and mainstream economics, the lessons of development economics gradually filtered into Western thinking. In turn, the new interest in growth in the West has obviously influenced development economics with the result that some now believe that the distinction between development and mainstream economics has become redundant. The diversification and very divergent development experiences of the developing countries and the adoption of Western economic policy thinking in the former communist countries also suggests that the distinction is no longer helpful.

Growth is also given far more priority in the political and business worlds. Periodic economic performance reports based on GDP growth are eagerly awaited by stock markets, finance houses, commercial enterprises, politicians and everyday investors. However, much economic thinking in the West still reflects a view, long challenged in development circles, that economic growth is synonymous with social progress and inevitably results in improvements in standards of living for the population as a whole. While few would reject the claim that economic growth is needed to eradicate poverty and raise the standards of living of the mass of the population, most development scholars no longer accept that it is sufficient to achieve this goal.

The narrow conception of development as involving little more than economic growth has been challenged by many scholars. One of the most forceful was the British development economist Seers (1969) who famously argued that national income growth can only be legitimately linked to the notion of development if it is accompanied by sustained improvements in living standards for all. He pointed out that economic growth in many parts of the world has not been accompanied by steady reductions in poverty and improvements in social welfare. His argument has since been widely accepted, and the view that economic development should produce tangible social benefits for the mass of the population now characterizes most definitions of the term. These benefits include improvements in income as well as nutrition, health status, education, housing, employment opportunities, recreation and other dimensions of the quality of life.

Some scholars have augmented this approach by claiming that development should create opportunities for people to maximize choice and realize their potential. Others have incorporated egalitarian ideals into their definition of development arguing that development requires the redistribution of resources and the creation of just and equitable societies. Some have objected to the materialist elements in development thinking, insisting that development involve a proper regard for the natural environment and ensures that growth is sustainable. These critics believe that while economic growth raises incomes and standards of living, governments should ensure that growth does not harm the environment or that it fosters a consumerist and acquisitive culture.

On the other hand, some thinkers reject the very idea of development and particularly its economistic connotation. Scholars of the post-development school (Escobar, 1995; Rahema, 1997) argue that development effort over the past century has been infused with Western acquisitive and materialist values that have served neo-imperialist, capitalist interests and brought few benefits to the masses of the developing world. Others such as Sachs (1992) view development as a colossal failure. They claim that development has not only failed to raise the standards of living of the poor and dispossessed in the Global South, but also often worsened their condition. The idea of development, they believe, stands as a monument to delusion, ineptitude and corruption. Writers such as Daley (1996) are less pessimistic but nevertheless believe that the relentless pursuit of economic growth and the exponential increase in consumption is unsustainable. It has not only damaged the environment but also created a consumerist culture that will eventually devour itself. Obsessed with the acquisition of material possessions, people have become self-obsessed and insensitive to the welfare of others. The current commitment to unrelenting growth needs to be reversed, and steady-state policies that meet social needs without harming the environment and the quality of life should be adopted.

While the post-development school and steady-state environmentalists question the need for continuous economic growth, most development scholars today take a middle position that recognizes the importance of economic growth in raising incomes and alleviating poverty. Many are persuaded that the goal of poverty eradication can be attained through the adoption of policies that enhance production, create employment and raise standards of living. However, they do not dismiss the criticisms of those who believe that a slavish commitment to growth has generated social and environmental problems. But, far from opposing the adoption of growth policies, they believe that judicious regulation of the economy through government intervention as well as policies that protect the environment, foster sociability and maintain traditional cultural commitments can be used to direct the growth process for the benefit of all.

The achievements of economic growth should also be recognized. Many believe that progress over the past half century have been unprecedented. Already by the 1950s, Myrdal (1957) claimed that efforts to promote economic growth for the purpose of bringing about sustained improvements in the standards of living of ordinary people was historically unprecedented. While political and economic elites had in the past taken measures to enhance their own well-being, the idea that the masses should be the primary beneficiaries of economic policy is relatively new. However, Myrdal was hardly sanguine about the impact of economic growth and, in the 1960s, urged the adoption of redistributive policies that ensure that the benefits of development have a positive and tangible effect on the welfare of ordinary people. His views were subsequently endorsed by many leading development economists including Seers.

Myrdal's efforts gave rise to the notion that economic and social development should be closely linked. The United Nations (1996)became a major champion of this idea insisting that the economic and social dimensions of the development process should be harmonized. An awareness of ecological concerns has subsequently broadened the concept of development to include the requirement that economic growth should be environmentally sustainable and that it does not deplete the world's natural resources. The concept has also been broadened by the less clearly articulated notions of political and cultural development which refer loosely to the strengthening of democratic political institutions and the allocation of resources to preserve the cultural heritage.

The idea that the economic, social, political and cultural aspects of development should be given equal emphasis is widely accepted but not realized in practice. This is particularly true with regard to the social effects of economic growth. In many countries, growth has produced a distorted process of development that has benefited a relatively small proportion of the population while many in the rural areas and the informal economy have been left behind (Midgley, 1995). Similarly, some regions of the world, such as East Asia, recorded impressive rates of economic growth while others have stagnated. In the latter decades of the twentieth century, East Asian countries such as Korea and Taiwan have become urbanized and industrialized, and many of their citizens are engaged in wage employment enjoying a comparatively good standard of living. Despite the adoption of development policies and the injection of international aid, other regions of the world such as Sub-Saharan Africa have not fared well and the incidence of poverty has increased. In Latin America and the Caribbean, a highly unequal pattern has emerged in which persistent poverty among a large proportion of the population coexists with conspicuous manifestations of wealth among the urban middle class and the rich. This pattern of distorted development is not uncommon in the Global South and, of course, it characterizes a number of high-income countries such as the United States as well. Nevertheless, real social progress has accompanied economic development around the world. The incidence of global poverty has fallen by about 80 million people since 1990 and there have been significant gains in life expectancy, nutrition, literacy and educational attainment. Infant mortality rates have also declined even among the poorest developing countries (World Bank, 2001).

The nature of development, the relationship between economic growth and social welfare and the gains of development progress over the past few decades are only some of the issues that are currently being debated by development scholars. There are sharp disagreements about the role of the state in directing the development process and promoting people's well-being. While much development thinking has reflected a preference for government involvement, this position has been more frequently challenged by neoliberals who claim that government intervention will inevitably retard progress. They contend that governments should restrict their involvement to creating the conditions for entrepreneurs and investors to pursue the profit motive unhindered by burdensome regulations and taxes. By creating a climate in which business interests flourish, the market will not only reward those who are motivated by self-interest but bring widespread prosperity.

In addition to the neoliberal critique, development thinking has also been informed by an anti-statist, communitarian approach that emphasizes the role of ordinary people and local communities in development effort. This approach has a venerable history and has played a major role in development in many parts of the world. In many developing countries, this approach resonates with popular sentiments, traditional beliefs and populist politics. It also finds expression in the work of international non-governmental organizations and in the activities of official organizations such as UNICEF that have long advocated for a community-based approach to development.

More recently, the statist, neoliberal and community approaches have been augmented by an emphasis on individual and household engagement in small-scale entrepreneurial activities. Since the 1990s, community-based development initiatives have placed more emphasis on small enterprises funded through microcredit and microenterprise programmes. The popularity of this approach is reflected in the award of the Nobel Peace Prize in 2006 to Muhammed Yunus for his work with the Grameen Bank. Proponents of the microenterprise approach have also argued that informal economic sector activities are a dynamic locus for development effort. Advocates of local enterprise such as de Soto (1989) believe that poor people have the entrepreneurial acumen and abilities to raise their incomes and standards of living if governments desist from regulating or suppressing their 'informal' economic activities. Similarly, Mafeje (2001) believes that small-scale enterprises are much more likely to foster economic development than macroeconomic policies based on industrialization and economic modernization. Development, he contends, can be achieved through a 'trickle-up' strategy.

The current vogue for microenterprise and small-scale development effort is, of course, compatible with the market-liberal belief that development goals can best be achieved through entrepreneurship, ambition and hard work. The populist elements in the writings of de Soto and other proponents of local economic development are well matched with macroeconomic neoliberal approaches that extol the virtues of capitalism and limited government intervention in economic affairs. These ideas currently dominate the world of development policy. However, interventionist ideas are still influential. Despite the decline of Keynesianism, many development scholars and policymakers continue to believe that judicious government regulation of the economy, appropriate economic stimuli and public investments play a major role in fostering economic growth. Nevertheless, few would deny that market-liberal thinking exerts a powerful influence in the world of development policy today. Although many academic departments, government aid agencies and international development organizations remain committed to a centrist, mixed-economy approach, powerful Western governments and institutions such as the International Monetary Fund and the World Bank use their political influence and control of resources to promote the neoliberal agenda.

The diverse perspectives of development studies have obvious implications for debates about the relationship between social security and economic development. Although it is often implied that development involves a single set of coherently formulated policy recommendations, the preceding account has shown that there are many different definitions of what development entails and policy prescriptions about how economic growth can be promoted and sustained. Although neoliberalism enjoys a uniquely popular position today and often shapes development debates, particularly in international aid circles, its hegemonic influence continues to be challenged. This is also true of the field of social policy where attempts by neoliberals to shape debates about social security and economic developments are being challenged by alternative perspectives that have mustered increasing evidence to show that government income maintenance and support programmes are not only compatible with economic developments but actually facilitate the development process.

The scope of this book

This book discusses the relationship between social security and economic development by first examining a number of different interpretations of this relationship offered in the literature and second by reviewing developments in several countries. The country case studies are illustrative and also highlight different dimensions of the issue. They also report on policy innovations that clarify social security's role in economic development. For example, in South Africa social security is being purposefully employed by the government as a poverty alleviation strategy. In Singapore, social security has long been used as an investment instrument and key element in the country's economic development efforts. Despite intentions to partially privatize social insurance in the United States, recent policy developments reveal the potential benefits of using alternative mechanisms such as tax credits and asset accounts to meet income-protection needs.

The book is divided into two parts. *Part I* deals with definitions and with historical and conceptual issues. *Part II* contains country case studies that examine the issue of social security and economic development with reference to the experience of each country. The country case studies hope to transcend a basic descriptive account by addressing different aspects of the argument. This approach is designed to examine a particular dimensions of the wider issue in some depth and to discuss innovations in each country that enhance social security's contribution to economic development.

In *Part I, Chapter 1* provides a historical overview of the development of social security and describes its key features. This chapter provides a broad introduction to the field by defining key terms and concepts relating to social security. It also discusses some of the issues and challenges facing social security. It shows that social security has come under increasing criticism and that the support it once enjoyed among of political leaders, policy analysts and members of the public has waned. *Chapter 2* considers the relationship between social security, economic growth and development. It reviews four different normative perspectives on social security's relationship with economic development and discusses their respective merits.

As noted earlier, the *country case study chapters in Part II of the book* are intended to illustrate arguments about the relationship between social security and economic development and to provide examples of policy innovations that show how social security programmes have been linked to development efforts. *Chapter 3* discusses social security in South Africa and shows how the use of social assistance as an explicit poverty alleviation strategy has contributed positively to the country's development efforts. *Chapter 4* traces the record of economic development following the privatization of social security in Chile. Contrary to the claim that privatization would contribute significantly to economic growth, the record has been decidedly mixed and the economic as well as social goals of the reform have not been realized. *Chapter 5* describes recent social security innovations in China and considers their relevance to economic development in the light of country's extraordinary rates of economic growth. *Chapter 6* examines recent policy innovations with regard to income maintenance and support in the United States. It shows that the attack on social security has been narrowly focused on some forms of social security and neglected other forms of government income protection that patently contribute to economic development. *Chapter 7* reviews the social security policies of recent Korean governments in the light of the country's rapid economic development and attempts to forge a unique productivist approach to social welfare. It shows how social security has formed an integral part of what has been called 'developmental social policy'. *Chapter 8* discusses the use of welfare-to-work programmes in Norway and examines their contribution to the country's economic development efforts. Recent developments in social security policy in the United Kingdom are examined in *Chapter 9* with reference to the Labour government's commitment to address the problem of child poverty. The author pays particular attention to the economic consequences of the failure to properly address the issue. *Chapter 10* discusses social security in Singapore and the role of the country's Central Provident Fund and housing policies in mobilizing capital for investment and promoting economic growth development. *Chapter 11* examines the issue of how informal sector workers, who make a major contribution to economic development in many low-income countries, can be brought into the social security system. It examines the issue with reference to India where efforts have been made to include the country's many informal sector workers into the national social security system.

References

Arndt, H. W. (1987). *Economic Development: The History of an Idea*. Chicago, IL: University of Chicago Press.

Daley, H. (1996). *Beyond Growth*. Boston: Beacon Press.

Escobar, A. (1995). *The Making and Unmaking of the Third World*. Princeton: Princeton University Press.

Mafeje, A. (2001). 'Conceptual and Philosophical Predispositions'. In F. Wilson, N. Kanji and E. Braathen. *Poverty Reduction: What Role for the State in Today's Globalized Economy*. London Zed Books, pp. 15–32.

Midgley, J. (1995). *Social Development: The Developmental Perspective in Social Welfare*. London: Sage Publications.

Myrdal, G. (1957). *Economic Theory and the Underdeveloped Regions*. London: Duckworth.

Rahnema, M. (1997). 'Towards Post-Development: Searching for Signposts, a New Language and New Paradigms.' In M. Rahnema and V. Bawtree (eds), *The Post-development Reader*. New York: Zed Books, pp. 377–403.

Rostow, W. W. (1990). *Theorists of Economic Growth from David Hume to the Present*. New York: Oxford University Press.

Sachs, W. (1992). *The Development Dictionary: A Guide to Knowledge and Power*. London: Zed Books.

Seers, D. (1969). 'The Meaning of Development', *International Development Review*, 3 (1), 2–6.

de Soto, H. (1989). *The Other Path: The Invisible Revolution in the Third World*. New York: Harper and Row.

United Nations (1996). *Report of the World Summit for Social Development: Copenhagen, 6–12 March 1995*. New York, UN.

World Bank (2001). *World Development Report, 2000/2001*: Attacking Poverty. Washington, DC.

Part I

Issues of Social Security and Development

1
The Origins and Features of Social Security

Kwong-leung Tang and James Midgley

Although the term 'social security' is generally associated with income maintenance and support programmes, it was noted in the introduction to this book that social policy scholars in different parts of the world have used the term in different ways. In some countries, notably the United States, it is used narrowly to refer exclusively to the federal government's social insurance retirement programme. Similarly, in many Anglophone developing countries where provident funds are the primary form of income maintenance, social security also has a very specific meaning. On the other hand, in Europe and in many other Western nations, the term is used broadly to connote a variety of income protection programmes including means-tested social assistance, contributory social insurance, employer mandates and demogrant or universal social allowances. In several continental European countries, it also refers to health insurance. The term has an even broader meaning in many Latin American countries, referring not only to income protection but to the provision of health care, social work services and even educational and recreational facilities.

Whether broad or otherwise, all definitions of social security have problems. A narrow definition suffers from the fact that it is unlikely to have universal application since it is likely to exclude some provisions that are known as social security in some countries. The broader approach, on the other hand, suffers from the weakness that it is too general to be of much use for comparative purposes. Of course, accounts of social security within specific countries often overcome the problem by formulating an operational definition based on local provisions. But definitions that seek to describe the general features and principles of social security are far more difficult to formulate. It is for this reason that many social policy scholars use the term loosely

17

but nevertheless recognize the different ways it is defined in different national contexts.

This chapter provides a broad introduction to the field by examining some of the ways the concept of social security has been defined. It also elaborates on the typology of the different types of social security programmes outlined in the introduction to this book. It focuses primarily on social security's income protection and support functions and will not, therefore, deal with health and other social services in much detail although it should be noted that some of the book's country case study chapters do refer to health issues and related services when discussing trends in social security. Finally, the chapter concludes by discussing some of the issues and challenges facing social security. In particular, issues touching on the long-term viability and financing of social security will be examined.

The concept of social security

The idea that statutory income protection programmes seek to address the problem of income insecurity is a common feature of many definitions of social security. It is reflected not only in the way many academics use the term but also in many official definitions. In the United States, the Roosevelt administration originally used the term 'economic security' which was more suggestive of income protection than the term 'social security' which was subsequently adopted. The International Labour Organization or ILO has also emphasized the role of social security in minimizing the income insecurities and risks facing people in modern, industrial societies. In one document, the ILO (1958) describes modern social security programmes as meeting people's natural 'craving' for security. Another ILO document (2001) concurs by stressing the role of social security in protecting people against low or declining living standards arising out of a number of risks and needs.

Some scholars have elaborated on this approach by stressing social security's role in meeting people's innate needs for security, protection and nurturing. These scholars emphasize the historical role of the family and kin as well as local community supports in providing security and care. They note that all societies have culturally institutionalized norms and values that obligate families and communities to provide security not only to the vulnerable such as small children, people with disabilities and the elderly but also to all members of the community. These norms and values have an ancient provenance and express themselves in different ways in different cultures. In addition, familial and community obligations in many societies are augmented by religiously mandated requirements to provide support and care, and often more elaborate institutions such as almsgiving have evolved to encourage the provision of support to strangers. These archetypical institutions are widely believed to have laid the foundations for the subsequent emergence of modern social security programmes and particularly social insurance.

Indeed, the dislocation resulting from rapid industrialization is often cited by social historians as a major reason for the introduction of the first social insurance schemes in European countries in nineteenth century. As the rural areas were denuded of the young who migrated to the rapidly expanding cities to work in manufacturing industries, the numbers of able-bodied family members who could ensure the family's livelihood declined. This problem had a particularly serious impact on peasant families comprised of elderly people, widows and small children. However, despite being drawn into the wage economy in the cities and towns, urban migrants also faced new risks. The prospect of accidental injury or death in the factories was a major contingency as was the possibility of becoming ill and of being deprived of an income. Unemployment was an ever-present possibility since no restrictions were imposed on employers who could use labour on a casual basis or dismiss workers at will. For many migrants, the attraction of earning cash wages and improved standards of living was offset by the insecurities of industrial employment.

As the insecurities of industrial life affected many more people, governments were prompted to respond. In addition to restricting the exploitative nature of wage employment, legislation was enacted to ensure that workers were protected against the risk of industrial injury and that those who became ill would continue to have an income. As more workers survived into old age, governments also responded to the problem of retirement insecurity by introducing statutory pensions. In time, as the cyclical nature of capitalism was recognized, the risk of unemployment itself was addressed. Social insurance was widely used to address these contingencies. Many scholars believe that modern day social insurance thus replaced the traditional institutions that had been weakened by urbanization and industrialization.

Although these ideas are popular in academic circles, the view that modern social insurance programmes were introduced in response to the social insecurities of industrial societies underemphasizes the role of political, cultural and economic factors in the genesis of social security. It also neglects the role of older forms of income protection such as social assistance. While social security is often equated with social insurance, and particularly with social insurance retirement pensions, social assistance had been used for centuries prior to the emergence of social insurance to supplement familial and communal supports and to address the problem of income insecurity which had existed long before the emergence of urban industrial societies.

In addition, some scholars place less emphasis on the role of social security in providing income security and stress its role in promoting altruistic behaviours and social solidarity. This was a particularly strong theme in the writings of Richard Titmuss (1971, 1974) who believed that social security and, indeed, all forms of statutory social welfare give expression to innate helping and caring motives. Because complex industrial societies provide limited opportunities for people to engage in effective reciprocal giving, collective forms of provision are used to realise these ideals. In turn, collective forms of provision such as social security foster social solidarity. Although Titmuss's ideas have been widely challenged, particular by writers on the political right, they have been resurrected by legal scholars such as Pieters (2006) who see social security as a means for shaping solidarity among people facing the threat of income insecurity arising from the termination or interruption of earnings or other particular costs. The notion of solidarity features prominently in accounts of the evolution of social security in Europe. These stress the importance of finding collective solutions to societal problems through consensus and cooperation between governments, business firms, worker's representatives and other civil society actors (Dickinson, 1986; Neaman, 1990).

Another approach emphasizes the idea of social security as a social or human right. This approach gained popularity when social security became the subject of international legal conventions and treaties. These instruments infuse definitions of social security with a formalistic, rights-based connotation. In addition to seeing social security as an institutional response to the problem of risk and insecurity, the ILO has also promoted the view that access to an adequate level of social protection is a basic human right. As early as in 1944, the ILO's Declaration of Philadelphia recognized that economic security should be a right for all people and that the nations of the world should develop programmes to achieve the extension of social security measures to provide a basic income to all in need of such protection. Social security is also identified as a right in the Universal Declaration of Human Rights of 1948, which states that

> Everyone, as a member of society, has the right to social security and is entitled to realization, through national effort and international

co-operation and in accordance with the organization and resources of each State, of the economic, social and cultural rights indispensable for his dignity and the free development of his personality. (Article 22)

Subsequent ILO Conventions and United Nations charters such as Section 9 of the International Covenant on Economic, Social and Cultural Rights reiterate the principle that social security is a basic human right. The right to social security has also been written into the constitutions of many countries, including those of many developing countries of the Global South. A case in point is Communist China, where the constitution stipulates that the state shall establish and improve a social security system corresponding to the level of economic development. However, apart from identifying its significance, these international and regional human rights treaties, as well as national constitutions, seldom offer a precise definition of social security. Nevertheless, their requirement that state parties to these international instruments have an obligation to provide income protection to their citizens clearly links the concepts of security and protection to specific policies and programmes.

The emphasis on statutory authority and public provision is a key feature of most definitions of social security. However, as Midgley and Sherraden (1997) point out, there are significant differences in the way public sponsorship is defined in different countries. In some countries, social security programmes are administered by a single, governmental agency; while in others, a number of organizations are responsible for different social security schemes catering for different groups in the community. In several continental European countries and in Latin America, different social insurance organizations, or funds as they are known, provide income protection for different categories of workers. In some countries, the state's role is limited to the enactment of legislation and the regulation of these programmes, while implementation may be delegated to quasi-public or even private agencies. The privatization of social security in Latin American countries such as Chile created new opportunities for commercial providers to be involved in the administration of the country's retirement programme although, as will be shown in Chapter 4 of this book, the marketization of social security has not significantly diminished state involvement or reduced public social security spending.

Another aspect of the statutory nature of social security is the extent to which their administration is centralized. In some countries, these services are operated directly by central government; while in others, different types of social security provisions are administered by central, state and municipal authorities. In China, for instance, the newly introduced social assistance programme (the Minimum Living Standard Guarantee) is administered and mainly financed by local governments, although the central government guides and monitors its implementation. In federal systems, states may operate different types of schemes under the overall guidance of the federal authority, but there may be marked differences in the contingencies covered and the benefits paid.

Social security has also been defined with reference to different types of programmes and the different functions and goals of these programmes. This 'operational' approach to defining social security is less concerned with sociological or legal notions than with the actual income, health and other social service programmes provided by governments. Although social security programmes provide income, health and other social services, the term will be operationalized in this book to refer to income programmes and specifically to programmes that provide for the maintenance of income when specific contingencies arise or otherwise supplement the incomes of those who experience particular needs or demands on their incomes. The twin functions of income maintenance and income support are thus central to most operational definitions of social security. Typically, income maintenance and support is provided through the four major types of social security described in the introduction to this book, namely, social insurance, provident or savings funds, social assistance, employer mandates and social allowances.

However, as noted earlier, social insurance is most often equated with social security. In the United States and in many Latin American countries, the term social security refers exclusively to social insurance programmes. It is also the case that social insurance is often regarded as the most desirable form of social security by many social security experts and by international organizations. For example, the International Social Security Association or ISSA places far more emphasis on social insurance than on other types of social security. The ILO also favours social insurance and has played a major role in promoting the adoption of social insurance programmes around the world. Since the 1990s, the World Bank has become quite active in promoting retirement savings accounts, which are its preferred type of social security. In addition, it believes that those who are not able to accumulate sufficient savings to meet their retirement needs should have recourse to social assistance. The Bank's preference for savings accounts and social assistance stands in stark contrast to the conventional preference for social insurance among social security experts at the ILO and ISSA.

In addition to referring to these different types of social security, the ILO (1958) operationalizes the concept by identifying three criteria that must be satisfied before a scheme or service can be considered a part of social security. First, it requires that the objective of the system must be to grant curative or preventive medical care, or to maintain income in case of involuntary loss of earnings or of an important part of earnings, or to grant supplementary incomes to persons having family responsibilities. Second, the system must have been set up by legislation which attributes specified individual rights to, or imposes specific obligations on, a public, semi-public or autonomous body. Third, the system should be administered by a public, semi-public or autonomous body. These three criteria will be kept in mind when considering the different types of social security programmes referred to above in more detail.

A typology of social security

Various ILO conventions and formal documents offer classifications of social-security schemes. Despite its preference for social insurance, the organization recognizes that social-security goals can be achieved through different approaches including social insurance, social assistance, employer mandates and social allowances as well as provident funds and other mechanisms. The ILO's *Social Security (Minimum Standards) Convention* (No. 102 of 1952) identifies social security generally with the statutory provision of (1) medical care, (2) sickness benefit, (3) unemployment benefit, (4) old-age benefit, (5) employment injury benefit, (6) family benefit, (7) maternity benefit, (8) invalidity benefit and (9) survivors benefit. In a subsequent convention of 1958, the ILO pointed out that social security included 'compulsory social insurance, certain voluntary social insurance schemes, family allowance schemes, special schemes for public employees, public health services, public assistance and benefits granted to war victims' (ILO, 1958, p. 2).

One of the most comprehensive typologies of social security provisions was developed by Kaim-Caudle (1973) in his study of social security in ten industrial countries. It was noteworthy because it included both statutory and non-statutory provisions. Drawing on an earlier analysis of the social divisions of welfare by Titmuss (1958), Kaim-Caudle argued that social security not only includes organized income maintenance services provided by the state, but also indirect benefits provided through fiscal measures, those provided by voluntary organizations as well as occupationally linked benefits provided by employers. Examples of non-statutory social security schemes include the payment of sickness benefits, retirement pensions, and a variety of 'perks' to workers by their employers and the provision of benefits by charitable societies. Although this attempt to expand the definition of social security and comprehensively incorporate a wide variety of income protection programmes is commendable, it has proved to be too broad and is not often cited today.

Nevertheless, his typology of statutory social security inspired subsequent typologies which included social insurance, means-tested social assistance schemes, demogrant allowances and a variety of mandatory benefits provided by employers, as well as tax allowances and concessions. Kaim Caudle's inclusion of employer mandates and the use of tax advantages by governments was particularly helpful in that it publicized the need to transcend the emphasis placed on social insurance as the primary and most desirable form of social security at the time. It is certainly recognized today that fiscal measures should be included in any account of social security. As is shown in Chapter 6 of this book, the tax system is now being used quite extensively by the government of the United States to provide income support, and there are signs that other countries, such as the United Kingdom, are also placing more emphasis on the use of fiscal measures.

Following the ILO classifications, many comparative accounts of social security now classify social security into four or five different types of schemes. In his formative study of social security in the developing countries, Midgley (1984) argued that the classification of social security schemes as social assistance, social insurance, employer liability schemes, social allowances and provident funds is a convenient way of proceeding and offers a reasonably comprehensive framework for analysis. Similarly, in his prodigious account of international trends in social security, Dixon (1999) also classified social security programmes in this way. The typology presented in Table 1.1 not only adopts the standard five-fold classification of social security but also recognizes the importance of the fiscal system in providing income maintenance and support.

Social assistance

Of the different approaches to social security, social assistance is the oldest. Its origins can be traced back to the charitable activities mandated by religious and cultural beliefs. For example, it is well known that the custom of giving charity to the poor is an integral part of

Table 1.1 Basic features of major social security schemes

	Primary source of funding	Coverage	Particular entitlement qualifications
Social assistance	Public revenues	Persons in designated categories who have low income	Means test domicile
Social insurance	Contributions from employee, employer and public revenues	Members of social insurance schemes	Contribution record
Provident fund	Employer	Employees in designated categories	Employment criteria
Employer mandates	Payroll contribution	Employees in designed categories	Employment criteria
Social allowances	Public revenues	Persons in designated categories	Domicile

Source: Adapted from Midgley (1984).

Judaism, Christianity, Hinduism, Buddhism and Islam. Obviously, the giving of charity is based on an assessment, however informal or subjective, of the recipient's needs. It is this assessment that has been formalized in social assistance through the use of what is generally referred to as an income or means test. Although the use of the means test is historically associated with the English Elizabethan Poor Law of 1601, its use is far older. The Byzantians provided state-sponsored poor relief in addition to religious charity, and during the time of the Islamic caliphates, public treasuries or *beit- ul-mal* were created to aid the needy. Similar funds were subsequently established by various municipal authorities in Europe and formal assessment of the needs and circumstances of applicants for assistance was made. Poor relief was generally reserved for those who had no relatives to care for them and only those who were believed to be deserving of aid were assisted. This definition usually applied to widows with small children, the elderly and people with disabilities. The able bodied were usually excluded.

The Elizabethan statute is particularly important because it created the first centralized, nation-wide system of public poor relief. It recognized that traditional forms of familial and community support were not always able to cope and that religious charity needed to be augmented by public provision. In addition, the Elizabethan law strengthened earlier statutory sanctions against vagrants and able-bodied beggars and required that they be apprehended and put to work. It prescribed punishments such as whippings to control vagrants and those who refused to work. Many social policy scholars believe that the Elizabethan Poor Law marked an important phase in the history of social security and that it shaped its subsequent evolution. It also served as a model for many social assistance programmes that were subsequently created in the United States and in many parts of the developing world. The Elizabethan statute was replicated in the Massachusetts Bay Colony in 1642 and in Virginia in 1646. It was also adopted in other parts of the British empire beginning with Jamaica in 1682. Although social assistance was originally intended to provide limited and meagre benefits to a small proportion of the population who were in dire need, it has also been used more generously to fund old-age pensions for a sizable proportion of the elderly population in countries such as Australia and South Africa. In Mauritius, it was originally used to pay child benefits to low-income families, but it has since been replaced with a universal family allowance scheme. An interesting development is the use of what are known as conditional cash transfer schemes in some Latin American countries. These schemes pay benefits to poor families on condition that their children attend school and that their parents ensure that they are immunized.

The ILO (1942, p. 84) defines social assistance as a service or scheme which 'provides benefits to persons of small means granted as of right in amounts sufficient to meet a minimum standard of need and financed from taxation'. Three distinctive features of social assistance are emphasized in this definition. First, it is available only to those who fall below a defined minimum level of income, and the means test is used to determine eligibility. Other eligibility criteria such as invalidity, old age, widowhood or desertion may be employed as well. Second, social assistance is financed entirely from public revenues. Third, because social assistance schemes have a legislative basis, there is a right to entitlement. Once assessed as qualifying for aid, applicants have a legal right to be helped. Although it has been argued that the notion of right to entitlement is more firmly established in social insurance and social allowances, it also applies to social assistance.

Although widely used, social assistance has been subject to much criticism over the years. Critics on the political right believe that social assistance programmes are widely abused by indolent and irresponsible people who are able to persuade the authorities that they are unable to work and earn a living. The media often portrays social assistance recipients in a negative way and cases of abuse are often sensationalized. Critics on the left believe that social assistance is an ineffective form of income protection because it stigmatizes those who seek aid and provides meagre and limited benefits which do not meet the income needs of those experiencing financial difficulty. Although they recognize that claimants have a legal right to be helped, they contend that social assistance is often administered in ways that deny these rights or otherwise limit the ability of claimants to receive benefits. They believe that the stigmatization of claimants is a major deterrent and an important reason why many elderly, disabled and other needy people fail to apply for benefits. It is for this reason that social insurance is usually preferred by those on the political left who believe that the right to benefit is more effectively enshrined in these programmes.

Social insurance

Social insurance schemes are distinguished from other forms of social security in that they are financed from the regular contributions of those who participate in these schemes. Although these contributions are sometimes said to be similar to commercial insurance premiums, contributions to public social insurance schemes differ from insurance premiums in that they are obligatory and, unlike private insurance, contributions are usually supplemented by employers and the state (Burns, 1936). Also, benefits are not usually assessed on an actuarial basis. While it is generally assumed that benefits are directly linked to contributions, this is frequently not the case. For these reasons, it is recognized that social insurance contributions are a form of taxation or, more precisely, that they comprise a payroll tax on labour income.

Social insurance schemes have been described as 'occupationalist', because they cater for designated categories of workers on the basis of occupational status (Pavard, 1979). These categories are comprised of workers in regular wage employment and, with the exception of a few countries, benefits are restricted to the members of the scheme and their dependants. Membership of social insurance schemes is defined by legislation, and it is compulsory for those who fall into the designated categories to join. Coverage is said to be universal or comprehensive when all workers, including those who are self-employed, are members of social insurance schemes. However, with the exception of the Western countries, universal coverage is rare.

However, social insurance schemes are similar to commercial insurance in that they have a connotation of indemnity against contingencies or risks. As noted earlier, the notion of protection against risk is closely associated with industrial employment and the loss of income that wage employees experience when incomes are interrupted, reduced or terminated because of illness, injury at work, invalidity, maternity, retirement, death and other reasons. Most authoritative definitions of social insurance refer to these contingencies. Recommendation 67, adopted at the 26th International Labour Conference in 1944, encouraged governments to extend social insurance rather than other forms of social security. These schemes, the organization pointed out, protect workers against the contingencies which prevent persons in wage employment from earning a living whether by inability to work or inability to obtain remunerative employment or in which the worker dies leaving a dependent family. The recommendation urged that contingencies which 'involve an extraordinary strain on limited income in so far as they are not otherwise covered' should also be included.

Today many social insurance schemes provide protection against the contingencies enumerated in the ILO Social Security (Minimum Standards) Convention of 1952. As noted previously, nine contingencies are covered by this convention. The principles anchored in the Convention are four-fold in that they define and guarantee benefits, require the participation of employers and workers in the administration of the schemes, accord general responsibility to the state for the due provision of the benefits and the proper administration of the institutions and finally require the collective financing of benefits by way of insurance contributions or taxation. Social insurance is widely used today to provide old-age retirement, sickness, invalidity, unemployment and survivor's benefits. To qualify for benefits, claimants (or their dependents) must have paid contributions for a specified period of time. There are also obvious eligibility conditions that apply in the case of illness, accident, invalidity and retirement. Claimants must also meet other qualifying conditions such as citizenship or lawful residence. Social insurance benefits are usually paid in cash although, as was noted earlier, the insurance method is also used to provide medical and other services in some countries, particularly in Latin America.

The link between social insurance and industrial employment is revealed in the historical origins of these schemes. As is well known, Germany was the first nation in the world to introduce a national, mandatory social insurance programme in 1883. This programme provided sickness benefits to low-income workers who were temporarily unable to work because of illness and who were often summarily dismissed by their employers. This practice had caused great resentment, and promises by the Social Democratic Party to address the issue mobilized a great deal of working-class support. It was largely for this reason that the Chancellor, Otto von Bismarck, used both repressive and conciliatory measures to attack the Social Democrats and their union allies. The creation of a statutory, mandatory sickness insurance programme sought to out-manoeuvre the Social Democrats and to neutralize the threat they posed to the government and established interests.

The insurance idea had actually emerged much earlier among non-formal mutual associations, the unions and neighbourhood savings and burial associations. Prior to Bismarck's introduction of sickness insurance, thousands of small sickness funds operated in Europe. Similar associations known as the friendly societies had also emerged in Britain and, as in the rest of Europe, they laid the foundations for both commercial and statutory insurance. Germany's sickness insurance programme was supplemented in 1884 by a work injury insurance programme and in 1889 by an old age retirement insurance scheme. Unemployment insurance was introduced in 1927. Britain was the first country to establish an unemployment insurance scheme in 1911. It also established a retirement insurance scheme in 1925. Several other European nations also introduced old-age insurance and other forms of social insurance in the early decades of the twentieth century. In the United States, retirement pensions were originally provided through social assistance by the states but, with enactment of the Social Security Act by the Roosevelt administration in 1935, these programmes were replaced with a federal retirement programme that now covers the vast majority of the country's workers (Karger, 1996; Leiby, 1978).

Social insurance has also been used to provide medical care. Although Britain and the Soviet Union funded their health services from general revenues, most other industrial nations have used the insurance mechanism for this purpose and, as was noted earlier, many countries, particularly in Latin America, include the provision of medical care in their definition of social security (Roemer, 1997). In non-European countries, Japan took the lead in offering health insurance in 1922, finally providing universal coverage by 1946. Japan was also an early pioneer of social insurance retirement pensions as was Chile, which was the first developing country to establish statutory social insurance funds in the 1920s. However, different groups of workers in Chile and other Latin American countries were covered by different insurance funds. Because the different funds had different eligibility requirements and paid different levels of benefits, social insurance in Chile became quite fragmented causing administrative and fiscal difficulties that eventually undermined the system's credibility.

As is well known, the Chilean social insurance system attracted international attention when General Pinochet's military dictatorship sought to privatize the system in 1981 by introducing commercially managed retirement accounts. Although social insurance had long been the preferred social security funding mechanism in international circles, the involvement of the World Bank in social security debates in the 1990s (World Bank, 1994) offered an alternative to the standard ILO social insurance model which had been adopted in many parts of the world. Through its policy influence and lending resources, the Bank aggressively promoted savings accounts as an alternative to social insurance claiming that they were a far more effective approach to income maintenance especially during retirement. A number of Latin American countries have emulated the Chilean innovation, and recently Hong Kong established a retirement security system based on personal savings. On the one hand, the governments of several other developing countries have elected to introduce or retain social insurance and, as shown in Chapter 4 of this book, the Bachelet government in Chile is reassessing the merits of the privatized retirement savings account system. On the other hand, as shown in Chapter 5, developments in China are noteworthy for introducing a combined social insurance and savings account approach.

As will be shown later, funding is a major issue in social insurance policy debates today. It was shown earlier that social insurance is funded from special payroll taxes known as contributions that are levied on workers and their employers. Often, these contributions are supplemented by governments. The revenues raised by social insurance contributions are pooled and may be placed in a trust fund administered by a special government agency. The accumulated revenues are invested and the income is used to pay benefits. However, in most Western countries today, trust funds have not maintained a reserve and revenues are immediately transferred to pay benefits. In this case, the social security programme is described as a pay-as-you-go system. In the former case, it is known as a funded system. Critics of social insurance claim that these programmes are not sustainable because of the growing income needs of the increasing numbers of retired people and others claiming benefits and the declining numbers of workers who contribute to social insurance funds. Although this problem applies largely to the Western countries, it has been argued that it is only a matter of time before similar demographic and fiscal challenges will arise in the developing world. In addition, social insurance is said to pose a major challenge to economic development. As will be shown in Chapter 2, social insurance schemes are said to stifle investments, distort labour markets and negatively affect work incentives.

Provident funds and commercial savings accounts

The introduction of a system of commercially managed mandatory retirement accounts in Chile was viewed by many as a daring policy innovation, which was in keeping with the needs of dynamic capitalist economy and suited to the times. However, few advocates of this approach recognized that mandatory retirement accounts known as provident funds had been established in many Anglophone developing countries in the middle decades of the twentieth century. These provident funds have many similarities with the commercial savings account except that they are managed by public bodies and do not provide opportunities for their members to choose from a variety of investment options (Dixon, 1982, 1993).

Provident funds have certain similarities to social insurance in that they are financed by regular payroll contributions but, unlike social insurance, contributions are not pooled. Instead, a personal, designated account into which workers pay contributions is established and usually contributions are matched by employers. Accumulations in the personal account is accessed when a specified contingency arises. Most provident funds are designed to provide retirement pensions. Contributions paid into the account are invested by a public or quasi-public body, and the total accumulated amount plus interest is withdrawn when the worker retires either in a lump sum or as phased payments. Lump sum payments have been used in many countries and are generally preferred by the members of these schemes. Sometimes the lump sum is used to purchase an annuity from a commercial provider. In addition to paying retirement pensions, provident funds are also used to cover disability. If the worker becomes unemployed, and is unable to find work, the accumulated contributions may also be withdrawn prior to retirement. In many cases, partial withdrawals are also permitted in the case of temporary unemployment.

Provident funds were established in many British colonial territories in the middle decades of the past century in the period preceding independence. Unfortunately, little historical information has been obtained to clarify the reasons for this decision or to highlight the role of

British politicians and civil servants in promoting the spread of provident funds in the Anglophone developing world. However, it appears that the nationalist independence movements were exerting growing pressures for the creation of social security, particularly in the light of the publication of the Beveridge report, which attracted international attention. The British authorities were mindful that the proportion of the labour force engaged in regular wage employment was relatively small, and they were reluctant to establish social insurance programmes for a small minority of the population. In addition, the ILO conventions required that social insurance funds be supplemented by government, and because of these costs, an alternative form of income protection was sought. It is also likely that the provident fund was modelled on similar retirement pension programmes that had been established in Britain. They were also reminiscent of the civil service pension schemes that had been established for colonial administrators during the imperial period.

One of the first provident funds was created in India in 1952 to cover workers with low or moderate incomes in designated industries. The programme was administered at the state level, and a lump sum benefit was paid when the worker reached the age of 55 years. Other Asian countries such as Malaysia, Singapore and Sri Lanka emulated the Indian innovation, and in the 1950s and 1960s, provident funds were established in a number of African countries including Nigeria, Ghana and Uganda. Several Caribbean and South Pacific territories subsequently establish provident funds, and in the 1970 new funds were introduced in the Seychelles and Swaziland. The Singaporean provident fund is perhaps the best known, having been extensively documented in the literature, largely because of the effective use of accumulations by the government for housing construction and economic development projects.

In addition to the British territories, provident funds were also established in other developing countries including Indonesia and Taiwan (Dixon, 1982, 1993; Midgley, 1984). On the other hand, several British territories chose not to establish provident funds but instead opted to introduce social insurance to provide retirement pensions.

As the Singaporean experience reveals, provident funds have the advantage of accumulating substantial reserves which can be used for investment, and many governments have found them to be a useful source of credit (see Chapter 10 of this book). On the other hand, as the International Social Security Association (1975) pointed out, provident funds have the disadvantage of not providing adequate protection to those who have been in employment for a relatively short period before retirement or invalidity, and they are especially disadvantageous to the dependants of younger workers who die before they are able to accumulate adequate funds in their accounts. They have also been criticized for paying lump sum benefits and failing to ensure that members have a steady income during retirement. As Gobin (1977, p. 9) puts it, 'The lump sums paid at retirement are often frittered away by purchasing consumer goods and, in the long run, recipients must still revert to relief from the public assistance programme.' This observation has relevance for the private savings account retirement programmes that have been established in several Latin American and other countries.

As was mentioned earlier, a number of countries have adopted the provident fund approach to create commercially managed individual savings accounts since 1981 when the Chilean military government privatized the country's social insurance system. The privatized system created individual savings accounts into which the workers' contributions deducted from wages are accumulated and then disbursed when they reach retirement age. A distinctive feature of the approach was the use of commercial fund managers to invest accumulations. Unlike conventional provident funds which are entirely state managed, the Chilean system provided new opportunities for the financial services industry to participate in the social security system. Workers, it was argued, would benefit from this arrangement because they would choose which management firms to use, and thus faced with competition, these firms would minimize cost and seek the best rates of returns for their participants. The World Bank (1994) enthusiastically endorsed this system claiming that the involvement of the private sector would greatly enhance efficiency and meet the needs of workers and retirees by the effective use of the market mechanism. Since the Chilean privatization, a number of other Latin American countries have introduced commercially managed retirement savings account schemes, but as various studies have shown, the claim that the marketization of social security will inevitably enhance efficiency and coverage has not been realized. Recently, the government of Hong Kong established a retirement security system based on personal savings, but unlike the Latin American funds, it designated the scheme as a provident fund. However, like the Latin American funds, accounts are commercially managed. Despite the efforts of the World Bank to promote commercially managed accounts, other governments that have created provident funds have not shown much interest in privatization and their funds continue to be state managed.

Employer mandates

Social security also operates through the mandates imposed by governments on employers to meet the income needs of their workers. Generally, loss of income arising from employment injury, temporary illness and maternity is most frequently covered by these programmes. The term 'workmen's compensation' is often used to refer to programmes that mandate employers to pay compensatory benefits to workers who sustain injuries at work. Employer mandates are also used to require firms to pay terminated workers a lump sum, redundancy benefit. In some countries, employers are required to provide old-age retirement and disability benefits as well. In the Communist countries, the state enterprises were required to accumulate sufficient funds to meet the retirement and other income protection needs of their workers. In China, the state-owned enterprises were previously responsible for meeting the income protection and particularly the retirement income needs of their workers, but as shown in Chapter 5 of this book, many were unable to meet their obligations, and today the new social insurance system operated by the provincial governments under the direction of the central government has covered most workers in regular wage employment.

The employer liability approach to social security is based on the premise that the costs of meeting contingencies should be borne by employers, usually backed up by legislation which specifies what type, amount or level of benefit is to be paid under what circumstances. Although imposed by governments through legislative dictate, mandates are funded by employers. Unfortunately, employers are not always able to meet their obligations. Some evade payment and, in the case of employment injury, the costs of the compensatory benefit may be very large. Many employers complain that mandates impose significant costs which affect their profitability and even their commercial viability. For these reasons, many social security experts recommend that employer mandates be replaced with social insurance. However, in some countries, a hybrid employer mandate has emerged by which governments require employers to insure themselves with a commercial carrier to meet worker's claims. In some countries, insurance is provided by a government agency.

Like social insurance, employer mandates are historically associated with the risks of industrial employment. The first employer mandates sought to address the contingency of work injury and were known as worker's compensation. One of the earliest was established by the English Fatal Accidents Act of 1846 and required the payment of compensation to workers who died as a result of injuries sustained at work. The statute responded to the problem that industrial workers who were injured at work were compelled to litigate to secure compensation. It recognized that they were disadvantaged in having to establish employer negligence and incurred considerable legal expenses to press their claims. Although the statute made it easier for workers and their families to claim compensation, it upheld the principle that litigants had to prove negligence on the part of the employer and many still found it difficult to secure redress. As a result of growing dissatisfaction and union agitation, the government responded by enacting the Workmen's Compensation Act of 1897 which required the payment of compensation without proof of negligence. This statute inspired similar legislative developments in other countries – notably in the English-speaking world. New Zealand established an employment injury mandate in 1898, and similar statutes were enacted in several of the American states and in Australia in the years before the First World War. Denmark was the first continental European nation to establish an employer mandated employment injury scheme in 1898. However, employment injury provisions in many other countries were often based on social insurance principles. This was the case in Germany and in other European countries, and in time, employment injury mandates were either augmented by the practice of insuring employers or otherwise by replacing them with social insurance schemes funded by payroll taxes levied on employers.

Although employer mandates which require employers to insure themselves with a public carrier are very similar to employer-financed insurance provisions, the use of the payroll tax in the latter case is widely regarded as a key difference between the employer liability and social insurance approaches. Today, employer mandates are not particularly popular with social security experts and policymakers, but nevertheless governments continue to use this approach. It remains popular in the United States, where it is also been used to require the payment of minimum wages and to direct employers to provide leave when workers or immediate family members become ill.

Universal social allowances

Universal social allowances are funded directly out of government revenues and are paid to those who meet specified eligibility requirements. Income or wealth is not taken into account when determining eligibility, and benefits are paid to all who fall within a specific population category. Because social allowances cover specified demographic groups irrespective of their incomes or assets, they are also known as demogrant social security schemes. Merriam (1969, p. 56) reports that the term 'demogrant' was first used by Evelyn Burns in 1936. As she points out, the great strength of these programmes is that they do not divide people into 'those who have and have not'. Social allowances are designed to supplement the income of those who incur additional costs because of their needs or social obligations. Although the benefits paid through social allowance programmes are generally small, they nevertheless cover all of those in the population who are in the designated demographic category and provide a measure of income support to meet their additional income needs. They may be viewed as a form of collective compensation paid by the state to those who face additional demands on their income, whether or not they have the resources to meet this burden comfortably.

Child benefits are often paid as social allowances on the ground that families with children have greater demands on their resources than families without children. These programmes have conventionally been known as family allowances. In some countries, such as France, they were introduced to address the problem of a declining birth rate. On the other hand, family allowances were not established for pronatalist reasons in most other European countries but rather to supplement the incomes of families with children and particularly families with large numbers of children who were often among the poorest and most needy. In some countries, social allowances are paid to people with disabilities or to elderly people.

Despite their popularity with social security scholars who approve of their universal coverage, social allowances are not widely used around the world today. They are largely confined to European countries, although there are a few exceptions such as Canada and Hong Kong where they are used to fund retirement pensions. Another example is New Zealand which established an old-age allowance scheme in 1938. Originally, retirement pensions were based on social assistance principles, but coverage was extended to all residents over the age of 65 years irrespective of their income or assets. In 1965, Denmark enacted legislation, which replaced the country's social assistance pension scheme with a universal old-age allowance. In Hong Kong, elderly people over the age of 70 receive a small old-age pension (known as a social allowance) irrespective of their income. Those with low incomes may apply for social assistance to supplement their pensions. The contingency of disability is also met through universal social allowance programmes in a number of European countries, notably the Scandinavian nations and Finland. In Finland, social assistance payments are used to supplement the universal social allowance paid to people with disabilities. A social allowance scheme for people with disabilities was established in Britain in 1975 to provide income support to those who had not qualified for social insurance benefits and who were, therefore, left without any income in the event of disability.

Social allowances are championed by those on the political left, who believe that social security coverage should be extended to all irrespective of their incomes and assets. It was this idea that played a major role in the creation of family allowance schemes in the early twentieth century, although as was noted earlier, pronatalist motives were also relevant particularly in France. However, in most cases family allowances in Europe were created to meet the additional income needs of low income, large families. In Britain, the Beveridge Report of 1941 strongly urged the introduction of universal family allowances, because it was argued that they would subsidize the incomes of low-incomes families without stigmatizing them or creating a 'poverty trap' that would discourage poor families from working and thus losing their benefits. On the other hand, universal allowances are opposed by those on the political right who believe that it is wasteful to pay income benefits to those who have adequate income and assets. Instead they advocate the use of social assistance schemes that 'target' the poor and direct benefits at the most needy sections of the population. They reject the argument that social assistance unfairly stigmatizes claimants and contend the claim that people in need fail to apply for benefits because they fear stigmatization is grossly exaggerated. The poor and needy, they believe, will seek public assistance when they need it. The real issue is not the stigmatization of recipients but rather the need for adequate measures that prevent fraud and abuse.

However, despite their attempts to eliminate universal social allowances and replace them with social assistance schemes, social allowances have been quite resilient. This is largely because they have extensive coverage and are popular. They have also helped to reduce the incidence of poverty among those receiving these benefits (Tang, 1997, 2000). The idea that direct, universal cash transfers are an effective anti-poverty measure has also inspired advocates of the basic income approach who believe that universal benefits currently directed at certain demogrant groups such as families with children, elderly people and people with disabilities should be paid to all citizens irrespective of their incomes or assets and irrespective of whether they are employed or not (Fitzpatrick, 1999; van Parijs, 1992).

Fiscal measures and social security innovations

Kaim-Caudle's (1973) typology of social security, which was mentioned earlier, drew attention to the social security role of the tax system. Although social security has been primarily associated with direct income transfers and the provision of health care, Kaim-Caudle noted that governments have intentionally or unintentionally used the tax system to advantage different groups of people in ways that affect their incomes. The tax system is usually believed to mobilize resources to fund public services and the other activities of governments, but by creating concessions and advantages, it can also be used to transfer resources to different groups of people. The business community has historically benefited extensively from tax advantages of this kind, but they have also been used to benefit larger groups of people such as homeowners through mortgage tax relief. The use of the fiscal system in this way has numerous purposes. Often, governments grant concessions in response to political pressures, but they also use the tax system to create incentives. In the case of mortgage tax relief, the concession has the stated objective of promoting homeownership.

The tax system has also been used by governments to encourage employers to provide income protection and particularly retirement pensions. For example, after the federal government of the United States introduced tax concessions to reward firms that established retirement pensions, the number of occupational pension plans expanded significantly, so that by 1929 about four hundred occupational pension plans covering almost three million employees had been created (Howard, 1997). Tax incentives were again used during the Second World War by the Roosevelt administration to harmonize occupational pensions with the government's newly established retirement insurance programme, and as Hacker (2006) reveals, this decision strengthened both systems. Similarly fiscal policies facilitated the expansion of occupational pensions in Britain and, as was noted earlier, inspired Titmuss (1958) to stress the important contribution that the fiscal and occupational systems make to social welfare. More recently, the federal government of the United States has also used the tax system to encourage individuals and employers to establish commercially managed, retirement savings accounts.

Although fiscal incentives of this kind generally favour middle- and higher-income workers in steady wage employment, they can also be used to direct resources to low-income earners provided they are covered by the tax system. As is shown in Chapter 6 of this book, the tax system of the United States has been used since the early 1970s to supplement the incomes of low-paid workers through what is known as the Earned Income Tax Credit or EITC. In the early 1990s, the Clinton administration extended the credit to cover many more workers and increased it value. Wage earners who meet specified eligibility requirement may claim a tax refund which functions as an income subsidy. It is estimated that in 2000, approximately twenty million households benefited from the credit and that it lifted more than four million people out of poverty (Hoffman and Seidman, 2003). In addition to its positive social impact, there is evidence to show that the EITC has strengthened work incentives and also increased the number of workers covered by the tax system.

In addition to the more frequent use of the tax system to provide income support and protection, a number of innovations such as matched savings accounts and stakeholder accounts have attracted attention from social security policy makers who are advocating that they be more widely adopted. Matched savings accounts are also known as individual development accounts or IDAs. Developed in the United States by Sherraden (1991) they are targeted at low-income people who are encouraged to contribute to a restricted account which is then matched to varying degrees by the government or other sponsors. Accumulated funds can only be withdrawn for retirement or other approved social purposes such as meeting educational or housing costs. Although IDAs are now well known in the United States, they have not been widely adopted in other countries, and even in the United States, government sponsorship is still limited. Indeed, as it is noted in Chapter 6, most IDA projects are operated by non-profit organizations although many of them do receive federal funds. Nevertheless, IDAs are a potentially useful social security mechanism which can assist low-income families to save, attain credit worthiness and utilize established financial services, including subsidized public lending services such as special mortgages which avoid the predatory activities that characterize credit facilities in many low-income neighbourhoods. In addition, as Sherraden pointed out, they transcend social security's conventional emphasis on income transfers for consumption purposes. They seek to support asset development and promote investments among low-income people, who have not benefited from the various asset accumulation incentives available to higher-income earners.

Stakeholder accounts are similar to IDAs in that they promote asset accumulation, but they do not utilize the matching formula of the IDA. In addition, they are not usually targeted at people with low incomes but provide universal cash benefits. Most proponents of these accounts propose that they be created by governments for all children or young people. Ideally, these accounts are established with a lump sum provided by government into which subsequent deposits may be made (Ackeman and Alstot, 1999; Lindsey, 1994). However, although widely discussed in the literature, stakeholder accounts have not been introduced in many parts of the world. The major exception is Britain where the Labour government recently introduced a child savings account scheme for all children at birth. These accounts are opened with an initial deposit from the state and which may then be supplemented on a tax advantaged basis. Accumulated funds may be withdrawn on reaching maturity and may be used for various purposes.

Issues in social security

For many years after the Second World War, social security enjoyed strong support from both governments and the public. Governments believed that social security is an effective means of ensuring income protection and highly suited to the needs of industrial societies. Social security was also embraced by the governments of the developing countries, since it was believed that these countries were on the path towards industrialization and would soon need modern forms of income protection. However, support for social security has gradually lost ground partly because of the difficulties social security programmes have encountered, the extent of social and economic change and the ideological campaigns waged against state intervention by neoliberals and their allies. Supporters of social security have been slow to respond but, as was pointed out earlier in this chapter, the challenges presented by critics and by new social and economic realities are being more readily addressed. There is a greater recognition of the need to respond more effectively to new challenges and to deal with the issues facing social security. A readiness to debate and respond to these issues has strengthened the capacity of social security scholars and policy makers to address the challenges of the time.

Current social security debates are marked by more incisive analyses of the issues. While the field is now the subject of intensive disagreements, these disagreements have fostered a greater understanding of the issues and the formulation of policy responses that offer effective solutions. Of the many issues being debated in social security circles today, some merit further discussion. The first concerns the question of whether new demographic and economic realities will limit social security's long-term effectiveness and sustainability. The second issue concerns the sustainability and fiscal viability of social security programmes. The issue of whether ideological beliefs significantly influence social security decision-making or whether decisions are governed by rational, technicist approaches is yet another important issue. The question of managerial efficiency versus administrative incompetence is also widely discussed. Debates have also revolved around issues of equity. These debates are concerned with the coverage of social security programmes and the extent to which they treat everyone equally. Another issue concerns the relationship between social security and economic development, but since this topic is extensively covered in this book, it will not be discussed separately here. These issues affect social security in both the Western and developing countries. There are, as Tracy (1996, p. 144) pointed out, major issues facing social security internationally with regard to 'expanded coverage, credible administration, and sustainable economic development...and growing disparity in wealth both within and among countries'.

With regard to the question of whether demographic and economic changes have affected social security's relevance to current demographic, cultural and economic realities, some academic commentators claim that conventional approaches now have limited usefulness. They point out that modern social security programmes emerged in the context of rapid industrialization and urbanization in the Western nations. They contend that social security's occupationalist commitments, which were mentioned earlier, were specifically intended to address the challenges of industrial life. This was primarily the case with social insurance, but provident funds, employer mandates and social allowances were also closely linked with the rapid extension of wage employment in the late nineteenth century. Social security programmes also responded to the demographic and cultural realities of the new industrial world. Most wage workers were employed in industrial occupations and most remained with the same employer over their working lives. Although life expectancy was rising, comparatively few workers survived into old age in the early stages of social security expansion and only a small proportion were therefore dependent on retirement pensions. Initially, wage employees were overwhelming male and the 'breadwinner' approach to social security was compatible with cultural realities. Social security programmes were primarily designed to provide income protection to male-headed families in which adults were employed in industrial occupations.

Today, the situation has changed dramatically. As Sherraden (1997) puts it, industrial era social security programmes, based on mass wage employment and the male breadwinner model, do not fit the economic realities of the contemporary information economy. Demographic realities have also changed in that many more people are now living longer and drawing retirement pensions. This trend is expected to increase not only in the Western countries but in the developing countries as well. Changing demographic realities are also revealed in the sizable increase in the proportion of women who work, the rise in divorce rates, the numbers of lone-parent families and particularly the families headed by women. In addition, with rising incomes and rising expectations, many people now resent having to pay social security taxes and at the same time demand more of government. A more individualistic culture has also emerged in which notions of self-determination and self-reliance have become more important. The weakening of working-class solidarity and the undermining of trade unionism has also contributed to the growth of individualism and a disinclination towards cooperative endeavour that were characteristic of industrial era social security programmes.

The effects on social security policy of these and other changes are widely debated today, particularly with reference to the issue of whether the changes that have taken place pose new fiscal challenges that require new approaches. Some critics of social security contend that they do, and that entirely new approaches that require greater personal responsibility and the utilization of markets are needed to provide effective income protection in the future. They point out that conventional social security programmes in many countries now face fiscal obligations that have become increasingly difficult to meet and require ever-greater government subsidies. These critics argue that commercially managed income protection accounts that encourage people to save for their retirement, health care and the risk of unemployment offer a viable alternative to conventional, state managed social security programmes.

The fiscal pressures on social security have come largely from the increase in the proportion of elderly people in the population and the prediction that many more elderly retirees will live into their eighties or even nineties and require retirement pensions for many years. This demographic trend, it is argued, will severely stretch the resources of social security programmes and eventually even government subsidies will be insufficient to meet the demand. The problem is compounded by the funding mechanisms used in social insurance programmes. When these programmes were created, it was intended that sizeable reserve funds would be established to meet the future needs of retirees. But the funded approach was eventually replaced by the pay-as-you-go approach by which the use of actuarial predictions was undermined resulting in the immediate transfer of contributions to pensioners. Although it was believed that an expanding economy, full employment, rising incomes and a generally stable proportion of people in retirement would guarantee the viability of the pay-as-you-go approach, these optimistic assumptions have not been realised.

Other factors aggravated the fiscal problems facing social security. The increase in divorce and rise in single-headed families has meant that income needs have increased placing a higher burden on social assistance schemes. In addition, social insurance contribution rates have remained relatively unchanged in many parts of the world while benefits levels have increased. This is partly because politicians have used social security to garner electoral support and partly because of political pressures from workers and the trade unions. In addition, administrative inefficiencies and even corruption have undermined the fiscal viability of social security. Because social security programmes have been exploited by politicians for electoral gain and managed by inefficient bureaucrats, critics argue that there is an urgent need to privatize these programmes.

In some parts of the world, these fiscal realities are believed to be quite serious. Social security programmes in many Latin American nations face imminent insolvency, and this fostered the privatization of some programmes. In Britain, the Conservative Government (1979–1996) raised serious concerns about the feasibility of containing social security costs, and as Evans and Piachaud, (1996) pointed out, measures were taken to restrict both the scope and level of benefits. As they noted, a report of the Conservative Government asked, 'will the costs of social security outstrip the nation's ability to pay for it?' (p. 133). In the United States, much has been made of the looming crisis in social security funding despite the fact that the country actually has a sizable reserve fund. Nevertheless, some scholars such as Jackson (2004) claim that despite the system's $1.4 trillion of accumulated reserves, future obligations will soon deplete these reserves and the government will soon be required to transfer scarce resources to the system if it is to meet its obligations.

However, it should be noted that claims about social security's fiscal crisis usually come from those on the political right, while those on the left believe that the problem can be remedied through incremental changes such as adjustments to contribution rates and benefit levels and increases in the retirement age. Despite the claim that individual accounts offer an effective 'technical' solution to the problem, it is clear that this policy option is informed by neoliberal thinking. In fact, many commentators believe that debates attending social security issues are distinctly ideological. According to the neoliberal proponents of social security privatization, individuals should secure their welfare in the market, largely independent of subsidies or support from the state. The state should retain only a very minimal role by providing a last-resort safety net for the destitute. On the other hand, Social Democrats and social liberals believe that income security can best be provided through the collective agency of the state.

The neoliberal approach is being vigorously promoted by the World Bank and the International Monetary Fund, which have urged governments to abandon the insurance approach and replace it with commercially managed retirement accounts. In China, for example, the World Bank has made alarming estimates of the country's implicit pension debt which it puts at 141 per cent of national income. To ensure that this debt is met, and that viable pensions are provided to the country's elderly population, it estimated that additional pension costs of approximately $160 billion or seven per cent of national income will be incurred. Not surprisingly, it has urged the government to make a transition from the current pay-as-you-go system of social security to a fully funded system based on individual retirement accounts and, of course, a significant reduction in payroll taxes and employer's contributions. On the other hand, the ILO remains committed to a statist approach that emphasizes statutory social protection. It has opposed the World Bank's market-based approach and reiterated its commitment to government responsibility for social security (Deacon et al., 1997).

Nevertheless, it is clear that global trends in social security funding are indicative of a preference for market-based approaches and the privatization of social security. A recent study of pension policies in 15 Western countries (Rein and Schmahl, 2004) found that private-pension coverage has increased and that private provisions have been increasingly substituted for public programmes. This trend is also reflected in the decline of employer-provided occupational schemes and the growth of defined benefit pensions plans. In addition, public pension monopolies are weakening and there is a greater public-private mix in pension provision. These trends have been confirmed by Dixon and Hyde (2003) in their analysis of the privatization of social security, but the authors caution that the pattern is a complex one and does not involve a straightforward transition from public to private provision.

Another issue concerns the claim that social security schemes are failing to meet their stated goals due to poor budgetary decisions, inefficient management, political interference, the avoidance of contribution payments and other factors. Much has been made of the administrative inefficiency of social insurance funds in Latin American countries. In one of the first studies of social security in the region, Wolfe (1968) castigated the inefficiency of these schemes. He pointed out that social insurance claims took many months to process and that pension calculations were often inaccurate. Social insurance funds were governed by complex rules and bureaucratic procedures. Politicians frequently influenced decisions on behalf of constituents, and staff were often appointed on the recommendation of politicians and senior administrators rather than on meritorious searches for the best candidates. Writing 20 years later, Mesa-Lago (1989) reported that these problems had not been addressed. He also noted that the administrative costs of social security schemes in many Latin American countries exceeded those of Europe and North America. While European countries spent less than two per cent of revenues on administration, the comparable figure in many Latin American countries was in excess of ten per cent. The situation has apparently not improved as a result of privatization. As Borzutsky reveals in Chapter 4 of this book, the commissions and administrative costs incurred by commercial providers who manage individual savings accounts are extraordinarily high by international standards.

The issue of equity is given much more attention in social security debates today. Feminist scholars have challenged the breadwinner model on which social security programmes have traditionally been based, and they have drawn attention to the way many programmes discriminate against women (Charles, 2000; Lewis, 1993; Sainsbury, 1996; Wilson, 1977). Despite the claims of the proponents of individual retirement savings accounts, it is clear that privatization will not solve this problem since women earn less than men and are not able to accumulate as much in their accounts as men. Many women also leave their jobs to raise children and thus interrupts their working lives, again limiting their ability to accumulate sufficient funds in their savings accounts to adequately meet their retirement needs. The problem of inequity in conventional social security schemes is not likely to be remedied through privatization or any other quick-fix solution but rather through a careful assessment of the causes of these inequities and the formulation of appropriate policies that can address them.

However, the problem of inequity in social security has today been more widely recognized, and progress has been made in remedying some of the most obvious inequities in these schemes. The bias in conventional social insurance programmes towards the male breadwinner and the insistence that benefit levels for both genders be equalized has been corrected in a number of countries. However, the problem of limited coverage remains a major inequity in social security provision in the developing countries of the Global South. As Midgley (1984) revealed many years ago, social security schemes in many developing countries fail to address the needs of agricultural workers and those in the informal labour market. The problem is exacerbated by the fact that taxes levied on workers who are not covered by a social security are sometimes used to improve the benefit levels of workers in the modern wage-employment sector who are already advantaged by having regular cash incomes. Although social security coverage has improved in some parts of the developing world, van Ginneken (2003) notes that more than a half of the world's population is still excluded from any type of statutory social security protection and that in some regions, such as sub-Saharan Africa and south Asia, over 90 per cent of the population has no social security protection.

Recently, the ILO has renewed its commitment to improve the extension of social security coverage. The consensus between governments, employers and workers reached at the International Labour Conference in 2001 placed the extension of social security coverage high on the ILO agenda and was followed by the launch of the Global Campaign on Social Security and Coverage for All (Reynaud, 2002). In the face of globalization and structural adjustment policies, the Conference recognized that social security had become more necessary than ever, and it urged that that the highest priority be given to extending protection to the poor. In addition, specific efforts have been made in some countries to provide income protection to those in the agrarian and informal sectors. In India, about 400,000 mainly home-based *beedi* workers have been covered by the country's Employees' Provident Fund Act as a result of government action and innovative financing (Jain, 1999). However, it is clear that much more needs to be done to address current inequities. This will require innovative solutions as well as political will on the part of government to address the needs of the most disadvantaged groups. For example, crop insurance could be more effectively extended to peasant farmers to help them cope with the adverse effects of natural disasters if governments would provide the necessary leadership, subsidies and technical support.

Contrary to the claims of neoliberal advocates, it is clear that governments have the authority and resources to address these and other problems and are able to extend income protection to all citizens. This is not to deny that there are many different ways of responding to the challenges facing social security today. Indeed, many social security policymakers and academic researchers recognize that the challenges of insecurity in the modern world can be addressed in different ways and that the articulation of different approaches offers the most viable opportunities for ensuring effective income protection in the future. The idea that the state is the only agent capable of providing social security has been challenged, but the alternative argument that the market is the only viable means of achieving this goal is equally simplistic and misguided. Fortunately, the synergy of different partners in social security including the family, community, non-profit sector, the market and the state has been recognized. A carefully designed pluralistic social security system directed by the state and based on familial, community, occupational, fiscal and market-based approaches may indeed emerge to provide true security for all in the future. Needless to say, more debate on these issues will be needed if new and appropriate approaches are to emerge. An important question, which is addressed in the remainder this book, is how to provide income protection to the entire population and, at the same time, support national economic development efforts. The experiences of the different countries examined in this book will hopefully shed light on this critical issue.

References

Ackerman, B. and Alstot, A. (1999). *The Stakeholder Society*. New Haven, CT: Yale University Press.

Burns, E. (1936). *Towards Social Security*. New York: McGraw-Hill.

Charles, N. (2000). *Feminism, the State and Social Policy*. Houndmills: Macmillan.

Deacon, B. (with M. Hulse and P. Stubbs) (1997). *Global Social Policy*. Thousand Oaks, California: Sage Publications.

Dickinson, J. (1986). 'Spiking Socialist Guns: The Introduction of Social Insurance in Germany and Britain', *Comparative Social Research*, 9 (1), 69–108.

Dixon, J. (1982). 'Provident Funds in the Third World: A Cross-National Review', *Public Administration and Development*, 2 (4), 325–344.

Dixon, J. (1993). 'National Provident Funds: The Challenge of Harmonizing their Social Security, Social and Economic Objectives', *Policy Studies Review*, 12 (1/2), 197–1209.

Dixon, J. (1999). *Social Security in Global Perspective*. Westport, CT: Praegar.

Dixon, J. and Hyde, M. (eds) (2003). *The Marketization of Social Security*. Westport, CT: Quorum.

Evans, M. and Piachaud, D. (1996). 'Social Security in Britain: the Challenge of Needs Versus Costs.' In Midgley, J. and Tracy, M. B. (eds), *Challenges to Social Security: An International Exploration*. Westport, CT: Auburn House, Greenwood Press, pp. 103–140.

Fitzpatrick, T. (1999). *Freedom and Security: An Introduction to the Basic Income Debate*. New York: Palgrave Macmillan.

van Ginneken, W. (2003). 'Extending Social Security: Policies for Developing Countries', *International Labour Review*, 142 (3), 277–294.

Gobin, M. (1977). 'The Role of Social Security in the Development of the Caribbean Territories', *International Social Security Review*, 30, 7–20.

Hacker, J. S. (2006). *The Great Risk Shift*. New York: Oxford University Press.

Hoffman, S. D. and Seidman, L. S. (2003). *Helping Working Families: The Earned Income Tax Credit*. Kalamazoo, MI: W.E. Upjohn Institute for Employment Research.

Howard, C. (1997). *The Hidden Welfare State: Tax Expenditures and Social Policy in the United States*. Princeton, NJ: Princeton University Press.

International Labour Office (1942). *Approaches to Social Security*. Montreal.

International Labour Office (1952). *Social Security Minimum Standards Convention No. 102*. Geneva.

International Labour Office (1958). The Cost of Social Security, 1949–54. Geneva.

International Labour Office (2001). *Report of the International Labour Conference*. Geneva.

International Social Security Association (1975). 'Transformation of Provident Funds into Pension Schemes', *International Social Security Review*, 28 (4), 276–289.

Jackson, H. E. (2004). 'Accounting for Social Security and Its Reform', *Harvard Journal of Legislation*, 41 (1), 59–159.

Jain, S. (1999). 'Basic Social Security in India.' In van Ginneken, W. (ed.), *Social Security for Excluded Majority: Case Studies of Developing Countries*. Geneva: ILO, pp. 37–67.

Kaim-Caudle, P. R. (1973). *Comparative Social Policy and Social Security*. London: Martin-Robinson.

Karger, H. J. (1996). 'The Challenge of Financing Social Security in the United States.' In Midgley, J. and Tracy, M. B. (eds), *Challenges to Social Security: An International Exploration*. Westport, CT: Auburn House, Greenwood Press, pp. 19–34.

Leiby, J. (1978). *A History of Social Welfare and Social Work in the United States*. New York: Columbia University Press.

Lewis, J. (ed.) (1993). *Women and Social Policies in Europe*. Brookfield, VT: Edward Elgar.

Lindsey, D. (1994). *The Welfare of Children*. New York: Oxford University Press.

Merriam, I. (1969). 'Income Maintenance: Social Insurance and Public Assistance.' In Jenkins, S. (ed.), *Social Security in International Perspective*. New York: Columbia University Press, pp. 55–82.

Mesa-Lago, C. (1989). *Ascent to Bankruptcy: Financing Social Security in Latin America*. Pittsburgh, PA: University of Pittsburgh Press.

Midgley, J. (1984). *Social Security, Inequality and the Third World*. London: Wiley & Sons.

Midgley, J. and Sherraden, M. (eds) (1997). *Alternatives to Social Security: An International Inquiry*. Westport, CT: Auburn House, Greenwood Press.

Neaman, E. Y. (1990). 'German Collectivism and the Welfare State', *Critical Review*, 4 (4), 591–618.

van Parijs, P. (ed.) (1992). *Arguing for Basic Income: Ethical Foundations for a Radical Reform*. London: Verso.

Pavard, F. (1979). 'Social Security Financing through the Contribution Method', In International Social Security Association (ed.), *Methods of Financing Social Security*. Geneva: International Social Security Association, pp. 13–24.

Pieters, D. (2006). *Social Security: An Introduction to the Basic Principles*. The Netherlands: Kluwer Law International.

Rein, M. and Schmahl, W. (eds) (2004). *Rethinking the Welfare State*. Cheltenham: Edward Edgar.

Reynaud, E. (2002). *The Extension of Social Security Coverage: The Approach of the International Labour Office*. Geneva: ILO.

Roemer, M. I. (1997). 'Social Insurance for Health Service', *Scandinavian Journal of Social Medicine*, 25 (2), 65–66.

Sainsbury, D. (1996). *Gender, Equality and Welfare States*. New York: Cambridge University Press.

Sherraden, M. (1991). *Assets and the Poor: A New American Welfare Policy*. Armonk, NY: M. E. Sharpe.

Sherraden, M. (1997). 'Conclusion: Social Security in the Twenty-First Century.' In Midgley, J. and Sherraden, M. (eds), *Alternatives to Social Security: An International Inquiry*. Westport, CT: Auburn House, Greenwood Press, pp.121–140.

Tang, K. L. (1997). 'Noncontributory Pensions in Hong Kong: An Alternative to Social Security?' In Midgley, J. and Sherraden, M. (eds), *Alternatives to American Social Security: An International Inquiry*. Westport, CT: Auburn House, Greenwood Press, pp. 61–74.

Tang, K. L. (2000). *Social Welfare Development in East Asia*. New York and London: Palgrave.

Titmuss, R. M. (1958). 'The Social Divisions of Welfare.' In R. M. Titmuss, *Essays on the Welfare State*. London: Allen and Unwin, pp. 34–55.

Titmuss, R. M. (1971). *The Gift Relationship*. London: Allen and Unwin.

Titmuss, R. M. (1974). *Social Policy: An Introduction*. London: Allen and Unwin.

Tracy, M. B. (1996). 'Conclusion: Responding to the Challenge.' In Midgley, J. and Tracy, M. B. (eds), *Challenges to Social Security: An International Exploration*. Westport, CT: Auburn House, Greenwood Press, pp. 141–148.

Wilson, E. (1977). *Women and the Welfare State*. London: Routledge.

Wolfe, Marshall (1968) 'Social Security and Development: The Latin American Experience.' In Everet M. Kassalow (ed.), *The Role of Social Security in Economic Development.* Washington, DC: Department of Health, Education and Welfare, pp. 155–185.

World Bank (1994). *Averting the Old Age Crisis: Policies to Protect the Old and Promote Growth.* Washington, DC.

2
Social Security and the Economy: Key Perspectives

James Midgley

The expansion of social security in the middle decades of the twentieth century was generally welcomed. In the Western countries, memories of the Great Depression were still fresh and policies designed to maintain income in times of financial hardship were widely supported. At the end of the Second World War, many people subscribed to the view that poverty and deprivation could be ended through concerted collective action. After all, the war had shown that apparently insurmountable challenges could be overcome through cooperation and a commitment to common goals. Inspired by the New Deal in the United States and the Beveridge Report in Britain, many were persuaded that poverty could be eradicated through comprehensive income protection programmes.

In the newly independent countries of the Global South, governments also made plans either to introduce or expand existing social security programmes. Social security was regarded by the leaders of the nationalist independence movements as compatible with their efforts to transform their countries into modern, industrial states. Although fiscal constraints would obviously limit the scope of these programmes, it was believed that social security would, in time, cover the whole population. As these countries were transformed through economic growth, the mass of the population would be employed in the modern sector and, as is the West, be protected by social security.

By the end of the twentieth century, the original optimism that legitimated the introduction of social security had waned, and social security programmes were frequently criticized. Criticisms were directed at all forms of social security. For example, social insurance was attacked for accruing huge and unsustainable fiscal liabilities which, it was claimed, would prohibit these programmes from meeting their future obligations. Social assistance was condemned for paying generous benefits to indolent and irresponsible claimants and for creating a dependent welfare underclass. Employer mandates were accused of raising labour costs to unacceptable levels and undermining economic competitiveness. Social allowances were condemned for their high costs and for paying benefits to middle-class people who did not really need them. Accusations of managerial inefficiency were also levelled particularly at social insurance agencies in the developing countries. In addition, social security in these countries was criticized for having an urban bias and failing to address the more pressing problems of rural poverty and deprivation.

These criticisms were linked to the allegation that social security impedes economic development. This criticism is usually levelled by neoliberal economists in the United States, and it is most frequently directed at the so-called European 'welfare states' where excessively generous social security programmes are said to be responsible for sluggish growth and high rates of unemployment. In addition, complaints about mismanagement, inequity and the abuse of social security by unscrupulous claimants are also linked to economic factors and particularly to wasteful government social spending. By retrenching state involvement and marketizing social security, critics claim that these problems will disappear.

This chapter examines these and other arguments about the relationship between social security, the economy and development. However, it recognizes that the issues are complex and, as was noted in the introduction to this book, the tendency to simplify arguments is widespread but unhelpful. Similarly, the issues are often reduced to rhetorical statements that give expression to normative preferences about the merits of state versus commercial provision. While it is indeed appropriate to pay attention to the role of the state and market in social security, a more nuanced approach which is open to the possibility that welfare can be enhanced through the contributions of multiple agents and institutions is needed. This would foster a more accurate and incisive analysis. The issue then is not whether social welfare should be provided through the state or the market, but what mix of state and market involvement (and indeed other forms of income protection) is needed to maximize social well-being.

The following overview hopes to disentangle some of the issues attending the relationship between social security and economic development. It makes reference to different types of social security programmes and hopes to transcend a simplistic juxtaposition of market and statist preferences by reviewing different interpretations that have been articulated in the literature. Four major interpretations will be examined. Advocates of the first approach believe that social security should be an adjunct to an overall economic development strategy in which full employment is given high priority. Supporters of the second position reject the view that social security should be linked in any way to economic development and instead emphasize the humanitarian and welfare dimensions of statutory income protection. Those who favour the third position believe that social security harms economic development. They are informed by neoliberal ideas and are highly critical of state intervention in economic and social affairs. Supporters of the fourth approach take a diametrically opposite view claiming that social security promotes economic growth by investing in human capabilities and contributing to development.

It should be admitted that this typology is in itself open to the criticism that it oversimplifies complex realities. Certainly, it is reductionist in that it distils multiple normative interpretations down to a few basic categories. However, it is hoped that it will nevertheless facilitate analysis. In addition to clarifying the issues, the articulation of these four perspectives may also reveal the interesting normative and ideological perspectives that characterize debates on the relationship between social security and economic development today.

Social security as an adjunct to the economy

Although social security has often been linked to economic policy, scholarly accounts of the historical evolution and functions of social security have generally not emphasized its economic contribution, and instead they have often stressed its political role. Many social policy scholars believe that social security programmes were introduced to secure electoral advantage or exercise political control. Another popular approach is the view that social security gives expression to society's collective conscience and compassionate commitments. This approach views social security as a humanitarian innovation designed to foster welfare goals. However, despite the popularity of these approaches, many examples of the way social security programmes have been used to serve economic interests can be given.

For example, de Schweinitz's (1943) magisterial account of the evolution of social security in England, which placed much emphasis on the role of compassion in shaping social security's historical development, also recognized the way social security was used by governments at different times in the nation's history to foster economic goals. In addition to providing for indigent widows, orphans and the elderly, the Poor Laws were also designed to shape labour markets and promote work incentives. The earliest medieval statutes sought to preserve the feudal economy by preventing labour mobility, and this goal was subsequently reiterated in the Elizabethan statutes and their various amendments which used coercive means as well as incentives to affect labour supply. The Speenhamland amendment, which was temporarily adopted in the late eighteenth century, attempted to maintain employment during recessionary periods by supplementing the wages of low-income workers. It is one of the world's oldest welfare-to-work programmes. Similarly, the 1834 Poor Law amendments gave expression to the-then fashionable beliefs about the effects of social assistance on work incentives and economic growth.

Industrialization and the emergence of an urban industrial proletariat, on whom growth and profits depended, posed new economic challenges. Although many of the barons of late-nineteenth-century capitalism viewed labour as a commodity to be shamelessly exploited, others were persuaded that a different, gentler style of labour relations was needed. Some were concerned about the growing power of the unions and they sought to counterbalance union influence by introducing workplace benefits and supporting campaigns for reform. Others believed that the brutal exploitation of labour was counterproductive, fostering an adversarial relationship between workers and employers that would impede economic progress. Others were motivated by a paternalistic or religious concern for their workers to establish congenial working conditions and provide discretionary social welfare benefits. Nevertheless, all supported the view that industrial production would be enhanced by a stable, loyal and contented labour force. In addition, the realization that much of the labour force was ill-equipped for heavy industrial work because of chronic ill-health, malnutrition and other debilitating conditions spurred remedial action not only on humanitarian but also on economic grounds. The need for action became especially urgent with the disclosure that many recruits into the British army in the early twentieth century were physically unfit for military action (Bruce, 1961). The threat that this state of affairs posed to the nation's imperial interests caused widespread alarm and revealed the necessity for collective action.

The political motives of Bismark's social insurance innovations are usually stressed in the literature, but it is clear that economic motives were equally relevant in view of the need for a well-disciplined and committed labour force able to drive Germany's industrial machine and ensure the nation's economic ascendancy (Rimlinger, 1971). This was recognized by the Chancellor and his advisors and by many corporate leaders who were greatly concerned about the electoral prospects of the Social Democratic Party. The Social Democratic Party, which had championed social insurance, not only presented an electoral threat but also, if successful in its political ambitions, would challenge the entrenched economic interests and continued profitability of the country's industrial corporations. Bismarck's decision to create the world's first statutory social insurance scheme in 1883 not only served political interests by undermining the Social Democrat's electoral campaign but also had economic implications.

The Great Depression further strengthened the link between social security and economic development particularly in the United States where President Roosevelt's New Deal exemplified the use of social policy for economic purposes. However, the New Deal was not, as is widely believed, primarily concerned with retirement pensions or other social welfare programmes but with policies designed to address the pressing problems of unemployment and economic uncertainty that dominated events at the time. Priority was given to reflationary policies, job creation and unemployment insurance. The decision to introduce a comprehensive social security system emerged later and was regarded as of secondary importance to the goal of reducing unemployment. Nevertheless, the introduction of a federal retirement insurance system and other income protection measures in the United States were inextricably linked to the President's economic policies.

The economists working in the Roosevelt administration vigorously rejected market liberal ideas. Although familiar with the work of Keynes, their proposals were not directly based on his work, and it was only later that Keynesianism became widely accepted in the United States. Instead, most were inspired by the teachings of Thorstein Veblen and his followers, and drawing on Veblen's theories, they dismissed the contention that the economy would self-equilibrate and that the unemployment problem would be resolved without government intervention. Rexford Tugwell, one of the leading members of Roosevelt's Brains Trust, declared that the economy had never been directed by an 'invisible hand' and that the policies adopted under the New Deal would instead provide 'a real and visible guiding hand' to solve the economic problems of the time (Leuchtenburg, 1963, p. 34). Tugwell and his colleagues persuaded the President that the problem of mass employment could be addressed through reflationary measures. They recommended that a public works programmes that would absorb unemployed labour, increase consumption and stimulate production be established (Leighninger, 2007). They also recommended that a comprehensive, nationwide unemployment insurance programme be introduced. Unemployment insurance would mitigate the harsh realities of mass unemployment, engender a greater degree of trust and security among workers and, in turn, foster economic efficiency and growth. Social security innovations were intended to complement this approach. Indeed, social security programmes were originally referred to as economic security (Leuchtenburg, 1963).

Proposals for a nationwide unemployment insurance programme were formulated by a group of economists from the University of Wisconsin, led by Edwin Witte. These proposals were based on the ideas of their mentor, John Commons, who had earlier persuaded the Wisconsin legislature to establish an unemployment insurance programme which would reward firms that retained their workers during recessionary periods. The Wisconsin economists focused entirely on unemployment insurance and were not much interested in pensions. Accordingly, the task of drafting the retirement component of the Social Security Act was left to Barbara Armstrong, a Berkeley professor who had written about European pension systems. At the time, poverty in old age was of lesser urgency than the problem of mass unemployment. Linking employment policy with a comprehensive unemployment insurance programme became a central New Deal preoccupation.

Economic considerations were equally important in the Beveridge Report of 1942 (United Kingdom, 1942) and were, in particular, regarded as complementary to wider employment policies based on Keynesian theory. Keynes was regularly consulted during the drafting of the report and although he did not have much interest in its technicalities, he told Beveridge that he was 'wildly enthusiastic' about his social security proposals which were not only constructive but affordable (Skidelsky, 2000, p. 267). Other economists working in the government at the time, notably James Meade, agreed and supported Beveridge's contention that economic progress was impeded by the five giants of Want, Disease, Ignorance, Squalor and Idleness. The giants had a negative effect on the quality and productivity of the labour force and were a major impediment to sustained economic growth.

As Beveridge pointed out in a policy paper circulated among key government officials prior to the publication of the report, defeating the five giants would require the integration of social and economic policy. In particular, Beveridge insisted that his social security proposals would only be effective if combined with measures designed to promote full employment. These ideas were articulated in his subsequent work on employment policy (Beveridge, 1944). He was also determined that social security benefits should not have adverse work incentives and for this reason proposed the introduction of universal, tax-funded child allowances. Unlike means-tested benefits, universal child allowances would not trap low-income families in welfare dependency. He also urged the introduction of comprehensive health care and educational programmes. Both would improve the health, knowledge and skills of the labour force and, in this way, enhance economic efficiency. Although health, education, housing and other pertinent social issues were not the main focus of the report, Beveridge's proposals complemented the major policy innovations in health, education and housing that were introduced during and after the war. They gave expression to the idea that social security should support an employment-based development strategy, improve labour force quality and protect workers against the contingencies of industrialization.

As noted earlier, social security was not generally regarded as an adjunct to economic development in the newly independent developing countries, but rather as indicative of the state's commitment to modernize economic, social and political institutions (Midgley, 1984). Although modernization would serve economic objectives, social security programmes were not well integrated with economic development policies at the time. In addition, social security programmes had a relatively small economic impact, because they covered only a small proportion of the population. Social insurance was limited to the comparatively few workers who were in regular wage employment, and social assistance was generally confined to providing meagre benefits to the urban destitute. Although it was believed that a fully funded social insurance programme could complement economic policy by mobilizing capital for development, a careful study of social insurance programmes in a number of developing countries found that the contribution of these programmes to capital formation had been decidedly mixed (Revilgio, 1967). On the other hand, provident funds obviously contributed to capital mobilization, but here again their coverage was also small and of dubious relevance. The major exception was Singapore where the government not only succeeded in covering most of the population but also effectively used its provident fund to mobilize capital for industrialization (Sherraden, 1997). In addition, the fund was also used to control wages and depress inflationary pressures (Vasoo and Lee, 2001).

One example of the use of social security for economic purposes is crop insurance. In the developing countries, crop insurance is specifically intended to serve these purposes, although of course, it also functions to ensure the well-being of farming families by reducing the risks associated with agricultural production. Designed specifically to protect small farmers, 29 countries had established programmes of this kind by the 1980s (United Nations, 1981). Losses caused by natural disasters are often costly and may totally destroy the livelihood of small farmers. However, crop damage not only has a negative effect on the incomes and welfare of these farming families but also, if widespread, has severe consequences for a country's agricultural production. These economic effects are often long-lasting and it may take years before production levels are restored. By insuring farmers against the costs of disasters, governments facilitate an expeditious return to productive economic activity and thus sustain national agricultural output. In this way, crop insurance is not only a welfare measure but also serves obvious economic purposes.

Another example of the use of social policy for economic purposes is Denmark's 'flexicurity' approach which was introduced in the early 1990s by the country's social democratic government to respond to sagging economic growth rates and rising unemployment. The government responded by significantly easing labour regulations such as facilitating the hiring of workers, permitting greater use of part time and temporary employment, and more readily allowing the termination of workers . However, to accompany this more flexible labour policy, the government strengthened unemployment insurance and other social programmes to ensure that income was maintained during periods of unemployment and that workers are provided with a range of supports as well as job placement and retraining services. These programmes maintain workers' livelihoods and help them to find gainful employment. Unemployment benefits are paid at 90 per cent of termination wages and are maintained for a period of up to four years provided that the worker participates in job placement and training programmes. The country's former Prime Minister Poul Nyrup Rasmussen (2007) claims that these policies have worked, reducing unemployment from 13 per cent in 1994 to less than 4 per cent by the end of the decade. By this time, average annual growth rates of 5 per cent were being recorded, and the country's economy was ranked as one of the most competitive in the world. Nevertheless, Denmark maintains high levels of social spending, and it also has comprehensive social welfare, educational and other social programmes. The Danish experience, he contends, shows that it is possible to have a dynamic, open economy supported by comprehensive social welfare and income protection programmes. Social security, he points out, can play a major role in a dynamic, high-growth economy that also maximizes the well-being of the population.

Of course, many social policy scholars have long maintained that the use of social policy to support economic objectives amounts to little more than the perpetuation of capitalism, support for the accumulation of profits by corporate and other elites and the heightening of inequalities. Although workers may benefit from social programmes introduced to support capitalist economic development, their long-term interests are hardly served by a system designed to enrich those who already have power and wealth. This was a common theme in social policy writing in the 1970s and 1980s when Marxist social policy scholars attacked the social democratic 'welfare state' approach to social policy for achieving little except to legitimize capitalism and perpetuate the exploitation of workers (Ginsberg, 1979; Gough, 1979; O'Connor, 1973; Offe, 1984).

Despite the close link that emerged between social security and economic policy in the middle decades of the twentieth century, it weakened during the post-war years as social welfare programmes expanded and consumed an increasing share of public resources. The fiscal significance of the welfare sector and its growing political importance undermined the notion that social security would support economic initiatives and play an adjunct role to economic development. Instead, social security acquired greater autonomy and emerged as a major, independent social institution that would be legitimated not on economic grounds but on its own terms. As social security expanded and consumed a large proportion of public revenues in the Western countries, the issue was not whether social security would serve economic objectives but whether the economy could generate the resources needed to maintain the social security system. By the 1980s, this issue dominated debates about the relationship between social security and economic development. At this time, however, the view that social security should support economic policy was challenged by scholars who rejected the argument that social security should be linked to economic development and legitimated in terms of economic criteria. As their ideas became ascendant, the issues became even more complicated.

Social security as delinked from the economy

As was mentioned earlier, the view that social security gives expression to society's collective conscience and compassionate commitments has been popular in academic social policy circles, particularly in Europe. Proponents of this approach believe that social security is rooted in deeply held non-economic, humanitarian values and should not be used to serve economic policy objectives. Governments, they believe, should not use social security programmes to promote economic development, or indeed other ulterior goals, but should instead provide benefits solely on the basis of meeting social needs.

This idea reflects the well-established religious and charitable traditions found in many cultures. Almsgiving is practised in most of the world's great religions including Buddhism, Judaism, Islam and Christianity. The virtues of charitable giving were articulated with particular effect in Franciscan teaching which exemplifies the ideals of compassionate giving and now exert a powerful influence not only among Catholics but Protestants as well. Charitable beliefs subsequently found expression in Christian socialism in the nineteenth century, where they fused with the Marxist view that social need should be the overriding criterion for the disbursement of income benefits and welfare services.

Interpretations of the reasons for the expansion of social welfare programmes in the twentieth century have also emphasized the role of altruism and compassion. During the post-Second World War decades, scholars often claimed that the modern social welfare programmes emerged because of the humanitarian concerns that citizens have for the less fortunate and that the 'welfare state' represents the highest form of charitable giving (Breul and Diner, 1980; Morris, 1986; Prigmore and Atherton, 1979). This 'social conscience' explanation of the origins of modern-day social welfare has, as Baker (1979) pointed out, been a popular theme in the social policy literature.

T. H. Marshall was an influential proponent of the idea that social policy should be based on non-economic motives, but he made little reference to the role of altruistic giving in social policy and instead offered a legalistic, rights-based rationale for welfare provision. In a series of lectures given at the University of Cambridge after the Second World War, Marshall (1950) observed that history had been characterized by a long and arduous struggle to secure human rights. This struggle had resulted in major gains including the recognition that people had the right to participate in the political process as well as rights against the arbitrary exercise of state power. Subsequently, the struggle for political and civil rights was augmented by the struggle for social rights and, by the mid-twentieth century, the governments of many Western liberal democracies had accepted that all citizens were entitled to social security benefits as of right. This was in keeping with the commitment at the time to extend human rights throughout the world. The adoption of the United Nations Universal Declaration on Human Rights in 1948 and other human rights conventions and treaties gave impetus to these efforts. Human rights, Marshall argued, would be fulfilled when it was recognized that social needs should not be met on the basis of market participation, political loyalty, conformity to cultural and social expectations or any other requirements but exclusively on the basis of the rights enshrined in citizenship.

Richard Titmuss (1971, 1974) was one of the most eloquent exponents of the role of altruism in social welfare. He argued that social security benefits should be provided exclusively on the basis of need and that social security and other forms of welfare provision should be regarded as the collective expression of society's altruism and concern for its members. He believed that the desire to care for others is deeply rooted in human nature. In simpler, agrarian times, instinctive altruism was expressed through the extended network of kin and community relationships and through local religious institutions. Since it is difficult to utilize these traditional caring institutions in modern, industrial societies, Titmuss believed that altruism is best discharged through the agency of the state. Despite its imperfections, the state is the most efficient institution for promoting people's welfare. However, political leaders should be mindful of the state's role as a moral agent and should be suspicious of the technicist tendency to base social policy decisions on rational decision-making criteria alone. Instead, they should emphasize social policy's wider values and social commitments. By ensuring that social security serves humanitarian and welfare goals, social security reinforces altruistic feelings and enhances social reciprocity and solidarity. In addition, it redistributes resources and promotes greater equality.

Titmuss was strongly opposed to the use of the market in social welfare. Although he believed that the market is an appropriate mechanism for distributing economic commodities, it was an inefficient way of allocating welfare resources. He devoted a good deal of effort to demonstrating the inefficiency of markets in social welfare and famously contrasted the distribution of blood through voluntary donation and commercial provision (Titmuss, 1971). His conclusion that the commercial distribution of blood, particularly in the United States, denied this life-giving necessity to those who could not pay, had a powerful moral impact even though it was hotly disputed by his detractors. Despite his frequent criticisms of the marketization of social programmes in the United States, his ideas were well received and provided a rationale for liberal American politicians advocating for the expansion of social security and other social programmes.

Titmuss vigorously rejected the argument that social welfare should serve economic purposes. He was highly critical of social policy in the Soviet Union and in some European countries where social security benefits were linked to work performance and meritocratic achievement. This undermined social security's true social and humanitarian purposes. Also, because the value of social insurance benefits was linked to income, they reinforced inequalities. For this reason, he urged that higher contributions be levied on those with higher incomes, but that flat-rate benefits be paid to all so that those in lower paid and onerous occupations were adequately rewarded. In his typology of different approaches to social policy, he criticized what he described as the industrial achievement-performance or 'handmaiden' model which posits that social needs should be met on the basis of merit, work performance and productivity (Titmuss, 1974). Since this model was based on economic theories about social security's role in creating incentives and supporting productivity, it undermined the moral basis of social welfare. Accordingly, it should be rejected.

Titmuss and Marshall's writing dominated social policy thinking for many years after the Second World War and subverted the economistic elements in New Deal and Beveridgian social policy. The argument that social security and the other social services should be provided solely on the basis of need and as of right was widely accepted well into the 1980s. Eventually, however, it was challenged by scholars on the political right, particularly in the United States. For example, Mead (1986) questioned the notion that social security benefits should be provided unconditionally, pointing out that rights obligate reciprocity and the fulfilment of duties. In the United States and other Western countries, those who receive benefits are expected to fulfil their obligations to society by behaving responsibly, conforming to social norms and seeking, if able, to work and secure an income for themselves and their families. Others such as Murray (1984) challenged the moral dimensions of Titmuss's argument observing that unconditional gift giving by the state had neither solved the problem of poverty nor created a more equal and solidaristic society. On the contrary, it had made things worse by producing an alienated underclass of poor people who depended on welfare and whose attitudes and behaviour undermined core social values.

These criticisms reflected a wider disenchantment with social assistance in the United States, Britain and other Western countries at the time. These programmes were widely believed to promote indolence and welfare dependency, particularly among immigrants and people of colour. Although they gathered some momentum in academic circles and dented the dominance of welfarist thinking, it was primarily in the policy world, and especially in the United States, where a significant shift in thinking emerged. President Reagan quoted Murray's work in his political campaigns, and Mead exerted considerable influence on the creation of American welfare-to-work programmes. His contention that benefit payments should be specifically linked to work performance was widely accepted and adopted in the welfare reform legislation of the mid-1990s. These initiatives replaced the needs- and rights-based approaches that traditionally characterized social assistance in the United States with a work-first model that required immediate job placement and work participation.

Although challenges to social security's humanitarian rationale have undoubtedly had a major impact, welfarist thinking has not been entirely eclipsed. The notion that social security should be delinked from economic considerations continues to be popular and, indeed, has been reinforced by Esping-Andersen's (1990) contention that social welfare should demodify labour by removing conditionalities on the provision of benefits. Proposals for a basic income to be paid unconditionally to all citizens irrespective of means, labour-force participation or other requirements have also been resurrected (Fitzpatrick, 1999; Standing, 2002; Van Parijs, 1992).

Social security as economically harmful

The argument that social security harms economic development is associated with the recently resurgent market liberal or neoliberal school of economics as it is more commonly known. However, as Eltis (1984) points out, contemporary neoliberalism has archaic origins, reflecting the ideas of the discipline's founders and particularly those of the Physiocrats, Adam Smith and David Ricardo. Central to their work is the belief that markets are the source of prosperity and that economies function most effectively when markets are competitive and driven by the investment and production decisions of entrepreneurs and the choices of consumers. The founders also believed that productive economic activities generate surpluses and, if correctly reinvested, will stimulate more growth and promote prosperity. If expropriated by the state and used for unproductive purposes, stagnation can be expected.

The core elements of classical economic liberalism have been resurrected in the writings of contemporary neoliberal and rational choice economists who have refined these ideas and made extensive use of mathematical modelling and empirical data to support their arguments. Although their accounts do not comprise a unified body of thought, they share a common disdain for state economic regulation and management. Rational choice economists have used complex game theories to demonstrate that individuals will inevitably pursue their own self-interests rather than engaging in collective action. Collective welfare efforts, they contend, will inevitably fail. Public choice theorists argue that politicians and bureaucrats will similarly pursue their own interests rather than those of the people they claim to serve. Rational choice and the natural pursuit of self-interest will inevitably nullify efforts to create collective social welfare programmes. Neoliberal economists have stressed the superiority of markets over the collective action and warned of the dangers of state intervention in the economy. Social welfare, they believe, should be left to individuals and families, faith-based and voluntary organizations and community support networks. In addition, leading neoliberal scholars such as von Hayek (1944) and Friedman (1962) have augmented the strictly economic aspects of neoliberalism by highlighting the political role of markets, and their claim that democratic institutions can only flourish in a market society has been widely accepted. Societies that seek to control the market will, as Hayek famously declared, inevitably travel down the road to totalitarianism.

These principles form the basis of contemporary economic critiques of social security which, as noted earlier, are a part of a wider set of complaints about social security's allegedly deleterious demographic, social and fiscal consequences. They also form a part of a wider attack on government social programmes and policy attempts to improve welfare conditions. It is common wisdom today that government social spending is a major cause of economic stagnation. Media as well as scholarly analyses of low rates of economic growth in Europe during the past 15 years invariably attribute a large part of the problem to generous welfare spending. European countries, it is claimed, spend far too much on social programmes and intervene excessively in the economy (Alesina and Gianvazzi, 2006). Similar conclusions were drawn when the British and American economies recorded low rates of economic growth and high levels of unemployment in the 1970s. Both Mrs Thatcher and President Reagan were able to persuade a sizable proportion of the electorate that economic stagnation was caused by profligate government spending and excessively generous welfare programmes.

In Britain, these ideas were formalized by Bacon and Eltis (1976) in their widely cited claim that Britain had too few producers. The British economy, they explained, had bifurcated into a shrinking productive or 'marketed' sector and an expanding unproductive state sector. They pointed out that social security is widely used by the state to transfer resources out of the productive economy to fund unproductive activities. As resources are transferred out of the marketed sector to the unproductive state sector, the economy will further decline. If these resources were instead allocated through the market, they would naturally gravitate towards the productive economic sector and generate the surpluses that can be reinvested to promote economic growth. Although they recognized that governments can mobilize social security resources for economic purposes such as stimulating consumption and mobilizing capital for productive investments, state managers are believed to be notoriously incompetent and unlikely to achieve this goal.

The argument that social security transfers resources from the productive to the unproductive sector applies to various types of social security. However, it is believed to be particularly relevant to social insurance in the Western industrial countries where the proportion of elderly people dependent on benefits continues to grow and now approaches 20 per cent of the population. In addition, social insurance and social assistance programmes in these countries pay benefits to the unemployed and those with disabilities who are also defined as 'unproductive'. To make matters worse, many European countries also provide universal social allowance in the form of child benefits. As a shrinking proportion of the working population supports an ever-growing number of unproductive people, market liberal scholars predict that economic output will be further retarded.

A somewhat different but equally pessimistic analysis was offered by Okun (1975) who used the insights of rational choice theory to emphasize the incompatibility of market efficiency and democratic egalitarianism. Although markets require inequality to function efficiently and produce high rates of economic growth, democratic politics will result in demands for greater equality. Egalitarian welfare programmes are inevitably in conflict with economic objectives, and governments must struggle to find a balance between the need for economic growth and popular demands for social programmes. However, governments seldom manage to balance the trade-off between growth and welfare, and by giving in to demands for ever increasing social spending, they sacrifice the economic dynamism needed to create prosperity for all.

Similarly, many neoliberal commentators have argued that when governments provide generous social security benefits, incentives to work hard, save and act responsibly are undermined. The issue of social security's negative impact on work incentives is, of course, an old one forming a key element in early-nineteenth-century debates about the role of the Poor Law in fostering indolence and other undesirable behaviours. It was for this reason that the 1834 Poor Law reforms in England imposed harsh conditionalities on claimants and that sympathetic although often moralistic charities emerged to give relief to the 'deserving' poor. The argument that the poor will invariably prefer to receive social security benefits rather than work has frequently been resurrected since then. More recently, Gilder (1981) claimed that the poor needed the 'spur' of poverty to compel them to work, and Mead (1992, 1997) has urged the adoption of strict paternalistic policies that will require poor people to work.

Although the negative effects of social assistance and social insurance on work incentives has been a perennial issue ever since, it has taken different forms in different places at different times. In many European countries, social insurance is often blamed for paying generous benefits to the unemployed and for encouraging workers to take early retirement. In the United States, on the other hand, little attention is paid to the disincentive effects of unemployment insurance and instead social assistance programmes, which are known as 'welfare', are widely condemned for their allegedly deleterious impact on work incentives. The case against social assistance in the United States has been directed primarily at single women with children and has been not too subtly linked to issues of race. When President Reagan famously caricatured the typical social assistance recipient as a 'welfare queen', the insinuation was widely understood. As noted earlier, similar messages are communicated about social assistance recipients in European countries where media reports focus on the abuses committed by allegedly parasitical immigrants who, it is often claimed, have an incentive to migrate because of the generosity and availability of social security benefits. In Europe, attention is also focused on young men who drop out of school and apparently live comfortably on social security benefits. These images have powerfully reinforced the argument that social security dampens work incentives and underwrites indolence.

Critics of social security have argued that media reports about social-security abuse understate the seriousness of the problem. They do not reveal the extent to which claimants are able to access multiple social security programmes which, in the aggregate, provide a very comfortable income. For example, it is claimed that in the United States, social assistance beneficiaries not only receive a cash payment but also are eligible for food vouchers known as food stamps, free school meals, medical assistance and housing benefits. In the mid-1990s, the total value of these benefits often exceeded the minimum wage, and in some states, such as Hawaii, where generous benefits are paid, claimants earned as much as $27, 700 per annum (Payne, 1998). Besharov's (1995) study showed that while a typical unwed mother would earn approximately $15,500 from regular employment, she would receive a total of about $17,400 in social assistance benefits if she chose not to work. These studies provide empirical support for Murray's (1984) widely cited case example of a hypothetical couple named Harold and Phyllis who came to the conclusion, after a careful calculation, that they would be better off if they stopped working and drew benefits instead.

In addition, Murray (1984) argued, social security programmes foster unsocial behaviours that involve high social as well as economic costs. Generous social assistance benefits may be intended to alleviate poverty, but they encourage worklessness as well as illegitimacy, crime, drug taking and other undesirable behaviours. The costs to society through increased law enforcement, correctional services and remedial education is immense. The costs of wasted lives, missed educational opportunities and welfare dependency found among the underclass are also huge. The effects of these costs have been stressed by many scholars but particularly by Mead (1992), who contends that worklessness is one of the most serious social problems in the United States.

Another problem is the negative effects of social insurance on savings and capital mobilization. Because readily accessible capital fosters investment and economic growth, governments should obviously adopt polices that encourage domestic capital accumulation. Although investment capital can be obtained internationally, it is obviously preferable for firms to utilize domestic capital. One of the aims of capital mobilization policy is to encourage personal savings. This can be done not only by creating savings incentives but also by removing disincentives to save. One of the disincentives of this kind is social security which retards the propensity to save. Since people are assured of a state retirement pension, they have no incentive to save and the supply of domestic investment capital is accordingly reduced. The link between social insurance and a low-savings rate was first demonstrated by Feldstein (1974), who estimated that the American social security system had significantly impeded domestic capital formation with adverse economic consequences.

A related concern is social security's role in fostering consumption and fuelling inflation. By transferring resources from those engaged in productive economic activities to those who are unproductive, consumption increases and exerts inflationary pressures. Of course, Keynesian theory is based on a diametrically different set of assumptions contending that it is economically beneficial to stimulate demand for goods and services. This was one reason why Keynesian economists supported the expansion of social security in the middle decades of the twentieth century and why demand management formed a key element of post-war economic policy. However, the emergence of stagflation in the 1970s confounded this approach and, following the popularization of monetarism in the 1980s, economic policy has been characterized by an almost obsessive preoccupation with inflation management. Of course, price inflation is only one aspect of the problem and, during the 1970s, controlling wage inflation became a major policy objective. Here too, social security is accused of exacerbating matters. Since social security taxes reduce disposable income, they are accused of playing a significant contributory role in fuelling worker demand for higher wages. Social security also reinforces the expectation that governments will meet income and other social needs. These expectations create electoral pressures that politicians are unable to resist and contribute to the inexorable growth of an already bloated public sector which requires punitive tax increases that stifle entrepreneurship and economic development.

Neoliberals often claim that social security distorts labour markets. By fostering worklessness, social security limits the supply of labour needed for a productive and efficient economy. Social security also raises the costs of labour and inhibits the expansion of employment opportunities. However well-intentioned, government policies designed to stimulate employment or to protect workers from exploitation usually have the opposite effect. These policies distort the natural, smooth workings of the labour market, impose excessive costs on employers and have a negative impact on employment. Since productive employment is the most effective way of raising standards of living, policies that retard employment opportunities and hamper the effective utilization of labour are extremely harmful.

Labour distortions are also said to affect productivity within commercial enterprises. Since workers know that they are protected by labour regulations and cannot be easily dismissed, they have little incentive to work hard. This situation is exacerbated by the fact that workers are covered by a generous social security system which protects them if they are dismissed. In addition, social security has perverse incentives such as encouraging unproductive union activities and strikes. They whet appetites for even more generous benefits and, by maintaining the incomes of striking workers, impede efforts to resolve grievances. Another cause of labour market distortion is the way social security programmes reduce labour mobility. A dynamic economy requires a highly flexible and mobile labour force that responds to market opportunities and the needs of employers for workers with particular knowledge and skills. Generous benefits provided through employer mandates are likely to deter workers from seeking new opportunities that may have positive long-term benefits not only for themselves and their families but also for the economy as a whole. A lack of mobility and flexibility, it is argued, contributes to economic stagnation.

While social insurance and social assistance programmes are believed to interfere with the spontaneous functioning of the labour market, employer mandates are said to have the most direct and pernicious impact. Employer mandates require firms to provide a variety of costly services and benefits to their workers. Corporations in many parts of the world are required by law to provide benefits to those who are injured at work, or to grant sickness or maternity leave or to pay severance benefits to those who are invalided, dismissed or made redundant. In some cases, such as work injury, governments have created funding mechanisms that ease the costs of these programmes but in many other cases, such as sickness or maternity leave, employers are not compensated. In addition to these more conventional social security mandates, governments have imposed other requirements on employers that raise labour costs and distort labour markets. These include minimum wage payments, ergonomic and environmental safety requirements and a host of regulations relating to the recruitment, appointment and termination of employees. To make matters worse, employers are required to use their own resources to administer these programmes and to defend themselves when charges of non-compliance are levied. These costs are exacerbated by the contributions that employers are required to make to social insurance payroll taxes when corporate taxes in many countries are already prohibitively high and deter investment. The overall costs of these mandates have risen steadily and, many believe, are now unsustainable, particularly in Europe where economic stagnation is said to be endemic (Alesina and Gianvazzi, 2006).

Social security is also believed to contribute to unemployment. As the governments of the Western countries have imposed higher costs on employers through mandates and payroll tax contributions, many firms have sought to reduce the number of workers they employ either through using labour replacement technologies or through relocating or outsourcing production to other countries where labour costs are lower. Although unemployment is often attributed to globalization, market liberals point out that rigid labour regulations, high taxes and costly mandates within the Western industrial nations are also to blame. Commercial enterprises would have no desire to relocate abroad or out-source production if governments refrained from making it unprofitable for them to do business. This requires the relaxation of employment and labour regulations and reductions in taxation. On the other hand, it should be noted that many corporations have welcomed the expansion of government income protection programmes that do not impose requirements on them or negatively affect their profitability. For example, as the costs of providing non-mandated health, retirement and other occupational benefits in the United States have increased, impeding the competitiveness of large corporations, calls for governments to assume responsibility for health and retirement obligations have become more common.

However, policy proposals to address the economic problems allegedly caused by social security have generally stressed the need to reduce government involvement and replace current social security programmes with commercial provisions. Because government spending and economic decline are believed to be highly correlated, the reduction of public spending became an overriding policy objective for many Western governments in the 1980s. The governments of many developing countries also sought to reduce spending, often at the behest of the International Monetary Fund and the World Bank, which required major retrenchments in public expenditures as a condition for aid. However, despite pursuing these policy objectives, public spending in the Western industrial countries has remained high. This is true even in the United States where policymakers have often stressed the need to shrink the public sector.

However, the argument that governments' social spending harms economic growth has been challenged on numerous occasions, and a great deal of empirical evidence has been collected to show that there is no inevitable trade-off, as Okun (1975) claimed, between social welfare and economic development. As Mares (2007) shows in her extremely thorough summary of many research studies, there is little solid comparative evidence to support the argument that social spending has a negative effect on economic growth. Indeed, several studies found a positive relationship suggesting that increased government spending fosters growth. Many other arguments presented by neoliberal and rational choice scholars have also been challenged. For example, the claim that social security harms work incentives and creates dependency has been challenged by Piachaud (1997), while the contention that social insurance deters savings and prevents capital accumulation, has been questioned by numerous researchers. Summarizing this research, Butare (1994) found little evidence to support Feldstein's (1974) claim that social insurance schemes have depressed savings and lowered the availability of investment capital. The frequent criticism that European governments interfere excessively in the economy and provide generous but ruinous social programmes has also been refuted. The example of Denmark cited earlier and the chapter on Norway (Chapter 8) in this book question the assumption that there is an irreconcilable trade-off between growth and social welfare. Numerous studies have claimed that policies designed to enhance economic competitiveness, growth and full employment are, in fact, facilitated by social programmes that create security, promotes employment and invest in the capacities of people to participate in the productive economy (Cichon and Hagemejer, 2007). In fact, research by Galbraith and his colleagues (1999, 2007) has reached the conclusion that European and other countries wishing to promote economic development should not adopt American-style neoliberalism.

Social security as an economic investment

The New Deal and Beveridgian view that social security policy should be integrated with economic policy and support economic objectives has been augmented by the claim that social security programmes can and should function as investments that contribute to economic development. This claim obviously challenges the arguments of social security's neoliberal opponents. It also appears to be counter intuitive. In the industrial countries, social security is funded by taxes levied primarily on workers in wage employment which are then transferred to those who are not in employment, particularly the elderly, to support or maintain their income and meet their needs for food, shelter, clothing and other consumable goods and services. Social security is by its very nature designed to meet consumption rather than investment goals.

Although proponents of the social investment approach do not disagree that social security plays a major role in maintaining consumption, they point out that consumption is an important element in economic development. They also note that the distinction between consumption, production and investment is not as clear-cut as many believe. For example, it is an elementary economic principle that increased consumption creates demand which in turn stimulates production. Similarly, increased production creates new investment opportunities. Although dictionary definitions make a clear distinction between consumption, production and investment, they are closely interlinked and complementary.

As was shown earlier, social security has been used in the past to complement economic development policies by fostering consumption. This was an important policy objective of New Deal and Keynesian economic thinking. Although social security was not regarded as a primary mechanism for stimulating demand, it was believed that it would support the massive public works programmes introduced for this purpose (Leighninger, 2007). It would also have positive economic consequences by enhancing the quality of the labour force and creating employment security. Beveridge's proposals were strongly committed to this goal. Although the effects of these policies have been hotly disputed, Keynesian interventionism has since become unpopular particularly on the ground that the injection of resources into the economy without commensurate increases in production fuels inflation. As noted earlier, Friedman's theoretical insights and the experience of stagflation in the 1970s severely dented the Keynesian approach. Nevertheless, many economists continue to believe that governments can judiciously manipulate the economy and various techniques ranging from tax cuts to interest-rate adjustments are currently used for this purpose even in economies that are heavily influenced by neoliberal ideas.

It is in this context that some social policy scholars believe that social security policies can be explicitly designed or reconfigured to function as investments that generate both private and public rates of return and contribute positively to economic development. Drawing inspiration from a body of thought, known variously as social development, developmental social policy or welfare developmentalism, proponents of this approach urge governments to play a proactive role in shaping social and economic policy, harmonizing economic and social policies, and giving priority to social programmes that promote participation in the productive economy and demonstrably generate social rates of returns. These arguments have been extensively informed by the experiences of

developing countries, which sought to develop innovative social programmes that complement economic development policies and contribute to efforts to raise standards of living (Midgley, 1995). Although
social development is a largely 'Third Worldist' approach to social policy, it has attracted growing attention in the industrial countries, particularly as a result of the United Nations World Summit for Social
Development which was held in Copenhagen in 1995 and the subsequent adoption of the United Nations Millennium Development Goals
(Midgley, 2003; United Nations, 1996, 2005).

Three principles guide welfare developmentalist thinking. First, they
urge that social and economic policy should be closely integrated and
organizational arrangements should be established at the national level
to ensure that this is achieved. Second, macroeconomic policies that
promote employment and raise standards of living for the population
as a whole should be given high priority. These policies should be 'people centered', participatory, focused on meeting basic needs and emphasize the goal of poverty eradication. Third, social welfare policies and
programmes, including social security, should be investment-oriented or
'productivist' by generating rates of return both to individuals and the
economy. Welfare developmentalists believe that there will always be a
need for remedial and maintenance oriented social welfare programmes,
but they should not dominate the social welfare system as is currently
the case but be focused on meeting the needs of those who cannot participate in the productive economy.

The importance of integrating these principles within a comprehensive development process is also emphasized by advocates of the welfare
developmentalist approach. They are critical of attempts to implement
productivist social programmes in a vacuum and contend that these
programmes will be most effective when implemented within a macro
political economy framework committed to planned economic growth,
interventionism, participation, universalism and egalitarianism.
Although productivist social policies can obviously be deployed in all
social, political and economic environments, they function most effectively when the problems of inequality and distorted development are
purposefully addressed (Midgley, 1995, 1999).

Some types of social security are highly productivist in that they
accumulate resources that can be used for investment purposes. This is
obviously the case with provident funds. As was noted previously, the
government of Singapore has used the resources of the country's
provident fund to mobilize capital for economic development. However,
it has also used them for social purposes such as funding its massive

housing programme which, most experts believe, played a key role in the country's impressive record of economic development (Vasoo and Lee, 2001). The government also encourages the use of these funds to meet education and health needs and, in this way, it has sought to enhance human capital and the quality of the labour force.

Although the Singaporean experience offers useful lessons for other countries, it should not be assumed that mandatory retirement savings accounts automatically have positive investment implications. As noted earlier, provident funds in many countries have remained small and governments have not effectively used them for development purposes. The experience of Chile, which replaced its social insurance programme with commercially managed individual retirement accounts in 1981, also demonstrates the limitations of this approach. Although the Chilean funds have indeed mobilized sizable amounts of capital for investment, the transition costs have created a significant economic burden. Borzutsky (2001) reports that the costs of privatization produced a deficit of 3.8 per cent of GDP in 1981, which grew to 6.1 per cent of GDP in 2000. The deficit is funded from public borrowing which has reached very high levels. In addition, there is a good deal of information to show that the programme's welfare effects have been mixed. Many workers are unable to accumulate sufficient funds to meet their retirement needs and many rely on supplementary social assistance payments. In addition, contribution avoidance is widespread with the result that many workers will rely on social assistance to meet their retirement needs in the future, imposing continued costs on the public sector (Borzutsky, 2002).

Another type of social security programme with a strong social investment effect is the Individual Development Account or IDA. As was noted earlier in this book, IDAs are savings accounts that are matched by governments or non-profit agencies. Participation is voluntary and the match is intended to create a savings incentive. Although these accounts can function like provident funds and be used to accumulate funds for retirement, most IDA projects are designed to support short-term savings, and participants normally save for periods ranging from one to four years. Accumulated funds are usually used for education, job training, home ownership and the establishment of micro-enterprises.

An evaluation of a demonstration project in the United States designed to test the effectiveness of the IDA approach found that the project's 1,326 participants had saved almost $380,000 and this amount had been matched by about $740,000 making a total of $1,120, 000 or a per capita accumulation of about $845 (Sherraden, 2001). Participants saved an average of $33 per month and the median length of participation was nine months. About two thirds had contributed regularly and more than 70 per cent were meeting their savings goals. Ninety-two per cent of the participants had made approved withdrawals of which a third were to finance small business start-ups, 27 per cent for home purchases, 20 per cent for home repairs and 13 per cent for education. Although some will regard the amounts saved as meagre and of limited consequence, the demonstration project reveals that people with low incomes can indeed accumulate assets which can be used as investments if incentives and matches are provided. Sherraden and other advocates of IDA accounts believe that these accounts are more effective than traditional income maintenance schemes such as social assistance that maintain poor people at basic subsistence levels and do little to promote self-sufficiency (Shapiro, 2001; Sherraden, 1991).

Although social assistance programmes have been widely criticized for fostering consumption, creating worklessness and harming economic development, they can also be used to foster investments and promote economic development. Indeed, growing evidence about their developmental impact has recently been collected. Some governments have expanded social assistance to complement wider economic development programmes by using these programmes to inject resources into poor communities to increase consumption and reduce poverty. This was the case in South Africa after the Mandela government came to power in 1994 (Patel, 2005). Under the apartheid regime, the programme had been used primarily to pay means-tested retirement benefits to elderly white and mixed race people, and many elderly African people were excluded. Those who were able to participate received meagre benefits. Following a major review of the programme, the government equalized benefits and initiated a major drive to expand the programme to cover more poor elderly Africans, and particularly to those living in the countryside. Since most of these elderly people live in extended families, pension payments are not hoarded but circulated within the household. By expanding the programme, and injecting resources into the household economy, the incomes of poor families have increased. Their nutritional status and housing conditions have also improved. As a result of higher family incomes, children are also sent to school regularly with positive implications for human capital formation (Edmonds, 2006). Studies have shown that the programme has not only reduced the incidence of poverty but stimulated the local economy particularly in rural areas (Johnson and Williams, 2006).

Social assistance has also been purposefully used to enhance human capital investment and, in this way, it contributes to economic development. This is the case in several Latin American countries where, Rawlings (2005) reports, conditional cash transfer programmes, as they are known, have been redesigned to pay benefits to poor families on condition that children attend school regularly. The Mexican government's *Opportunidades* scheme, which was established in 1997, is one of the largest programmes of this kind. It targets poor households with children between the ages of eight to eighteen years who are enrolled in primary or secondary schools. It pays a cash benefit as well as providing support for books and educational materials. The programme also provides a nutritional cash benefit to poor families with young children and to pregnant and lactating mothers (Levy, 2006). Another well-publicized conditional social assistance programme is Brazil's *Bolsa escola* (or educational grant) scheme, established by President Fernando Henrique Cardoso, which has since been augmented by the *Bolsa família* scheme introduced by President Lula de Silva in 2003 (Silva, 2006). In addition to requiring regular school attendance, children must be immunized, and pregnant mothers must regularly attend prenatal clinics.

Rawlings reports that these programmes have raised school enrolments. In Mexico, enrolment increases are estimated to range from 7.2 per cent to 9.3 per cent for girls and from 3.5 per cent to 5.8 per cent for boys. In Nicaragua, a similar programme is reported to have increased primary enrolment rates by nearly 22 per cent, although here, the initial enrolment rate was significantly lower than in Mexico. In Brazil, the government plans to extend the programme to 11.2 million poor families by the end of 2006. By the end of 2005, approximately 8.7 million families had been covered at a total cost of more than US$3 billion. When the programme meets its target, all families with incomes below the official poverty line will be covered. In addition to improving educational and health conditions and thus the human capital needed for development, these programmes also inject resources into the household incomes of poor families and have a direct impact on poverty. In addition, they increase consumption and stimulate the local economy.

Although these data are impressive, the extent to which education, nutrition and health conditions among children actually improve depends on the quality of schools, health and other social services. It is widely agreed that much more needs to be done to enhance these programmes in low-income communities and particularly in rural areas. Another problem is that it is difficult to ensure compliance especially since school attendance among many poor families is often intermittent. This is often the case when children are needed to help with agricultural tasks or participate in the informal labour market to augment family income. Also, it should be noted that the cash benefit is generally small. Nevertheless, these programmes show that social assistance programmes can be reconfigured so that they do not merely pay meagre cash benefits to destitute people on a limited basis but function to alleviate poverty, enhance human capital formation, stimulate the local economy and play an important investment role.

Social insurance programmes can also be used for investment purposes. One example is crop insurance which was mentioned earlier. In addition to addressing the risks associated with agricultural production, crop insurance invests in agriculture by maintaining and enhancing production. A recent study in Tanzania elaborates on this argument by showing that crop losses have negative effects on school enrolments and human capital formation and impede economic development in agricultural communities (Beegle, Deheja and Gatti, 2006). Although children make a significant contribution to agricultural production in many parts of the Global South, farming families now increasingly send their children to school. By attending regularly, they increase their knowledge and skills and contribute to their country's future economic development. However, the study found that when crop losses occur, children are frequently removed from school. Child labour is typically substituted for adult labour as adults leave the farm to seek employment in the informal economy, particularly in the urban areas. The study found that school enrolments in the country's rural areas typically run at 70 per cent but that agricultural shocks reduce average enrolments to about 50 per cent. Although the majority of children will continue to attend school, attendance becomes much more intermittent. The authors contend that an effective crop insurance programme could prevent enrolment and human capital declines, both of which are inimical to economic development and play an important investment role in low-income rural communities.

Conclusion: policy implications

These different perspectives on the relationship between social security and economic development reveal that the debate cannot be reduced to a simple juxtapositioning of two points of view about the respective merits of market and state provision. This dichotomy clearly fails to capture the complexities of the issues. It is also clear that the different perspectives reviewed in this chapter have very different policy implications, particularly with regard to government involvement. While those who believe that social security harms economic development obviously favour minimal state intervention, the often repeated argument that governments should allow the market to function spontaneously belies the fact that neoliberals frequently advocate policy interventions that facilitate market activities. This is clear when the privatization of social security in Chile is examined. Despite the claim that the Chilean government successfully turned income protection over to commercial providers, and significantly reduced public expenditures, the government did not, in fact, abrogate its responsibility for social security. Instead, as Borzutsky (2001, 2002) has shown, it actively shaped the privatized system through legislative initiatives, meeting its transition costs and providing extensive subsidies. Today, it ensures that the country's privatized social security system functions effectively. It also underwrites the programme by maintaining a sizable and expensive social assistance programme to provide income benefits to those who have not accumulated insufficient funds in their retirement accounts. The costs to the taxpayer and the economy remain substantial.

The argument that governments should divorce social policy from economic issues and pay benefits solely on the basis of need or citizenship rights may be beguiling, but it fails to take account of the economic consequences of what are huge public expenditures. It is also questionable whether governments can ignore economic considerations in today's globalized world where economic issues are a critically important part of political discourse. This is not to reject the role of needs and rights in social security policy. Indeed, they can and should be incorporated into a comprehensive rationale for social security that also takes economic factors into account. This is particularly important at a time when the need to justify government spending and to demonstrate its effectiveness is being stressed.

As the country case studies in the remainder of this book will demonstrate, policy options that more effectively link social security to economic development are not based exclusively or dogmatically on normative conviction but reflect current realities, historical trends, ideological struggles and political compromises as well as demographic, cultural and social factors. Values and ideological beliefs need to be rooted in a pragmatic understanding of current realities and should be more effectively expressed within a wider pluralistic context in which the diverse contributions of different welfare agents and institutions are recognized. An approach of this kind is more likely to succeed in improving human well-being through harmonizing social security and economic development policies.

A pluralistic social policy approach also allows the insights of different perspectives to be coherently harmonized. Different types of social security programmes should be more effectively linked to other social programmes to maximize welfare outcomes. In some countries, commercially managed savings accounts have supplemented occupational and statutory retirement schemes, creating an effective multipillared mix of provision. Many reasonable analysts will agree that this is a more effective policy approach than one that dogmatically insists on the privatization of statutory programmes and their replacement with commercial provision. Similarly, social assistance programmes can be effectively linked to human capital and other interventions to enhance their contribution to economic development. Although welfare-to-work programmes are frequently criticized, they too can play a useful role if properly integrated into comprehensive income maintenance and economic development policies. It is also clear that asset savings accounts need not operate in isolation from other social security programmes. Indeed, they can complement social assistance and social insurance schemes and provide opportunities for people on low incomes to accumulate funds that can be used for a variety of productive purposes.

Although the remaining chapters of this book reflect the policy insights of welfare pluralism, they nevertheless accord a vital role for the state in formulating comprehensive policies that shape social security programmes and harmonize different types of provision. It is hoped that these case studies will provide useful and interesting lessons for linking social security more effectively to economic development in the future and, in this way, maximize efforts to raise standards of living and improve social conditions for all.

References

Alesina, A. and Giavazzi, F. (2006). *The Future of Europe: Reform or Decline*. Cambridge, MA: MIT Press.

Bacon, R. and Eltis, W. (1976). *Britain's Economic Problems: Too Few Producers*. London: Macmillan.

Baker, J. (1979). 'Social Conscience and Social Policy', *Journal of Social Policy*, 8 (2), 177–206.

Beegle, K., Rajeev, D. and Gatti, R. (2006). 'Child Labor and Agricultural Shocks', *World Bank Research Digest*, 1 (1), 5.

Besharov, D. (1995) 'Using Work to Reform Welfare', *Public Welfare*, 53 (3), 7–16.

Beveridge, W. (1944). *Full Employment in a Free Society*. London: Allen and Unwin.

Borzutsky, S. (2001). 'Chile: Has Social Security Privatization Fostered Economic Development?' *International Journal of Social Welfare*, 10 (4), 294–299.

Borzutzky, S. (2002). *Vital Connections: Politics, Social Security and Inequality in Chile*. Notre Dame, IN: Notre Dame University Press.

Breul, F. and Diner, S. (eds) (1980). *Compassion and Responsibility: Readings in the History of Social Welfare Policy in the United States*. Chicago: University of Chicago Press.

Bruce, B. T. (1961). *The Coming of the Welfare State*. London: Batsford.

Butare, T. (1994). 'International Comparison of Social Security and Retirement Funds from the National Savings Perspective', *International Social Security Review*, 47 (2), 17–36.

Cichon, M. and Hagemejer, K. (2007). 'Changing the Development Policy Paradigm: Investing in a Social Security for All', *International Social Security Review*, 60 (2/3), 169–196.

de Schweinitz, K. (1943). *England's Road to Social Security*. Philadelphia: University of Pennsylvania Press.

Edmonds, E. V. (2006). 'Child Labor and Schooling Responses to Anticipated Income in South Africa', *Journal of Development Economics*, 81 (2), 386–414.

Eltis, W. (1984). *The Classical Theory of Economic Growth*. London: Macmillan.

Esping-Andersen, G. (1990). *Three Worlds of Welfare Capitalism*. Cambridge: Polity Press.

Feldstein, M. B. (1974). *Social Security and Private Savings*. Cambridge, MA: Harvard University Institute of Economic Research.

Fitzpatrick, T. (1999). *Freedom and Security: An Introduction to the Basic Income Debate*. New York: Palgrave Macmillan.

Friedman, M. (1962). *Capitalism and Freedom*. Chicago: University of Chicago Press.

Galbraith, J. K. (2007). *Maastricht 2042 and the Fate of Europe: Towards Convergence and Full Employment*. Annandale-on-Hudson, NY: Levy Economics Institute of Bard College.

Galbraith, J. K., Conceicao, P. and Ferreira, P. (1999). 'Inequality and Unemployment in Europe: The American Cure', *New Left Review*, 237 (1), 28–51.

Gilder, G. (1981). *Wealth and Poverty*. New York: Basic Books.

Ginsberg, N. (1979). *Class, Capital and Social Policy*. London: Macmillan.

Gough, I. (1979). *The Political Economy of the Welfare State*. London: Macmillan.

Hayek, F. von (1944). *The Road to Serfdom*. London: Routledge & Kegan Paul.

Johnson, J. K. M. and Williamson, J. B. (2006). 'Do Universal Non-contributory Old Age Pensions Make Sense for Rural Areas in Low-income Countries?' *International Social Security Review*, 59 (4), 47–90.

Leighninger, R. D. (2007). *Long Range Public Investment: The Forgotten Legacy of the New Deal*. Columbia, SC: University of South Carolina Press.

Leuchtenburg, W. (1963). *Franklin D. Roosevelt and the New Deal*. New York: Harper and Row.

Levy, S. (2006). *Progress against Poverty: Sustaining Mexico's Progresa-Opportunidades Program*. Washington, DC: Brookings Institution Press.

Mares, I. (2007). The Economic Consequences on the Welfare State', *International Social Security Review*, 60 (2/3), 65–82.

Marshall, T. H. (1950). *Citizenship and Other Essays*. Cambridge: Cambridge University Press.

Mead, L. M. (1986). *Beyond Entitlement: The Social Obligations of Citizenship*. New York: Free Press.

Mead, L. M. (1992). *The New Politics of Poverty: The Nonworking Poor in America*. New York: Basic Books.

Mead, L. (ed.) (1997). *The New Paternalism: Supervisory Approaches to Poverty*. Washington, DC: Brookings Institution Press.

Midgley, J. (1984). *Social Security, Inequality and the Third World*. New York: Wiley.

Midgley, J. (1995). *Social Development: The Developmental Perspective in Social Welfare*. London: Sage.

Midgley, J. (1999). 'Growth, Redistribution and Welfare: Towards Social Investment', *Social Service Review*, 77 (1), 3–21.

Midgley, J. (2003). 'Social Development: The Intellectual Heritage', *Journal of International Development*, 15 (7), 831–844.

Morris, R. (1986). *Rethinking Social Welfare*. New York: Longman.

Murray, C. (1984). *Losing Ground: American Social Policy, 1950–1980*. New York: Basic Books.

O'Connor, J. (1973). *The Fiscal Crisis of the State*. New York: St. Martin' Press.

Offe, C. (1984). *Contradictions of the Welfare State*. Cambridge, MA: MIT Press.

Okun, A. (1975). *Equality and Efficiency: The Big Trade-off*. Washington DC: Brookings Institution.

Patel, L. (2005). *Social Welfare and Social Development in South Africa*. Johannesburg: Oxford University Press.

Payne, J. L. (1998). *Overcoming Welfare: Expecting More from the Poor and from Ourselves*. New York: Basic Books.

Piachaud, D. (1997). 'Social Security and Dependence', *International Social Security Review*, 50 (1), 41–55.

Prigmore, C. S. and Atherton, C. R. (1979). *Social Welfare Policy: Analysis and Formulation*. Lexington, KY: Heath.

Rasmussen, P. N. (2007). 'The Danish Model of Flexicurity', *The Magazine*, American Association of Retired People (AARP, April 2007, p. 3).

Rawlings, L. B. (2005). A New Approach to Social Assistance: Latin America's Experience with Conditional Cash Transfer Programmes', *International Social Security Review*, 58 (2/3), 133–162.

Reviglio, F. (1967). *Social Security: A Means of Savings Mobilization for Economic Development*. Wshington DC: International Monetary Fund Staff Papers.

Rimlinger, G. (1971). *Welfare Policy and Industrialization in Europe, America and Russia*. New York: Wiley.

Shapiro, T. M. (2001). 'The Importance of Assets.' In T. M. Shapiro and E. N. Wolff (eds), *Assets for the Poor: The Benefits of Spreading Asset Ownership*. New York: Russell Sage Foundation, pp. 11–33.

Sherraden, M. (1991). *Assets and the Poor: A New American Welfare Policy*. Armonk, NY: M. E. Sharpe.

Sherraden, M. (1997). 'Provident Funds and Social Protection: The Case of Singapore.' In J. Midgley and M. Sherraden (eds), *Alternatives to Social Security: An International Inquiry*. London: Auburn House, pp. 33–60.

Sherraden, M. (2001). 'Asset Building Policy and Programmes for the Poor.' In T. M. Shapiro and E. N. Wolff, (eds), *Assets for the Poor*. New York: Russell Sage Foundation, pp. 302–323.

Silva, M. O. da S. (2006). 'The Family Scholarship Programme: Unification of Income Transfer Programmes in Brazil's Social Protection System.' *Social Development Issues*. 28 (3), 101–114.

Skidelsky, R. (2000). *John Maynard Keynes Volume Three: Fighting for Britain 1937–1946*. London: Macmillan.

Standing, G. (2002). *Beyond the New Paternalism: Basic Security as Equality*. London: Verso.

Titmuss, R. M. (1971). *The Gift Relationship*. London: Allen and Unwin.

Titmuss R. M. (1974). *Social Policy: An Introduction*. London: Allen and Unwin.

United Kingdom (1942). Social Insurance and Allied Services: Report by Sir William Beveridge. HMSO, Cmnd 6404.

United Nations (1981). *Crop Insurance in Developing Countries*. New York.

United Nations (1996). *Report of the World Summit for Social Development: Copenhagen, 6–12 March 1995*. New York.

United Nations (2005). *Investing in Development: A Practical Plan to Achieve the Millennium Development Goals*. New York.

Van Parijs, P. (ed.) (1992). *Arguing for Basic Income: Ethical Foundations for a Radical Reform*. London: Verso.

Vasoo, L. and Lee, J. (2001). 'Singapore: Social Development, Housing and the Central Provident Fund', *International Journal of Social Welfare*, 10 (4), 276–283.

Part II
Diverse National Experiences

3
South Africa: Social Security, Poverty Alleviation and Development

Leila Patel and Jean Triegaardt

Since the inception of democracy in 1994, the social security system has been refashioned to meet the country's constitutional mandate to promote social and economic justice and to address the legacy of its apartheid past. In addition to addressing this country's legacy of inequality and discrimination, South Africa's tax funded, non-contributory social assistance programme has been reshaped specifically to reduce income poverty and promote social development. It is now widely recognized to be the government's most successful poverty reduction strategy. It has also been described as exceptional for a country of this level of development and in a global context where public welfare systems have been under political and economic pressure to curtail their growth (Seekings, 2002). The South African experience of using social assistance to create a more just society, reduce poverty and promote social and economic development is also regarded as a model for other countries, particularly in the Global South, to emulate.

Social security enjoys a high level of visibility in South Africa today, and it has strong political and public support with high uptake rates. While it is acknowledged that social security contributes significantly to poverty reduction, the exponential expenditure growth in real terms of the programme of about 70 per cent has drawn some criticism from opposition political parties, commentators and researchers about the rise of state welfare and its negative consequences for employment and savings, the fostering of dependency on the state and the creation of perverse incentives to become or remain eligible to the grants. At the same time, government is also under increasing pressure from civil society groups to expand the social security net to incorporate excluded groups such as the unemployed, to address mass poverty and inequality and the social costs associated with the growing HIV/AIDS pandemic. The nation's constitutional mandate to realize the right to social security and other social and economic rights also provides a powerful substantiation for the retention and the expansion of the system.

In this chapter, the authors use the South African experience to argue that social security constitutes an important investment which contributes substantially to the overall social goal of the society to reduce poverty and to promote economic development. The chapter is structured in three parts. It begins with an overview of the South African situation and shows how social security evolved over many years in the context of colonialism and apartheid and in a post-apartheid society. It then outlines the nature and scope of the social security system and attempts to reform the system in contemporary South Africa. Finally, it examines the inter-relationship between social security and economic development. The social and economic impact of social security is examined by drawing on recent empirical research focusing on the reduction in income poverty, its development impact and its labour market and macroeconomic effects.

The South African context

Colonialism and apartheid shaped the political, economic, legal, social, cultural and welfare system of the society. South Africa was a Dutch colony from the mid-seventeenth century to the early eighteenth century when the British acquired sovereignty over the Cape colony in 1814. Colonial administrators adapted the socio-economic organization of the colonies to their own interests with the primary aim of creating the conditions for economic development. The colonizers also aimed to 'civilize' the indigenous people and justified their racial superiority on religious grounds. These attitudes permeated social policies which were racially discriminatory and laid the foundation for a welfare system that favoured whites as a welfare elite for more than two centuries.

The Nationalist Party came to power in 1948 with support from Afrikaners and white workers and ruled the country for 46 years. They set about implementing their policy of apartheid which was founded on the principle of separate development for each race group; namely, Africans who were the majority of the population and other race groups that were in the minority, that is, coloureds who were people of mixed race, Indians who were of Asian origin and whites. Apartheid was a system of institutionalized racial discrimination and all economic, political and social policies were fashioned to give effect to this policy. Political resistance to apartheid was spearheaded by political parties formed in the first half of the century of which the African National Congress (ANC), the South African Communist Party (SACP) and the Pan African Congress were most notable. These organizations were banned and exiled in the 1960s as a result of repression by the state. Student and other mass opposition movements and trade unions emerged in the 1970s and 1980s culminating in the unbanning of political organizations in 1990 followed by a process of political negotiations which resulted in the adoption of an interim constitution and a national general election in 1994. The ANC in an alliance with the SACP and the Congress of South African Trade Unions won the first democratic election and two subsequent general elections. The ANC government led by former President Nelson Mandela commenced the process of dismantling the old and reconstructing a new democratic society.

The history of resistance characterized by opposition to colonialism and apartheid over many generations advocated the political, economic and human rights of all South Africans in a common society. This political tradition shaped the nature of the constitution, *The Constitution of the Republic of South Africa Act* (Act 108 of 1996), and post-apartheid policies and legislation. The constitution recognizes a common South African citizenship, universal adult suffrage, multiparty democracy, free press and judicial review of government. Civil and political rights, language and cultural rights, children's rights, the right to social security, education, health care, food, water and housing are among the social and economic rights upheld in the *Bill of Rights*. The right to equality is designed to protect or advance persons or categories of persons who were disadvantaged or discriminated against in the past on grounds of race, gender, age, disability or ethnic or social origin among others. The constitution in Section 36, however, makes provision for limitations to these rights to the extent that its implementation is reasonably practicable and justifiable in an open and democratic society. The right to access social assistance, health care, food and water is protected, but the *Bill of Rights* states that this right is subject to available resources and that the state should demonstrate that it is taking reasonable steps to realize this right progressively.

In addition to being a constitutional democracy, South Africa has a three-tier system of government and an independent judiciary. National, provincial and local levels of government have legislative and executive authority which is distinct although inter-related, and they are required by the constitution to govern in a cooperative manner. The ANC government's strategy for transformation, the *Reconstruction and Development Programme* (RDP), was adopted in 1994, and it focused on the provision of basic services, development of human resources, rebuilding of the economy and democratization of the state and society. The RDP under the direction of a Ministry without Portfolio faced numerous institutional challenges which impacted on its successful roll-out and resulted in waning public confidence in the programme. In 1997, the RDP Ministry and office was disestablished and its programmes were mainstreamed through government departments led by ministers responsible for their portfolios. The RDP office achieved great visibility for government's social goals. However, in the years following the closure of the RDP Ministry and office, the government's commitment to its social goals were constantly questioned, especially since its closure coincided with the adoption of the *Growth, Employment and Redistribution* (GEAR) policy in 1996. The GEAR strategy aimed to (a) integrate the economy into the regional and global economic system; (b) achieve an economic growth rate of 6 per cent; (c) create employment, reduce inflation and the budget deficit and (d) curtail fiscal expenditure. Amidst growing criticisms of the policy from the left, the government argued that these measures were necessary to address the long-term structural economic crisis that faced the South African economy and that the strategy could aid in ending international isolation and promote investor confidence. It was also envisaged that GEAR would stabilize the economy. Critics of the government's GEAR policy argued that government sacrificed its social goals for conservative neoliberal free market economic policies in response to pressures from the private sector and economic globalization. A tension was perceived to exist between the social and economic goals of the state and its macroeconomic vision (Patel, 2005).

During the first decade of democracy, economic growth rates averaged about 1.7 per cent per annum between 1990 and 2001 – less than the population growth rate (Gelb, 2003). While inflation rates declined, the employment growth was limited and poverty levels decreased marginally during the latter part of the 1990s. Some researchers argue that it, in fact, increased during that period (see van der Berg et al., 2005). However, income poverty according to van der Berg et al. (2005) declined significantly since early 2000 as a result of the expansion of social assistance and economic growth. The debate as to whether poverty increased or decreased is discussed further in the final section of this chapter.

In the first decade of democracy overall social spending expanded amounting to nearly half of total government spending and increased from 46 per cent to 49 per cent. Social security and education received the largest increase, while housing and other services declined over the same period. Welfare services which include individual, family and community services also decreased in real terms in order to fund the large and growing social security system. This had the effect of limiting the reorientation of the delivery of remedial welfare services to a developmental approach (Triegaardt and Patel, 2005).

South Africa has a population of 47.4 million people (Statistics South Africa, 2006) and is considered to be a middle-income country. Since 2004, economic growth rates expanded significantly and in 2006 a growth rate of 4.9 per cent was achieved with inflation averaging 4.6 per cent in the same year (Manuel, 2007; National Treasury, 2007). Employment growth has been noted in the non-agricultural sector, but this has not been sufficient to absorb the new entrants to the labour market. In the 2007 fiscal year, a budget surplus is projected due to higher growth rates and improved tax collection methods. Surpluses in future will be directed to support social security reforms, education and infrastructure development as well as improving the competitiveness of the economy (Manuel, 2007).

Despite these positive developments, poverty and unemployment remain significant challenges. Unemployment, using a narrow definition, was estimated to be 25.5 per cent in 2006 with youth unemployment being by far the largest group of unemployed nationally (70 per cent). South Africa is one of the countries in the world with the highest HIV/AIDS prevalence rates. Poverty has race, gender, family-type and spatial dimensions. The Human Development Index and the Human Poverty Index measured in terms of life expectancy, education and income worsened between 1995 and 2002 (UNDP, 2003). Unemployment and the effects of AIDS on life expectancy are the main reasons cited for the declining human development situation. About half of the country's population has an income that falls below the poverty line of R533 per adult per month, and 10.5 per cent of the population is estimated to earn less than US$1 per day (UNDP, 2003). In 2002, poverty of coloureds was eight times greater than that of whites and single-parent families and 'couples with children' were over-represented among the poor. Just over a quarter of the poor are single-parent families (UNDP, 2003). Poverty levels among young children (0–14 years) and female-headed households are much worse off than that of the general population (van der Berg and Bredenkamp, 2002). The growing numbers of children under 14 years of age who have lost a parent/caregiver due to AIDS is placing great pressure on public, family and community systems of support.

While South Africa has made great strides in establishing a constitutional democracy and in developing policies and strategies to meet basic needs, the country is faced with the dual challenges of, on the one hand, overcoming its apartheid legacy and addressing the risks to human security generated by its integration into the global economy on the other hand. Economic globalization has resulted in increased employment insecurity among low-income groups locally resulting in substantial job losses. The lower end of the labour market where people have the least skills have been most affected, which has increased their vulnerability to poverty. Lastly, institutional and capacity constraints continue to hamper government in meeting its commitments to the poor.

The South African social security system

The constitution provides the mandate for social security, and the policy and legislative framework is set by The *White Paper for Social Welfare* (1997) and the Social Assistance Act 59 of 1992/Act 13 of 2004. The policy advocated a comprehensive and integrated social security system, which includes social assistance and social insurance and co-responsibility between employers, employees, citizens and the state to ensure universal access and coverage of social security. It also promoted the idea of creating new models of social security, which combined social security with community and social development strategies and employment programmes such as public work programmes including social insurance (Department of Welfare and Population Development, 1997).

The new social security system is built on the redistributive nature of earlier social assistance policies and can be traced to the 1920s when maintenance grants for children and family support was introduced for whites. As part of a strategy to address the 'poor white problem', pensions and disability grants were implemented in the 1930s. Over the years, social assistance gradually expanded and incorporated other racial groups namely coloureds and later Indians and Africans. Benefits were racially differentiated with whites receiving the largest share and Africans the lowest. Some programmes were largely accessible to certain race groups only, such as child and family support. After years of exile, political organizations were unbanned and negotiations for a peaceful political settlement commenced in 1990. By 1993, parity in benefit levels between race groups had been achieved with 81 per cent of social old-age pensioners being black (van der Berg, 1998). In this regard, Seekings (2002, p. 5) points out that the 'new democratic government inherited a highly redistributive budget from the late apartheid state in 1994'.

Both the International Labour Organization (ILO) and South African welfare policy provide a framework for the public and private sectors to make provision for unexpected contingencies which will impact on the ability to earn an income and for individuals who are unable to mobilize resources to take care of themselves. Therefore, the generic definition of social security is taken to include the following: contributory (social insurance) benefits; non-contributory cash benefits; social assistance (means-tested) benefits and tax credits (Walker, 2005).

Following the publication of the *White Paper* and the overhaul of the country's discriminatory and limited social security system, social security is now defined in South Africa as covering the following:

A wide range of public and private measures that provide cash or in-kind benefits both, first, in the event of an individual's earning power permanently ceasing, being interrupted, never developing, or being exercised only at unacceptable social cost and when such person is unable to avoid poverty and secondly, in order to maintain children. The domain of social security is poverty prevention, poverty alleviation, social compensation and income distribution. (Department of Welfare and Population Development 1997, p. 48)

Indigenous informal or semi-formal systems of social security exist alongside the formal social security systems in developing countries (Ardington and Lund, 1995; Mukaka et al., 2002; Subbarao et al., 1997).

While some remnants of traditional systems have survived modernization and colonialism, others have evolved due to the lack of access to formal systems of social provision. Examples of traditional and informal systems of social security are credit and savings schemes, burial societies, cooperative arrangements, and remittances of migrant workers to relatives in rural areas, in-kind support, family and friendship networks, volunteerism and mutual aid and self-help groups. These informal systems are based on personal reciprocity, social solidarity, social networks of trust and direct face-to-face interaction between individuals, households and communities and are pertinent in poverty alleviation – especially in rural areas.

The expansion of the safety net has been prioritized during the past decade with beneficiary numbers increasing from 3 million in 1997 to 12 million in May 2007 which is a four-fold increase. The largest number of beneficiaries are poor children (65.4 per cent) followed by older persons (18.2 per cent), people with disabilities (12 per cent) and war veterans, foster children and caregivers of children with mental disabilities (4.4 per cent) (South African Social Security Agency, 2007). Social security forms 3.2% of Gross Domestic Product (GDP) and amounts to more than R62 billion (or US$434 billion) a year constituting 12.1 per cent of consolidated national and provincial spending (Department of Treasury, 2007). Social assistance is but one strategy to reduce poverty through cash transfers. Other redistributive mechanisms include a public education system, a progressive income tax system, and access to health care and welfare services, subsidized housing, public works employment, small enterprise development and basic services such as water, sanitation and electricity.

However, despite these achievements, there are numerous challenges facing the government in realizing the right to social security. Barriers to access to social security that have been cited are related to institutional inefficiencies, a lack of coordination between different governmental agencies, corruption and ineffective administration in the delivery of grants by national and provincial governments and eligibility requirements that make it difficult for the poorest to access the child grants (Leat et al., 2005). Further, means testing is used to determine eligibility, and thresholds of means tests are often not adjusted to keep up with the inflation which results in large numbers of people not qualifying for social assistance. The thresholds of Child Support Grants have not been adjusted since 1998 (Budlender et al., 2005). Researchers have also drawn attention to how the eligibility criteria of some of the programmes have had the unintended consequences of creating incentives for people to become or remain ill in order to access the disability grants (Nattrass, 2007). A gendered analysis of the scope, coverage and impact of social assistance in order to deepen our understanding of other factors beyond income that have a bearing on poverty and deprivation is also needed (Lund, 2006). Finally, the question is being posed as to whether this method of addressing poverty is nearing the boundaries of its effective use because of fiscal constraints (van der Berg et al., 2005).

Contemporary social assistance strategies

The Social Assistance Act 59 of 1992/Act 13 of 2004 provides for the implementation of different types of social assistance or social grants to be paid to older persons, people with disabilities, caregivers of children and caregivers of children with disabilities and war veterans. The types of social grants for the different target groups and the amounts of each grant are set out in Table 3.1 below. All the social grants are means tested and targeted at the poor and vulnerable – except social relief of distress, which is needs tested. In order to qualify, all beneficiaries should be South African citizens, should be resident in South Africa at the time of the application and should have the relevant identification documents. Each of the grants has particular requirements such as a qualifying age; in the case of disabilities, evidence is required confirming the nature of the disability. The grants are also aimed at caring for older persons, war veterans, people with disabilities and children in communities. There is a requirement that the beneficiary should not be maintained or cared for in an institution. In this way, the grants provide for support and care in the community. In the case of Child Support Grants, the grant is paid to a caregiver who does not have to be the biological parent of the child. This approach is innovative, as there is recognition that large numbers of South African children are cared for apart from their parents due to the migrant labour system and historical factors which resulted in the breakdown of family and community life. It is also responsive to the situation of orphaned and vulnerable children affected by the HIV/ AIDS pandemic.

The different social assistance strategies are discussed below in relation to their nature and scope. The first and best-known form of social assistance or social grant is the State Old Age Pension (SOAP). By 1998, social pensions reached about 75–80 per cent of the population

Table 3.1   Social assistance: type, target group, number of beneficiaries and amount paid

Social assistance	Target group	Amount of grant (R)	Number of beneficiaries
Social pensions	Women over the age of 60 years; men over the age of 65 years	870	2,198,541
Disability grants	Persons medically-diagnosed disabled over the age of 18 years	870	1,419,669
Care dependency grants	Parents, the primary caregiver or foster parent of a disabled child who requires permanent care or support at home by another person	870	98,920
Child support grant	Paid to the primary caregiver of a child/children up to 14 years	200	7,892,869
Foster-care grant	Foster families caring for children under 18 years old	620	408,283
War veterans grant	Veterans of the two world wars and the Anglo-Boer war	838	2,305
Grants-in-aid	A person with a physical or mental condition requiring regular attendance by another person	180	32,505
Total number of beneficiaries			12,053,092

Source: Adapted from South African Social Security Agency, Personal Communication. (May 2007); www.sassa.gov.za/services/grant amounts.asp

who were eligible in terms of age – women from age 60 years and men from age 65 years (van der Berg, 1998, p. 6). Old age pensions have a high take-up rate and the further extension of this grant will not significantly reduce income poverty (Samson et al., 2004). In 2007, just over two million older people received social pensions (see Table 3.1).

Another major provision is the disability grants programme. In 2002–2003, out of 12 million people who were economically inactive, 1.2 million people were people with disabilities (Development Bank of Southern Africa, 2005). Individuals are eligible for a disability grant if they pass a means test and if they are unable to work or provide for themselves because of a mental or physical disability. Nattrass (2007, p. 181) points out that the grant compensates the individual for the impact of their disability on earning potential and is based on the principle that those who are capable of working should not be eligible.

Disability grants have increased significantly from 60,000 in 2000 to 1.3 million in 2004 (Nattrass, 2007) and reached the 1.4 million mark in 2007 (South African Social Security Agency, 2007). This growth was facilitated partly by institutional changes in the grant-awarding process that adopted a wider social interpretation of disability and is increasingly being used as a poverty relief strategy (CASE, 2005). The growth is attributed to increases in the number of people who are HIV positive and who now qualify for the grant. A study by CASE (2005) found that the number of beneficiaries who were on treatment or identified as 'immuno-compromised' increased by 14 per cent between 2001 and 2004 (CASE, 2005). Nattrass (2007) argues that high unemployment rates and generous disability grants have resulted in creating incentives for people to become ill or to remain ill which could worsen the AIDS epidemic and undermine the government's roll-out of anti-retroviral treatment. Measures to broaden access to social assistance for the unemployed through job creation such as an employment guarantee scheme or alternatively a universal basic income grant is advocated (Nattrass, 2007). A large proportion of people with disabilities are in the lowest-income households with the lowest-education levels (CASE, 1998). Developmental welfare and community-based development, including skills development programmes to address the socio-economic conditions of people with disabilities in poor households, are needed. A recent analysis of disability grants shows that large numbers of women take-up disability grants with the majority of women taking-up grants later in life (Steele, 2006). Many in receipt of disability grants also access the child support grant. A small percentage of disability grant beneficiaries are not employed; the grant is well targeted and is used more as a poverty alleviation grant than a compensatory grant (Steele, 2006).

Care dependency grants are available to family members who take care of a child with severe mental impairment and/or severe physical disability. Growth in the number of Care Dependency Grants has been rapid. This growth may be ascribed to the number of people infected and affected by HIV/AIDS and will continue to impact on the increase in these grants. The number of care dependency beneficiaries expanded five-fold between 1998 and 2003 (Republic of South Africa, 2003, p. 103). Currently, 98,920 beneficiaries receive this grant which make up 0.82 per cent of the total number of beneficiaries in 2007.

Next, the Child Support Grant (CSG) was introduced in South Africa on 1 April 1998. This social grant is earmarked for the poorest children in South Africa and was initially targeted at children up to six years of age. Uptake of the grant started slowly and expanded rapidly as more people became aware of the grant and as administrative systems improved. Once the benefits of the grant became known, the government extended eligibility to children aged 0–14 years of age. Research findings revealed that the CSG has had a significant impact on poor children and poverty-stricken families and that it has been most beneficial in the poorest provinces (Triegaardt, 2005). The CSG is used mainly for food, clothes and education (CASE, 2000, p. 50). In addition to the CSG being paid as a cash transfer to the primary caregiver of the child, the safety net also includes free health care for children under 6 years and feeding programmes for children. The purpose of the Integrated Nutrition Programme is to provide an intersectoral and coordinated response to nutritional deficiencies among women and children through health and community-based nutrition services. Lloyd (2000) argues that the benefits of the CSG should be noted in four areas. First, the CSG ensures greater access for poor children to an integrated and sustainable social security system in the country. Second, it provides a grant on an equitable basis to those children in need regardless of their family structure, form, tradition or race. Third, it prevents children from unnecessarily entering statutory substitute care, and lastly, it keeps children off the streets and out of juvenile detention centres. The grant, although small, supplements household income and provides the poorest children with resources to meet basic survival needs. The uptake rate of the grant in 2005 was estimated to be 64.4 per cent with the majority of children coming from rural areas (77.1 per cent) (Budlender et al., 2005). Many advocacy groups continue to press for extending the grant to children up to age 18 years. Popular concern exists that the grant may lead to increased pregnancies especially among teenagers, and it is based on the fear that it will encourage permissiveness. However, research findings show that only 5 per cent of recipients of the grant were under

20 years of age (Steele, 2006). High teenage pregnancies also pre-dated the introduction of the grant.

Finally, there are a number of other social grants that merit discussion. War veterans' grants have declined over the past few years and will gradually phase out over time. Another social grant, which has increased steadily since 2000, is that of foster-care grants. The provinces of Limpopo and KwaZulu-Natal have experienced significant increases in the number of foster-care grants. This rise in the number of grants has also been attributed to the impact of the HIV/AIDS epidemic that has been greatest in these provinces. Foster-care grants are intended to provide some financial support to non-related caregivers that are willing to provide a child with a secure and nurturing home environment. The award is subject to a means test and a full investigation conducted by a social worker. This may lead to the placement of the child in foster care and a Children's Court makes the award. Once the court makes the award, ongoing supervision and reconstruction services are supposed to be provided to the foster family and the natural family of the child by a social worker. In the absence of other forms of alternative care for children affected by HIV/AIDS, foster care is increasingly seen as a means of caring for orphaned and vulnerable children. The majority of children currently receiving foster-care grants registered on the government's SOCPEN system are orphans – children who lost one or both parents – and the majority of foster parents are family members. Informal kinship care is a well-established practice in South Africa. Foster-care grants are increasingly used more as a poverty alleviation mechanism than a child protection measure (Steel, 2006). A more sustainable foster-care model is needed to meet the challenges of the HIV/AIDS pandemic. The search for solutions should be linked to more innovative home and community-care interventions.

Social security reform

The new democratic government initiated a review and restructuring of the social security system after 1994. The Committee of Inquiry into a Comprehensive Social Security System for South Africa (Taylor, 2002) – the Taylor Committee – was established and made recommendations on the restructuring and redesign of the system. The Taylor Committee concurred with earlier findings that the assumptions under-girding social security were based on European conceptions of social security that are not appropriate for the local situation. The Taylor Committee highlighted the gaps in the safety net as being no coverage for the structurally unemployed and limited coverage for children. The Committee also recommended retirement reform and the introduction of a mandatory earnings-related social security scheme that is presently under discussion.

Social insurance is provided to protect employees and their dependents, through insurance, against contingencies which interrupt income. These schemes are contributory for both employers and employees. The contributions are wage related, and the employees and the employers agree upon a percentage to be paid. Social insurance covers contingencies such as pensions or provident funds, medical benefits, maternity benefits, illness, disability, unemployment, employment injury benefits, family benefits and survivor's benefits. The pension and insurance sectors are estimated to be among the largest in the world relative to the gross national product (GNP). Private pension fund contributions are recorded to be about R54.3 billion a year – 14 per cent of total personal remuneration (Taylor, 2002, p. 93).

South Africa's social security system is evolving and it does not yet have a comprehensive social security system. Around 60 per cent of the poor are not covered by existing forms of social provision (Taylor, 2002). Approximately 45 per cent of the labour force is covered by the Unemployment Insurance Fund (UIF), but many people employed in the informal sector, the 'working poor', the self-employed and the unemployed are not covered by unemployment benefits and have no safety net. In 2003, the government extended its safety net to the unemployed by making provision for domestic workers in the statutory unemployment insurance scheme. The reform of unemployment insurance has made the system more progressive, in that low-income workers benefit more than other categories, and benefits are paid up to 58 per cent of prior earnings (van der Berg and Bredenkamp, 2002). The UIF has become more sustainable by including higher-income earnings in paying contributions, but its role in providing income maintenance for this group is limited.

Many of the working poor earn too little to save money and would not qualify for social assistance such as the CSG) because they earn too much. Recommendations from the Taylor Committee included a Basic Income Grant (BIG), but the government vetoed this recommendation in 2003 on the grounds that it was unaffordable, would create dependency and would be available to all citizens. The Taylor Committee and civil society advocacy groups are certain that the social grant, that is, BIG, would successfully reduce poverty (Samson, 2002). Arguments have been presented that BIG would be a universal grant, without a means test, and therefore the stigma of labelling the recipient as 'undeserved or poor' would be removed. The BIG would be an entitlement for all South African citizens. Samson (2002, p. 76) notes that 'Such an entitlement supports the right to social security as entrenched in the South African constitution, while furthering the vision of a comprehensive social security system as identified in the 1997 White Paper for Social Welfare.' Research commissioned by the ILO on a Review on Social Security Reform and the Basic Income Grant concluded that BIG is feasible, affordable and supportive of poverty reduction, economic growth and job creation (Samson, 2002). A cautionary note is made by van der Berg and Bredenkamp (2002) who note that fiscal and administrative constraints limit the potential for grand schemes such as the BIG.

Instead of adopting the BIG proposal, the government's approach has been to expand the safety net for children and to combine this with a productivist/investment approach, which includes strategies to accelerate economic growth, employment creation through expanding public works, national youth service programmes, small business development and skills development strategies. The full impact of these strategies has not been assessed. More recently an ambitious proposal was released by the Minster of Finance, Trevor Manuel, for retirement reform and wage subsidies (Manuel, 2007; Republic of South Africa National Treasury, 2007). A mandatory earnings-related social security scheme is being mooted to provide improved unemployment insurance, disability benefits and death benefits and a standard retirement savings arrangement funded through a social security tax. A wage subsidy will be introduced for workers earning below the income-tax threshold to include low-income workers. The wage subsidy is intended to lower the cost of creating employment. It is critical that the proposal also wrestles with how informal-sector employees, the self-employed and workers in small businesses will be accommodated. Nevertheless, these proposals could go a long way towards creating a comprehensive social security system that combines contributory and non-contributory schemes, private savings schemes and the tax system with other social development interventions.

Economic and social impact of social security

In view of South Africa's unique history of inequality, the violation of human rights, human agency and social action, its approach to welfare policy has been infused with both non-economic and economic ideas about promoting human well-being. Integral to the country's welfare policy are also political ideas about promoting democracy, participation and active citizenship, social transformation and a collaborative approach between the state, the market and the voluntary sector. Thus a multifaceted developmental welfare policy framework emerged that combined economic and non-economic aspects including social and political goals. One of the key challenges of the policy framework was to address mass poverty and inequality and to enhance human capabilities through creating opportunities for people to find pathways out of poverty. The positive distributive effects of social grants has stimulated the interest of academic researchers, advocacy groups and government which is under pressure to demonstrate the benefits of the grant in relation to poverty reduction. Drawing on this growing body of empirical research, the social, economic and developmental impact of social assistance is discussed below.

Social grants and income poverty

There has been considerable debate as to whether poverty and inequality have been reduced since the political transition. Household survey data provided by Statistics South Africa indicated that household income declined since the transition, thus resulting in rising poverty levels in the latter half of the 1990s. A small increase in the Gini coefficient from 0.56 to 0.57 was also identified suggesting that inequality worsened over the same period (Statistics South Africa, 2003). Subsequent research studies analysed data from existing income and expenditure household surveys between 1995 and 2000 including labour force surveys and confirmed these findings (Hoogeveen and Özler, 2004; Leibbrandt et al., 2004; Meth and Dias, 2004).

However, empirical work by Simpkins (2004), UNDP (2003) and suggest that poverty may have stabilized or declined since the transition. van der Berg et al., (2005) questioned the finding that poverty increased on methodological grounds. A comparison of income and expenditure was conducted between 1995 and 2000 based on the Income and Expenditure Surveys (IES) for the respective years by the researchers leading to their conclusion that poverty has increased. One of the problems with the data sets of the two surveys was that they were not comparable as the IES for the year 2000 under-represented the white population and over-represented the black population, thus distorting income trends. van der Berg and his colleagues used a different methodology by first considering income distribution over a longer period of time by including datasets from 2000–2002. Second, they used a range of other data sources such as national accounts, employment and labour force surveys among others and compared these with the survey data. Their finding was that the survey data underestimated income which in turn accounted for the finding by the previous researchers that income declined and therefore poverty worsened. van der Berg et al. (2005) argued that it is not plausible that poverty could have declined to the extent indicated by Leibbrandt et al. (2004) who estimated that real earnings declined by 40 per cent between 1995 and 2000. This according to van der Berg and his colleagues (2005) was not borne out when compared with other economic indicators as such a sharp decline would have created a worse shock in output than what was experienced in the Great Depression.

Van der Berg et al. (2005) used two poverty lines to identify the poor, a lower poverty line set at R250 per month and a higher one set at R281 per month. They measured poverty using the Foster-Greer-Thorbecke measure which includes the poverty headcount (Po); the poverty gap index (P1), which measures the depth of poverty; and the squared poverty index (P2), which assesses the severity of poverty. The comparisons were conducted respectively for 1993, 2000 and 2004. For all the measures referred to above, poverty increased somewhat in the later part of the 1990s but declined to well below the starting levels by 2004. In other words, the proportion of people living in poverty increased slightly between 1993 and 2000, and by 2004 it had decreased quite significantly. The researchers argued that increased poverty levels in the late 1990s may have been due to slower economic growth rates and the poor labour market situation. The lowered poverty levels in 2004 is attributed to higher economic growth rates leading to improved employment levels and most critically to the large-scale expansion of social grants since 2000. The per capita real income of individuals in the two poorest quintiles improved by 30 per cent over the same period, which is borne out by the significant increase in social grants of over 70 per cent which benefited the bottom 40 per cent of the poor the most (van der Berg et al., 2005).

Similar findings were derived from a study assessing the social and economic impact of social grants conducted by Sampson et al. (2004). These researchers found that the measurement of poverty reduction was sensitive to which methodology was used to measure poverty, but they nevertheless concluded that 'South Africa's social security system successfully reduced poverty, regardless of which methodology is used'

(Sampson et al., 2004, p. 1). Of the three social grants with the largest beneficiary numbers namely Social Old Age Pensions, Disability Grants and Child Support Grants, the greatest poverty reducing potential seems to lie with the progressive extension of the Child Support Grant. Sampson argues that the further extension of the eligible age for children from 14 years to 18 years could reduce the poverty gap by a further 21.4 per cent.

These studies confirm the significant contribution that social grants make in reducing income poverty in South Africa. However, in order to accurately measure the economic impact of social grants, a poverty line for South Africa is needed. Researchers have used a range of different poverty lines which are based on different assumptions resulting in different conclusions. A national poverty line will be piloted by government in 2007 (National Treasury, 2007).

The developmental impact of social grants

Although it has long been accepted in social policy circles that social security's economic implications are of secondary importance to its social welfare and humanitarian impact, there is growing interest in the question of whether social security can be viewed as a social investment rather than a social consumption and welfare measure. This issue is discussed in some length earlier in this book and need not be repeated here, but it is suffice to say that a number of economists and social policy scholars have paid much more attention in recent times to social security's positive role in economic development. The work of Amartya Sen (1999) and his emphasis on capability enhancement has attracted considerable interest in economics; while in the field of social policy, scholars such as Michael Sherraden (1991) and James Midgley (1995, 1999) have argued that greater efforts should be made to link economic and social policies and that conventional social policies should be refashioned to contribute positively to economic development. In South Africa, these ideas have been actively promoted by social policy researchers and advocates (van der Berg et al., 2005; Department of Welfare and Population Development, 1997; Lund, 2002; Patel, 2005; Sampson et al., 2004; Triegaardt and Patel, 2005).

As early as 1995–1996, researchers identified the positive outcomes of SOAP (Ardington and Lund, 1995; Moller and Sotshongaye, 1996). Social pensions they argued were gender sensitive, reached far into rural areas and supported extended families in impoverished circumstances. Without the contribution of social pensions, poor people, particularly in rural areas, would simply not survive. Households with pensioners were found not to be as poor as households that have no pensioners. At a personal level, it contributed to improved self-esteem and higher status of older persons in households. In this regard, Ardington and Lund (1995, p. 571) state the following about the old age pensions:

> A significant source of income with marked distributive effects, they are a reliable sources of income, which leads to household security; they are the basis of credit facilities in local markets, further contributing to food security; they deliver cash into remote areas where no other institutions are; they are gender sensitive towards women; and they reach rural areas as few other services do.

The above findings are consistent with recent research (Sampson et al., 2004) that shows that social grants are well targeted at the poor and vulnerable. Since grants make up a significant portion of household expenditure on food, it leads to improved nutritional and health status. A positive relationship between social grants and improved school attendance was evident as grant payments provide households with additional resources to finance education. In the case of old-age pensions, this was most significant as grandmothers are one of the main caregivers of children. A positive correlation was found between households with pensions and improved school attendance of school-age girls where 7 per cent of girls and 3 per cent of boys were more likely to be attending school (Sampson et al., 2004). Based on Microsimulation estimates, Woolard's (2003) analysis shows that without the CSG 48 per cent of children would be in poverty and 23.9 per cent would be classified as ultra-poor. All three social grants reduced the vulnerability to poverty of older persons, children and people with disabilities from 40 per cent to 24 per cent (Woolard, 2003), and it also benefited whole households where resources are pooled. Households receiving social grants reflected lower levels of indebtedness. Sampson et al. (2004) also found that social grant recipients also spent a greater proportion of their resources on food, fuel, housing and household operations. In the case of Child Support Grants (CSG), spending on overall household operations was greater with lower expenditure on tobacco, alcohol and gambling.

Increasingly the beneficiaries of grants are adult women. As on March 2007, women made up approximately 82.3 per cent of the total number of beneficiaries (South African Social Security Agency, 2007). This appears to be due to the large uptake in grants for children and the increasing number of women who are accessing the disability grants. Women represented just over half of the beneficiaries of disability grants with 98 per cent of the caregivers of the CSG being women. Three quarters of the CSG recipients were mothers who had never been married (Steele, 2006). More women than men also access the old-age pension (Lund, 2006). The 'feminization of social grants' is certainly a new trend which is not well understood.

There is some evidence of how social pensions have been used to support recipients and or members of households with start-up costs of small businesses and micro-enterprises or the provision of agricultural inputs (Lund, 2002). Pension day in remote rural communities is a vibrant economic, social and community event also known as 'pension-day markets'. On these occasions grant recipients receive their cash payments, which are delivered by privately contracted companies. The entire community is involved with local people trading in goods that they produced such as vegetables, honey, indigenous herbs or trading live stock. Adato, Lund and Mhongo (2004) observed that at one of the research sites better-off areas and larger and better quality houses were built close to the 'pension-day markets'. This improved wealth status appeared to be due to household members starting up small retail activities on pension day which grew into successful enterprises.

These findings confirm the idea that South Africa's social security system is a social investment that contributes positively to development. Not only does it reduce income poverty but it also contributes positively to economic development through higher consumption of goods and services, improved capabilities in terms of health, education and nutrition and in turn yields positive social and economic benefits for individuals and the households of which they are a part. Little is, however, known about intra-household allocation of resources and decision-making about resource allocation and especially in relation to gender equity. The social and intergenerational dynamics pertaining to age, gender, disability and the status of children in households need to be better understood as tensions between recipients of grants and other household members have been noted (Lund, 2006). Social grants, however, are not the only source of household income for the poor; other sources of income exist such as remittances, informal employment, self-employment, agricultural activities and from illegal activities such as the illegal sale of liquor. Lund (2006), however, cautions against overestimating income from grants in relation to other sources of income.

Labour market and macroeconomic considerations

Sampson et al. (2004) assessed the labour market impact of two grants, namely old-age pensions and disability grants. Workers in households in receipt of these two grants were more likely to be employed. Further, households in receipt of grants increased labour productivity which in turn increased the demand by employers for workers. Sampson et al. (2004, p. 19) argues that 'social grants support the accumulation of human capital by workers, and it supports the workers' productivity-bolstering consumption. Better nutrition, health care, housing and transportation can all support the increased productivity of the worker'. Prospective work seekers in households in receipt of grants also had a higher success rate in finding work. Income from grants was used to support workers in job searches, and it provided income security for the household while its members were looking for work.

The case has been made that South Africa's high levels of inequality between rich and poor which also coincides with race fuels social discontent, increases social and political instability and reduces economic growth and reduced investment. High levels of inequality of wealth and income are also positively associated with higher tax rates and lower economic growth rates (Woolard, 2003). Persistent and continuing inequality remains one of South Africa's most pressing challenges which have impacted negatively on economic growth and social stability. Social grants make a significant contribution not only in reducing income poverty but also in reducing inequality. Grants also contribute to lowering the Gini coefficient, which measures income differentials across the income distribution range. In 1994, South Africa had the second highest Gini coefficient in the world. Sampson et al. (2004) indicates that full take-up of grants could lower the Gini coefficient by 3 percentage points. Further, the link between improved education and economic growth also needs to be made. Sampson et al. (2004) argue that social grants are positively associated with improved access to education which in turn contributes to improved economic growth leading to fiscal expansion and redistribution through social investment.

The idea that social security complimented by a range of social welfare and development programmes is a social and economic investment that may contribute significantly to reducing poverty, inequality and enhanced human capabilities was outlined and explained in this chapter. First, the South African case illustrates what can be achieved in a short space of time in a middle-income country and a post-conflict society when governments prioritize poverty reduction as a social and economic goal. Second, it highlights both the complexity and challenges of adopting and implementing poverty reduction programmes on this scale. Third, it raises the issue of what should the balance be when making policy choices between cash transfer programmes and those that promote the enhancement of human capabilities. Finally, given global economic uncertainty and its impact on South Africa's economic growth prospects as well as national economic constraints, the long-term sustainability of South Africa's social security strategy needs to be better understood.

References

Adato, M. Lund, F. and Mhlongo, P. (2004). Capturing 'Work' in South Africa:Evidence from a Study in Kwazulu-Natal. Unpublished Paper, School of Development Studies, University of KwaZulu-Natal and IFPRI Washington DC.

Ardington, E. and Lund, F. (1995). 'Pensions and Development: Social Security as Complementary to Programmes of Reconstruction and Development', *Development Southern Africa,* 12, 557–578.

van der Berg, S. (1998). 'Ageing, Public Finance and Social Security in South Africa', *Southern African Journal of Gerontology,* 7, 3–9.

van der Berg, S. and Bredenkamp, C. (2002). 'Devising Social Security Interventions for Maximum Poverty Impact', *Social Dynamics,* 28, 39–68.

van der Berg, S., Burger, R., Burger, R., Louw, M. and Yu, D. (2005). Trends in Poverty and Inequality since the Political Transition. Working Papers: 1/2005. Bureau for Economic Research. Department of Economics. Stellenbosch: Stellenbosch University.

Budlender, D., Rosa, S. and Hall, K. (2005). *At All Costs? Applying the Means Test for the Child Support Grant.* Cape Town: Children's Institute and Centre for Actuarial Research, University of Cape Town.

CASE (Community Agency for Social Inquiry). (1998). *Social Security for People with Disabilities.* Researched for the Department of Welfare. June. Johannesburg: CASE.

CASE (Community Agency for Social Inquiry). (2000). *Phasing in the Child Support Grant. A Social Impact Study.* Researched for the Department of Welfare. July. Johannesburg: CASE.

CASE (Community Agency for Social Inquiry). (2005). *Investigations into the Increase in Uptake of Disability and Care Dependency Grants since December 2001.* Johannesburg: Case.

Department of Treasury (2007). *Estimates of National Expenditure*. Pretoria: Government of the Republic of South Africa.

Department of Welfare and Population Development (1997). *The White Paper for Social Welfare*. Notice 1108 of 1997. Vol. 386 (No. 18166). Government Gazette. Pretoria: Government Printers.

Development Bank of Southern Africa (DBSA). (2005). *The Employment of People with Disabilities in South Africa*. Compiled by the Employment Equity Unit. Development Paper no. 170.

Gelb, S. (2003). *Inequality in South Africa: Nature, Causes and Responses*. Dfld Policy Initiative on Addressing Inequality in Middle-Income countries. Braamfontein, South Africa: The Edge Institute.

Hoogeveen, J. G. and Özler, B. (2004). *Not Separate, not Equal: Poverty and Inequality in Post-apartheid South Africa*. Mimeo. Washington DC: World Bank.

Leatt, A., Rosa, S. and Hall, K. (eds). (2005). *Towards a Means to Live: Targeting Poverty Alleviation to Make Children's Rights Real*. Cape Town: Children's Institute, University of Cape Town [CD-Rom].

Leibbrandt, M. H., Poswell, L., Naidoo, P., Welch, M. and Woolard, I. (2004). *Measuring Recent Changes in South African Inequality and Poverty Using 1996 and 2001 Census Data*. DPRU Working Paper 05/94. Cape Town: Development Policy Research unit, Cape Town: University of Cape Town.

Lloyd, I. (2000). *Policy Performance of the Child Support Grant 1 April 1998 to 30 June 1999*. Unpublished MA Dissertation. Johannesburg: University of the Witwatersrand, Johannesburg.

Lund, F. (2002). 'Crowding in Care, Security and Micro-enterprise Formation: Revisiting the Role of the State in Poverty Reduction, and in Development', *Journal of International Development*, 14, 1–14.

Lund, F. (2006). 'Gender and Social Security in South Africa.' In: Padayachee, V. (*ed.*), *The Development Decade: Economic and Social Change in South Africa 1994–2004*. Cape Town: HSRC Press, pp. 160–179.

Manuel, T. (2007). Budget Speech. Minister of Finance, Manuel, T. MP. 21 February, 2007.

Meth, C. and Dias, R. (2004). 'Increases in Poverty in South Africa, 1999–2002', *Development Southern Africa*, 21 (1), 59–85.

Midgley, J. (1995). *Social Development. The Developmental Perspective in Social Welfare*. London: Sage Publications.

Midgley, J. (1999). 'Growth, Redistribution and Welfare: Towards Social Investment', *Social Service Review*, 77 (1), 3–21.

Moller, V. and Sotshongaye, A. (1996). '"My Family Eats This Money Too": Pension Sharing and Self-respect among Zulu Grandmothers', *Southern African Journal of Gerontology*, 5, 9–19.

Mukuka, L., Kalikiti, W., Musenge, D. (2002). 'Social Security Systems in Zambia', *Journal of Social Development in Africa*, 17, 65–96.

National Treasury. (2007) *Budget Review 2007*. Pretoria: Government of the Republic of South Africa.

Nattrass, N. (2007). 'Disability and Welfare.' In Buhlungu, S., Daniel, J., Southhall, R. and Lutchman, J. (eds), *State of the Nation South Africa 2007*. Cape Town: HSRC Press, pp. 179–200.

Patel, L. (2005). *Social Welfare and Social Development in South Africa*. Cape Town: Oxford University Press Southern Africa.

Republic of South Africa (1996). *The Constitution of the Republic of South Africa*. Act 108 of 1996. Pretoria: Government Printers.

Republic of South Africa, National Treasury (2003). *Intergovernmental Fiscal Review*. Pretoria: National Treasury.

Republic of South Africa, National Treasury (2007). Social Security and Retirement Reform. Second Discussion Paper. February 2007.

Samson, M., Lee, U., Ndlebe, A., Mac Quene, K., van Niekerk, I., Gandhi, V., Harigaya, T. and Abrahams, C. (2004). *The Social and Economic Impact of South Africa's Social Security System*. Pretoria: Department of Social Development.

Samson, M. (2002). 'The Social, Economic and Fiscal Impact of Comprehensive Social Security Reform for South Africa', *Social Dynamics*, 28, 69–97.

Seekings, J. (2002). 'The Broader Importance of Welfare Reform in South Africa', *Journal of Social Dynamics*, 28, 1–38.

Sherraden, M. (1991). *Assets and the Poor: a New American Welfare Policy*. Armonk, NY: M. E. Sharpe.

Simkins, C. E. W. (2004). What happened to the distribution of income in South Africa between 1995 and 2001? Unpublished draft. (available on line at www.sarpn.org).

South Africa Human Development Report (2003). *The Challenge of Sustainable Development: Unlocking People's Creativity*. United Nations Development Programme (UNDP). Cape Town: Oxford University Press.

South African Social Security Agency. www.sassa.gov.za/services/grant_amounts.asp. Accessed 4 May 2007.

Statistics South Africa (2003). *Census 2001*: Pretoria. Statistics South Africa.

Statistics South Africa (2006). Latest key indicators. Population (mid-year estimates). http://www.statssa.gov.za/keyindicators/keyindicators.asp. Accessed 3 April 2007.

Steele, M. (2006). *Report on Incentive Structures of Social Assistance Grants in South Africa*. Kesho Consulting and Business Solutions (Pty) Ltd., Geospace International, Department of Social Development. Pretoria: Department of Social Development, Republic of South Africa.

Subbarao, K., Bonnerjee, A., Braithwaite, J., Carvalho, S., Ezemenari, K., Graham, C., Thompson, A. (1997). *Safety Net Programs and Poverty Reduction: Lessons from Cross-Country Experience*. Washington DC: The World Bank.

Taylor, V. (2002). Committee of Inquiry into a Comprehensive Social Security System for South Africa. *Transforming the Present – Protecting the Future. Draft Consolidated Report*. Pretoria: Department of Social Development.

Triegaardt, J. (2005). 'The Child Support Grant in South Africa: A Social Policy for Poverty Alleviation?', *International Journal of Social Welfare*, 14, 249–255.

Triegaardt, J. and Patel, L. (2005). 'Social Security'. In Patel, L. (ed.), *Social Welfare and Social Development in South Africa*. Cape Town: Oxford University Press Southern Africa, pp. 122–153.

UNDP (2003). *South African Human Development Report*.s

Woolard, I. (2003). *Social Assisatnce Grants, Poverty and Economic Growth in South Africa*. Cape Town: Development Policy Research Unit, School of Economics, University of Cape Town.

Walker, R. (2005). *Social Security and Welfare. Concepts and Comparisons*. Berkshire: Open University Press.

4
Chile: Social Security, Privatization and Economic Growth

Silvia Borzutzky

The purpose of this chapter is to link Chile's complex social security history with the economic development of the country. It examines the way social security has evolved over the years and pays particular attention to the well-documented privatization of the social insurance system and the way privatization affected economic development. Contrary to the claims of the supporters of private retirement accounts, it shows that the relationship between privatization and economic development has been problematic. It discusses current attempts to create a combined private-public system under President Bachelet and concludes with an analysis of the country's current economic policies and their impact on inequality, which is a major challenge facing the country.

The case of Chile is particularly interesting for a number of reasons: First, Chile had one of the oldest, most comprehensive and most expensive social security system in Latin America based on a system of contribution by the employer, employee and the state. Second, Chile fully privatized its pension system in 1980, and as a result more than 25 years of data has been accumulated regarding the performance of this system and its impact on the state, the society, and the economy at large. Third, the Chilean economy has performed well in the past 15 years and has maintained fairly stable rates of economic growth. Fourth, Chile's economy is fully globalized and integrated into the world economy and is enjoying a sizeable trade surplus which could be spent on economic development. Finally, the market economic model has generated both economic growth and reductions in poverty since the end of the Pinochet regime but has also generated increased inequalities. Future economic development in Chile must be linked to reductions in inequality, and the issue of how economic development, inequality and the role that social security must play in both reducing inequality and sustaining higher levels of economic development must be addressed.

For the purpose of this chapter, economic development will be understood not only in terms of economic growth but also in terms of poverty and inequality reduction. As Midgley and Tang argue in the introduction to this book, economic development should produce tangible social benefits for the mass of the population. These benefits involve improvements in income as well as nutrition, health status, education, housing, employment opportunities, recreation and other dimensions of quality of life.

In the case of Chile, social security policy has been integrated into a larger economic model and, as a result, the effects of social security cannot be separated from the other policies that formed part of that model. Because it is possible to distinguish two distinctively different development models, the effects of social security on economic development at two different points in Chilean history will be analysed. First, the effects of social security at the end of the 1960s will be examined in order to assess the effects of the social insurance system which, in turn, was integrated into an import substitution industrialization (ISI) model. Second, the effects of social security at the end of the Pinochet regime will be discussed in order to assess the effects of the privatized system in the context of the market model implemented by the regime. Since President Bachelet (2006–2010) is in the process of reforming the system, an analysis of her policies is provided.

Economic and political background

From a political standpoint, Chile's well established democratic stability suffered a major blow on 11 September, 1973 when General Pinochet overthrew the constitutionally elected regime of Socialist president Salvador Allende. General Pinochet's regime (1973–1989) did not only transform Chile's political institutions but also changed the nature of the country's social and economic policies. Under General Pinochet's rule Chile adopted a radical market economic model which resulted in a reduction of the economic role of the state, a change in the scope of the state intervention and a dramatic change in the country's basic social and economic policies. The model emphasized the importance of the market and the subsidiary role of the state, and the private sector benefited from the Pinochet regime through a series of economic policies known as 'modernizations' that entailed the privatization of basic social services including education, social security and the partial privatization of health.

Since the end of the Pinochet regime, the centre–left coalition known as the Concertación has ruled the country. The most distinctive feature of the country's transformation has been a slow but steady process towards the democratization of society and its political institutions and the maintenance of the market model with some marginal modifications geared to reduce the abysmal rates of poverty inherited from the Pinochet regime (50 per cent of the population was below the poverty level, while 25 per cent was in extreme poverty). By 2005 the most authoritarian features of the constitution had been reformed and poverty rates had been cut at least in half (Borzutzky and Hecht-Oppenheim, 2006).

Today, Chile is a country of 16 million people which is placed among the mid-level developing countries. Its literacy rate is 98 per cent, life expectancy is 76.7 years, and its per capita income is $8,884. Economic growth in 2006 was 4.2 per cent. Exports reached almost $60 billion in 2006, and copper represented 56.5 per cent of the country's exports generating a surplus in 2006 of over $23 billion dollars. Total investment reached $28 billion in 2006, and corporate profits increased by 46 per cent during the year due to a boom in consumer demand and increased demand for Chilean products abroad, particularly in China and India. Unemployment declined from 9.7 per cent to 7.8 per cent, and average monthly income for workers enrolled in the pension system was $560 reflecting stagnation in the wages (they increased only about a dollar from the previous year). Health spending per capita has increased from $136 in 2000 to $207 in 2006, while education spending grew by 42 per cent between 2000 and 2006 ('Los grandes números del debut de Bachelet', El Mercurio.com, 4 March, 2007).

The Chilean social security system: the early years

Chile's first comprehensive set of social security laws were approved in 1924 and 1925. These laws established separate social insurance funds that provided pensions to blue and white collar workers, civil servants and the armed forces. The different funds offered old age and disability pensions, family allowances and health benefits. The quality of the pensions and the structure of the social security tax changed from one fund to another one.

Between 1924 and the early 1970s, the system's most important characteristic was the division of the insured population in a multitude of funds defined along occupational lines. Over the years, this process of division and subdivision of the population along occupational lines continued, creating a stratified system formed by over 2,000 laws and several hundred funds each with its own system of benefits and financing. The nature of the benefits and the type of financial arrangement received by the members of these funds were a direct reflection of the power that group was able to exercise over the political system. By the mid-1960s the system was in trouble. While the system had expanded enough to offer benefits to over 70 per cent of the population, it was entirely fragmented and very costly (about twelve per cent of GDP was spent in social security and related programmes). However, the fragmentation of the social security system was not only a product of the expansion of coverage but also was closely linked to the nature of Chile's political system which encouraged the formation of clientelistic relationships between specific interest groups and the members of Congress and the concession of special social security benefits to special groups in order to gain political support. This approach to policymaking produced an atomization of the system, which in turn had a number of negative effects including high administrative costs which made Chile's system one of the more expensive in the world with insufficient pensions for the majority of the workers, privileged pensions for a selected group of workers and a persistent financial crisis among others. In this context, the social security system only served to reinforce the very large class and socioeconomic differences that exited in the society at large (Borzutzky, 2002).

By the mid-1960s several commissions had clearly established the need for reform. The Frei Administration (1964–1970) unsuccessfully attempted to unify and rationalize social security provisions. Linking the nature of the system to the country's economic health and development was very much in the mind of president Frei. As he argued in his first State of the Nation Speech, in May of 1965,

> It is the decision of my government to undertake the integral reform of the social security system. The multiplicity, disparity, privileges, omissions and injustices of the present system not only constitute a permanent factor of unrest and disturbances, but they are a paralyzing obstacle to the achievement of the economic development plans and the social reforms that are part of our program ... this system will inevitably lead to the bankruptcy of the social security funds or the bankruptcy of the country. (Frei, 1965)

However, Frei's attempt to rationalize and unify the social security system did not succeed. His proposals clearly damaged the interests of the core constituencies of all the political parties including his own Christian Democratic party. Narrow political interest prevailed over the general interest of the nation, and the parties rejected the proposed reforms and continued enacting special laws geared to grant special benefits to special interest groups.

The election of Salvador Allende as President of Chile in 1970 did not change these practices. On the contrary, Allende's precarious political position prevented him from attempting a serious reform and enticed him to continue expanding the system to specific groups in order to gain much needed political support. Both the financial and the administrative crisis continued.

By the end of the Allende regime, the social security system had expanded to about 79 per cent of the population, but it was highly discriminatory both in terms of the benefits and financing; the majority of pensions were highly inadequate; the funds had been driven into bankruptcy by the legislators who constantly added new benefits and obligations to the system without creating the needed financial resources; the administration was expensive and inefficient. Moreover, Congress continually granted exemptions to the entrepreneurs in order to reduce their labour costs and get their political support, and the state constantly owed money to the funds. The social insurance system's financial crisis can be explained as a result of a number of processes including the 'massification' of benefits (Mesa-Lago, 1976), the massification of exemptions and the fragmented administrative system. 'In the final analysis the different societal forces that formed the populist coalition that governed Chile during the second half of the twentieth century pushed social security to the brink. Whereas the Frei administration tried to check those forces, the Allende regime only fed them.' (Borzutzky, 2002, pp. 148–149).

Social insurance and economic development

Did this system contribute to the economic development of the country? Between the 1930s and the early 1970s Chile's economic policies were defined by an ISI model which called for an expansion of the state's social and economic functions in order to deal with the disastrous effects of the Great Depression and dependence on external markets. While in its origins the social security system had been created as a mechanism to co-opt critical working-class groups and middle sectors, in the long run the provision of social security benefits constituted a core element of import substitution policies and the type of Latin American populism that is traditionally associated with these policies. Although, in Chile, populism took a somewhat different form, the analysis of the policies implemented during that period clearly indicates that the goals of the policies were to industrialize the country by using a state-sponsored model of industrialization and the provision of social benefits to the urban middle and working classes. These socioeconomic groups, were in turn, the critical constituencies of these regimes. In the context of this economic model, social security was expected to play a critical development role through the provision of retirement income to the urban classes. This retirement income was seen both as a condition for the development of the internal market, a critical social policy in the ISI formulation, a critical political mechanism, as well as policy that would satisfy the kind of humanitarian concerns typically associated with the provision of social security.

Like many other Latin American countries, Chile only partially achieved the import substitution model's ambitious goals. The country was able to develop a state-supported industrial sector limited to the production of consumer goods, electronic products and car assembly. By the early 1960s industrialization had become a difficult and expensive process because acquisition of technology was expensive, the market remained small, the state could support the process only by running massive budget deficit which quickly created massive inflation and the United States did not support this process. In the social arena, the government did implement a set of social programmes, including expansion of education and the provision of health and social security benefits to the urban classes, but the newly enfranchised groups continued to make demands that the country's dependent economy could barely afford. In the final analysis, the process of fragmented growth which characterized the expansion of social security benefits became unaffordable and chaotic. Just like President Frei argued in his 1965 speech, social security had the potential of making important contributions to the development of the country, but the atomization of the funds and the problems associated with this process were leading both the system and the country to bankruptcy.

The expansion of social security benefits during this period could have contributed to the economic development of the country. However, the particular form that the provision of retirement income took in Chile totally distorted and frustrated the possibility of any positive impact on economic and social development, because pensions only reinforced the already existing large income differences and the pensions received by the lower income groups did not entail an improvement of their standard of living.

Social security and the Pinochet privatization

The privatization of Chile's social security system was an integral part of the economic and political model imposed in Chile by General Pinochet and his economic advisors. The Pinochet regime's goals were not only the destruction of Chile's democracy but also the destruction of the ISI model that had become an integral part of that democratic process. In the minds of the new political and economic rulers, the ISI policies had led the country towards political and economic bankruptcy and totalitarianism. Inspired by the economic ideas of Milton Friedman and Fredrick von Hayek the regime quickly began to dismantle the economic underpinnings of the ISI model, reducing the economic and social functions of the state and increasing the power of the private sector (Borzutzky, 2005). Simultaneously, the regime constructed an authoritarian system built around General Pinochet's power, the elimination of the political institutions and massive repression.

Although the Chicago-trained economists had been planning their market reforms since the election of Salvador Allende, those reforms were not fully implemented until the late 1970s after General Pinochet had fully consolidated his power and economic policymaking was under the firm control of the 'Chicago Boys'. Thus, what one sees in Chile in the late 1970s and early 1980s is the state establishing a market system through a series of policies which 'modernized', or privatized, the social security, health, labour and rural property system among others. These modernizations revolutionized Chile's economy, changing the role of the state, setting new parameters for the relations between the private and public sectors, destroying organized opposition and attempting to establish a new belief system based on the combination of authoritarian and market ideas.

In the social security area, we see a series of modifications between 1973 and 1980 and the implementation of a sweeping reform in 1981. Among these partial reforms, the most important one was the enactment of the Law Decree 2448 in 1979 which equalized benefits, ended the system of privileged pensions and established a uniform system of pension readjustment. Important reforms to the Family Allowance system were also enacted during this period. These reforms resembled what President Frei had unsuccessfully tried in the 1960s and equalized benefits and contributions.

In 1978 the neoliberal economists, or Chicago Boys, consolidated control of the economic policymaking institutions. Consolidation of power was followed by what the Chicago economists called a series of modernizations which in fact entailed the application of neoliberal principles to critical public policies, including the labour law system, health, education, and land tenure among others. In charge of the social security reform was Mr Jose Piñera, a Harvard-trained economist, but an integral part of the Chicago Boys team.

The privatization of social security was designed by a commission handpicked by Minister Piñera which operated secretly and without consulting relevant interest groups. Piñera and his commission designed a privatized, defined contribution scheme geared to strengthen the private sector, reduce the role of the state and interests groups associated with the previous system and to do away with the 'collective concept of man and society which inspired the old system' (Piñera, cited by Acuña and Iglesias, 2001, p. 16). The reform introduced major changes to the financial and administrative structures, eliminating the employer's portion of the social security tax and creating a private, for-profit entities in charge of the administration of the funds and the provision of benefits. The most distinctive elements of the system are the financial and administrative systems. The next section contains a discussion of the financial and administrative systems and assessment of their impact.

Financial and administrative aspects

Key to the Pinochet reform was the elimination of the employer's portion of the social security tax, which in the view of the framers of the programme was going to directly affect economic development by reducing labour costs and unemployment. As a result, the employer's portion of the social security tax was eliminated, and the tax is paid entirely by the employee or insured people. The basic tax amounts to 10 per cent of wages. However, the employee also needs to contribute at least an additional 7 per cent to qualify for health and maternity benefits and between 2.5 per cent and 3.7 per cent to finance disability and survivor's benefits. In summary, the total compulsory contribution amounts to about 20 per cent of the earnings for those employed in the private sector (Mesa-Lago, 1998). A system of voluntary contributions was added in 2002. While the elimination of the employer's portion of the social security tax was explained as a way of reducing labour costs and unemployment, the critical principle here is that retirement becomes a personal endeavour, deprived of a social content and commitment.

The personal savings accounts are administered by private, for-profit entities known as Administradoras de Fondos de Pensiones (AFPs), or Pension Fund Administrators. The AFP charges a commission for the administration of the accounts. Pensions are provided either directly by the AFP or indirectly through an annuity bought from an insurance company or through a combination of both. In the case of disability and survivor's pensions the benefit is paid directly by the AFP. The creation of these institutions was seen as a key element in the development of a market economy and as a critical element in the new market development model proposed by the Chicago Boys.

The new system was made compulsory for the workers who joined the work force after December 1981. Those who were employed before December 1981 could choose between staying in the social insurance system or moving to the new one. Due to the effects of the propaganda that preceded the launching of the new system and the inadequacy of the pensions provided by the social insurance system, a large percentage of the working population moved to the privatized system.

The public funds of the past disappeared and the provision of pensions for those who remained in the social insurance system was transferred to a new bureaucracy, the Instituto de Normalización Previsional. This bureaucracy, in turn, administers the Bono de Reconocimiento or Recognition Bond, which represents the contributions made to any of the funds that existed prior to the reform. The monies accumulated in the old funds are transferred to the AFP at the time of retirement.

The effects of privatization

By its very nature, social security affects the entire society, the relations between state and society, as well as the state. Thus, to assess the effects of the reform one needs to look into its effects on a number of different sectors, including the retirees, the AFPs, the fiscal effects and the effects on the economy at large. What is clear is that the reform has produced very distinct effects on each of these sectors. Below, we will analyse the effects on the AFPs on economic growth, savings, capital markets and the insured. A distinction between winners and losers is made throughout the analysis. This distinction will also help us evaluate the effects of the privatized, defined contribution system on economic development.

The Winners: The clear winners from the establishment of a privatized, defined contribution system are the AFPs. There are only seven pension fund administrators in Chile, and contrary to the predictions of the system's founders there is little competition among them. Competition is further reduced by the fact that three of the seven concentrate on 79 per cent of the insured (SAFP, Boletín Estadístico Mensual, 2003).

The creation of the AFPs had an important effect not only in Chile but also throughout the world, since the Chilean model was heralded as one that had to be adopted by the rest of the world. However, this perception has changed as a result of new World Bank assessments about their performance. Thus, while in the past the World Bank had promoted the establishment of AFPs elsewhere, it is now quite critical of these institutions. A 2004 World Bank report found that the industry is highly concentrated, is not competitive, charges high commissions and has a captive audience distorting basic principles of a sound capitalist economy. If past trends are any indication of the future, the tendency in Chile, and the other countries that have adopted this system, has been towards further administrative concentration given the economies of scale that prevail in the industry and the lack of information that the insured has about the costs of the system (Gill et al., 2004).

Another World Bank report argues that persistent problems with this type of system such as the low level of coverage and the low level of the pensions – which are analysed below – are at least partly explained by the high commissions charged by the AFPs to administer the accounts (García, 2006). In fact, although the commissions have decreased from 3.57 per cent in 1982 to 2.26 per cent of the salary in 2003, they remain high and unequal. As proportion of the monthly deposit, the commissions have declined from between 24.1 per cent and 30.2 per cent of the deposit to 18 per cent in 2003 (Mesa-Lago, 2004; SAFP, Boletín Estadístico Mensual, 1998). According to a study, the AFPs' commissions are 67 per cent higher than the fees charged by the banks to manage savings and on time accounts (Mesa-Lago, 2001). The high administrative cost not only reduces the amount saved in the individual accounts but also results in pushing a sizeable number of insured people to the state-provided minimum pension, because they are not able to save enough to obtain a minimum pension. Marketing and advertisement account for about one fourth of the AFPs' administrative costs.

The World Bank also argues 'that AFPs profits have been persistently high with an average rate of return of about 30 per cent per year, double the rate of return of the commercial banks' (García, 2006). But this estimate is in fact quite low because the SAFP reported in 2001 that the rate of return was over 50 per cent (SAFP, 2001, Unpublished data), while another study argues that for the period 1999–2003 the average rate of return reached 53 per cent per year (Engel, 2005). For 2006 the rate of return for the AFPs was 46 per cent higher than in the previous year, amounting $255 million (García, 2007). The World Bank has proposed a restructuring of the AFPs organization in order to reduce costs.

Moreover, the current scheme has generated not only very high rates of return but has also allowed the AFPs to control about 60 per cent of the country's Gross Domestic Product (GDP). As can easily be imagined, the effects of the accumulation of 60 per cent or more of GDP in the hands of the AFPs go well beyond the insurance system and touch every single aspect of the country's economy. Most importantly, AFPs investments are a critical factor in the development and performance of the Chilean markets and stock exchange.

In a privatized, defined contribution system, the size of the pension is determined by the amount saved, the interest generated by the savings and the administrative costs. What has been the performance of the pension funds between 1981 and 2000? On average, the value of the funds have grown at a rate of about 10 per cent per year; however, during the same period the selected share price index or IPSA (Indíce de Precios Selectivo de Acciones) which measures the values in the Chilean Stock Exchange, increased by 21.9 per cent and the average interest rates produced by a savings account was 13.8 per cent. Thus, although the performance looks impressive, it was 11.9 per cent lower than the performance of the stock market and 3.8 per cent lower than the profits generated by saving deposits. Moreover, the funds' performance have showed a large degree of variation from one year to the next which has potentially negative effects on some of the retirees depending on the year they have retired or choose to retire (Acuña and Iglesias, 2001). For instance, while the funds did very well in 2006, obtaining a rate of return of 17 per cent (García, 2007), the decline of the stock market in February and March of 2007 meant that in a month the insured not only lost all the gains accumulated during the year but also actually showed a net loss of 0.9 per cent in one of the funds (El Mercurio.com, 10 March, 2007). One also has to keep in mind that the insured's profits are largely diminished by the very large commissions charged by the AFPs for the administration of the funds.

The Losers: Because the pension is based solely on the contributions made by the insured, among the losers are certainly those workers who cannot afford to contribute to the pension system and as a result are not getting a pension after retiring. The data indicates that the percentage of those contributing to the private pension system has been declining persistently since 1989, and by 2003 only 49.1 per cent of the workforce was contributing to the privatized system (in 1973, the social insurance system covered more than 79 per cent of the workforce). Data for 2006 shows that the coverage has remained at about the same level. Independent workers have remained largely outside the system, since only 5 per cent of these workers are contributing to an AFP (Mesa-Lago, 2004). The authors of the World Bank report also note that after gaining the right to a minimum pension most of those enrolled in an AFP stop contributing and prefer to use their resources in other items such as housing, education and others. Two serious problems have emerged after 25 years: the reduction in coverage and the growth in the state's responsibilities.

Thus, another major loser has been the state. Although the reform proponents argued that the privatized system was going to reduce the fiscal cost, data for the past 25 years indicate that the reality has been quite different. Government studies consistently show that the fiscal deficit produced by the privatized system increased from 3.8 per cent of GDP in 1981 to 6.1 per cent in 2000. By 2040 the deficit will be equivalent to 3.3 per cent of GDP (Arenas de Mesa, 1999). The deficit results from the state's obligation to pay the Recognition Bond, minimum pensions, and the payment of pensions to those who remained in the social insurance system. While the costs associated with paying pensions to those that remained in the public system and the Recognition Bond are going to decrease over time, the cost of the minimum pensions is expected to increase since a larger and larger proportion of the insured will be unable to save enough to have in their savings accounts the equivalent of a minimum pension. Some studies argue that by the end of this decade about 50 per cent of the retiree will be receiving minimum pensions.

Moreover, although Mr Piñera and his neoliberal colleagues argued that the establishment of the privatized, defined contribution system would improve the pensions received by the retirees, the data indicates that in fact pensions in the private sector have remained low and that they are not very different from those provided by the public sector. This issue is fully explained in the next section.

Coming full circle: effects on retirees

In 1980, the framers of the reform argued that existing system had to be replaced by the privatized, defined contribution system because the pensions generated by the social insurance system were low, the administrative costs were high and the financial burden for the state had become unbearable. It has already been shown above how 25 years after the reform the cost for the state is high and will continue to grow in the future, and the administrative costs are enormous. What about the value of pensions?

Because Chile's system is 25 years old, we have a variety of interesting and evolving data regarding the value of pensions. Using data for the first 12 years, Acuña and Iglesias argued in 2001 that the pensions generated by the private system were quite a bit higher than in the previous social insurance system – about 43 per cent higher for old-age pensions and 68 per cent higher in the case of disability pensions (Acuña and Iglesias, 2001). However, as Mesa-Lago argues, once you take into account the number of pensions provided under each rubric and their value, the end result is that pensions in the private system are only 3 per cent higher than in the social insurance system (Mesa-Lago, 2004). On the other hand, a 2001 governmental study concluded that while the value of an average old-age pension in the privatized system was 12 per cent higher than in the social insurance system, disability pensions were 23 per cent higher in the social insurance system than in the privatized system (SAFP, Boletín Estadístico Mensual, 2001).

In recent years, it has become evident that not even the old-age pensions provided by the privatized system are sufficient, and that this is true not only for low-income workers but also for the middle class. In fact, the World Bank experts have argued that the pensions provided by the system are clearly insufficient and that only 45 per cent of the pensions will be over the minimum pension (García, 2006). The same World Bank report also shows concern for the low level of participation and coverage, which are explained as a result of the high commissions charged by the AFPs and the low level of competition among the AFPs.

Because, as indicated above, the number of people receiving the minimum pension is very high and growing (in 2000 they amounted to about 43 per cent of the retirees and it is expected to reach 50 per cent in the not so distant future), the overall value of retirement pensions will be heavily determined by the value of the minimum pension. For the period between 1990 and 2000, the value of the minimum pension averaged 70 per cent of the minimum wage and only 24 per cent of the average wage in the private sector. Thus, there is little doubt that for at least 50 per cent of the population the pensions are highly insufficient and condemn the retiree to poverty.

In 2005, the *New York Times* reported that 'the government continues to direct billions of dollars to a safety net for those whose contributions were not large enough to ensure even a minimum pension approaching $140 a month. Many others [50 per cent of the work force]...remain outside the system altogether' (Rother, 2005). The article also argues that even for many middle-class workers who contributed regularly their pensions will be highly insufficient, because as much as a third of the original investment was consumed by the exorbitant fees charged by the AFPs. The example of a 66-year-old technician earning almost $1,000 per month who had to retire after 24 years of contributions because of medical reasons with a 20 year annuity of $350 is indicative of the malaise affecting the system. As he compared his very poor pension with that of his colleagues in the social insurance system the shock was even greater because his colleagues will obtain about $700 for life, not just $350 for 20 years. Moreover, a study by the National Center for Alternative Development Studies calculates that in order to get the equivalent to the maximum pension in the social insurance system (about $1,250 per month), a worker enrolled in an AFP would have to contribute more than $250,000 over their career, a target reached by fewer than 500 of the seven million past and present contributors. As argued above, government costs have remained high at 5–6 per cent of GDP, while about 50 per cent of the population will not be covered by the pension system (Rother, 2005).

Much like in the past, desperate pensioners have formed an Association of People with Pension Damage and much like in the past politicians began to focus on the need to reform the system, an issue that acquired a great deal of prominence during the 2005 presidential campaign. However, in some ways, the future looks even worse than the past because the privatized, defined contribution system not only reinforces income differences but also reinforces gender differences. Several studies have consistently demonstrated the negative effect of the privatized system on women's pensions. These studies have indicated that women pensions are on the average about 30 per cent lower than their male counterparts and that lower-income women are negatively affected by the structure of the commissions, job instability and simply having a limited income. As a result, it is estimated that about 60 per cent of the women contributing to an AFP will end up receiving only a minimum pension which is insufficient for the women and represents a burden for the state.

Here we have two critical problems reinforcing each other: female poverty and female pensions. There is long list of reasons that explain female poverty, and among them are the following: lower salaries (by about 30 per cent), women largely found performing low-paying jobs and enterprises tending not to invest in women's training as well as the 'glass ceiling' effect for professional women. Data for 2006 indicates that although women participation in the labour force has increased from 34.6 per cent to 38.5 per cent, it is still substantially lower than men. The data also indicates that unemployment among women is 1.4 times higher than male unemployment, and that although women are obtaining higher educational degrees their incomes are lower than men. On average, in 2005, women made 79 per cent of male salary and the gap increases if the comparison is made between women and men with higher education degrees. In the case of professional women, salaries are only 66 per cent of the men's salary (Castañeda, 2007b). In brief, for the reasons descried above the salary gap between men and women is about 30 per cent.

Once women retire, the situation becomes even worse. In a privatized system deprived of any solidarity mechanisms or state contribution, all that women have are the monies accumulated in the account. The data shows that women have less money accumulated not only because of lower salaries and higher unemployment rates but also because they have to take time out for child bearing/rearing reasons as well as other family obligations. Moreover, the smaller fund has to be distributed over a longer period of time because women live 4 to 5 years longer than men (Arenas de Mesa and Montecinos, 1996; Arenas de Mesa and Hernández, 2001). The end result is that women not only are able to save enough to have their own pension but in a growing number of cases they are also forced out of the system entirely because they have not contributed for a minimum of 20 years. In summary, on the average, funds accumulated in women's accounts are between 32 per cent and 46 per cent lower than the funds accumulated by men; replacement ratios fluctuate between 52 per cent and 57 per cent for females and 81–86 per cent for males, while pensions for old-age retirees fluctuate between 60 per cent and 87 per cent lower than men depending on the retirement age (Bertranou and Arenas de Mesa, 2003). This situation bears directly on economic development issues, because it discriminates against 50 per cent of the population, increases poverty and exacerbates inequality.

Effects on economic development

As argued above, to assess the effects of the privatized, defined contribution system on economic growth and development is a complex problem because the social security system does not operate in an isolated socioeconomic environment, but is intimately connected to the performance of the economy and the economic model that is guiding economic policies. Thus, the performance of the privatized system has to be linked to the effects of the other market-oriented policies implemented by the Pinochet regime.

The impact of a privatized social security system on the country's economic development can be assessed through its effects on savings, economic growth and the development of capital markets as well as the value of the pensions provided by the individual accounts. Both the authors of the reform and World Bank's proponents of the Chilean model indicated that privatization of social security was going to increase the country's savings generating a massive process of economic development spearheaded by an active and powerful private sector. What has happened after 25 years? It is clear that privatization has placed an enormous amount of resources in the hands of the AFPs but has not necessarily increased national savings. Arenas de Mesa, for instance, has concluded that for the period 1981–1997 the effects on national savings were negative, estimating a reduction in savings equal to 3 per cent of GDP. Arenas de Mesa also estimated that the fiscal cost will decline over a 20-year period, but given the reduction in savings produced by the current system, the country will need about 40 years to begin showing positive effects on savings (Arenas de Mesa, 1999). Thus, here again the expectations that the authors of the reform had have not materialized, and instead of generating a massive national savings the privatization of social security has generated a large fiscal deficit which offsets the gains made in the private sector.

Critical to the economic development model proposed by the Chicago Boys was the development of capital market. The impact of the privatized system on the capital markets has been positive and quite conclusive, because it has facilitated the development of a capital market, increased the depth and liquidity of the markets (Holzmann, 1997) and increased specialization in the investment decision-making process (Walker and Leffort, 2002).The World Bank analysis also makes the same claim; however, both Holzmann and the authors of the World Bank report argue that it is difficult to measure the real impact of the pension reform because Chile was carrying out a number of other macroeconomic reforms at the same time which also contributed to the development of the markets (Gill et al., 2004).

The extent of the pension system's impact on capital markets is at least in part determined by the degree of regulation of the investments.

In the case of Chile, since the inception of the system, the state has regulated the form in which the AFPs invest the funds. Different reforms over the years have introduced more flexibility in the investment decisions. By 2003, 29.1 per cent of the funds had to be invested in public instruments, 30.4 per cent in financial institutions, 19.9 per cent in foreign companies and 10.9 per cent in shares of Chilean companies (Mesa-Lago, 2004).

Lastly, while economic growth is different from economic development, data on economic growth should give the analyst some indication of the overall performance of the economy. Here again the picture is not that bright. A 1997 econometric study argued that the pension system increased the economic growth of the country at a rate of about 1–2.9 per cent per year (Holzmann, 1997); however, the author of the study also argued that, as one looks at this data, it is necessary to analyse the effects not only of the pension reform but also the other macroeconomic reforms carried out simultaneously by the Pinochet regime, which included the entire transformation of the economy and the establishment of market policies across the board.

What we do know about economic growth during the Pinochet period is that the implementation of a market economy produced a very large economic recession in 1975 and another one in 1982, and that as a result of these recessions the economy decreased by 12.9 per cent in 1975 and 14.4 per cent in 1985 (Borzutzky, 2002). The social data looks even worse since average wages in 1989 were 8 per cent below the 1970 level, while minimum income had decreased by 9 per cent. Income distribution data confirms that the model's effect were highly regressive, since between the 1970s and the 1980s the income of the highest 20 per cent of the population increased from 44.5 per cent to 54.5 per cent, while the lowest 60 per cent experienced a decline from 34 per cent to 25 per cent (Borzutzky, 2002).

Subsequent gains in economic performance were barely capable of offsetting the huge losses produced by the two recessionary processes. Economic growth improved after 1985 as a result of modifications made to the market model, and for the remainder of the 1980s economic growth remained at about 7 per cent and unemployment remained high at about 8.8 per cent The entire Pinochet period is also characterized by a large contraction in social spending and the growth in poverty. It is estimated that by the end of the regime, over 45 per cent of the population were below the poverty level and 27 per cent of those were defined as indigents or extremely poor. Poverty was undoubtedly linked to wage reduction, reduction in social spending and unemployment.

For the elderly, poverty was certainly linked to the privatization of social security. As noted above, the value of the pensions generated by the privatized system has not increased substantially, and for the majority of the population the choices seem to be between a government-provided minimum pension of about $130 per month or no pension at all, since about 50 per cent of the population are not contributing to the system (Borzutzky, 2002). Thus, the value of pensions remains low and insufficient; the system has generated a sizeable fiscal deficit, and it has also generated new inequalities along gender lines.

In conclusion, the privatized, defined contribution system has not generated a positive effect on the country's economic growth, which is what the framers of the system expected to obtain. The system has not had a positive effect on economic development if development is understood as improving the standards of living of the society. What it has done is to generate a very limited and unequal pension system which reinforces the existing income inequalities in the society.

The Bachelet administration's approach

Before discussing the specific policies proposed by the Bachelet administration, it is important to note that since the end of the Pinochet regime the country has been ruled by a centre–left coalition known as the Concertación and that the Concertación has maintained and reinforced the main characteristics of the market model designed by the previous regime while moving the country towards a process of democratization. Since 1990, the market model has not only been maintained but has also been reinforced through a number of policies, and probably the most important of these policies deal with Chile's integration into the world economy. Suffice it to say that Chile has liberalized international trade and signed free trade agreements with its major trading partners (Fermandois, 2006; Hecht-Oppenheim, 2006). Moreover, the major tenets of the market model, including the social security system, were not seriously questioned within the government coalition until the 2005 presidential elections. The fact that about 50 per cent of the population were not covered by the system and that the pensions received by the majority of the retirees were insufficient ignited the first national discussion about the implications of the pension system since its inception in 1981. What is even more remarkable is that both the candidate from the right-wing coalition, Sebastián Piñera (different from José Piñera) and Michelle Bachelet the Concertación's candidate, agreed on the need for reform.

The newly elected President Bachelet decided very early that reforming the existing pension system was a major priority. The President ordered the establishment of a commission (Consejo Asesor Presidencial para la Reforma Previsional, known also as Comision Marcel after the Commission's Director Mario Marcel, which is the name used here) charged with the task of studying the problems of the current system and proposing a set of solutions that would expand the coverage and improve the pensions. Mario Marcel, the Commission's director had previously been the National Budget Office's Director and has written extensively on social security issues. Other members were Alberto Arenas de Mesa, the current Budget Director and also very well known social security expert, the Ministers of Finance and Labor and about a dozen experts. While neither the AFPs representatives nor the labour representatives were part of the commission, the commission asked for testimony of national and international social security experts including international organizations such as the World Bank and the Inter-American Development Bank.

The Marcel Commission's report

The goals of the reform as stated in the Marcel Commission's report presented to President Bachelet in July of 2006 were to move towards the universalization of benefits, augment the pension system's replacement ratio until it becomes similar to the ratios existing in the developed nations, eliminate old-age poverty, reduce the variance in the replacement ratios and create a system that can sustain these goals over time. In order to reach these goals, the Marcel Commission proposed to structure a 'pilar solidario' or 'solidary pillar' which would guarantee basic state benefit to lower-income groups, augment competition among the AFPs, increase the rate of return and reduce investments risks, strengthen the private pillar and increase the transparency and predictability of the system. In order to achieve these goals the commission proposed to 'structure a multipillar system which would include a public, a contributive, and a voluntary pillar which would all be integrated and would complement each other' (Informe Comisión Marcel, 2006, pp. 99–101). The new 'solidary/public pillar' will be structured on the basis of a Universal Basic Pension, or Pensión Básica Universal, or Solidaria (PBU or PBS) for those who are unable to obtain a pension from the privatized, defined contribution system. According to the Commission's proposal, the new universal pension will be granted to all those who are 65 years or older and do not have sufficient resources to obtain a minimum pension. The universal pension is expected to replace the existing system of minimum and welfare pensions, which is seen as expensive and inadequate. The newly proposed system would also provide invalidity pensions to all those who qualify for a universal pension.

The new universal pension is designed to avoid old-age poverty and sustain an adequate level of consumption after retirement as well as to secure a decent pension to women, particularly those women who have participated in the labour market sporadically and to independent workers who today are basically deprived of any pensions. The goal of the proposed universal pension is to rapidly expand coverage by providing the pension to low-income workers who are unable to save enough or to save at all in the private system, workers that have been in and out of the labour market, including temporary and independent workers, and women. The commission estimated that about 65 per cent of those 65 years or older will benefit from the universal pension. Today only 15 per cent of those 65 years or older benefit from social assistance pensions, which leaves about 50 per cent of that population without any coverage (Informe Comisión Marcel, p. 108). The universal pension is expected to grow from $160 in the first year to about $330 per month by 2012; a sum that is expected to keep the retiree just above the poverty level, providing a replacement ratio of 84 per cent of the minimum net income of the workers over 65. The universal pension will also benefit those workers who due to an unstable employment history have a low density of contributions and as a result cannot obtain a pension under the current system. The government commission estimated that 56 per cent of those actually contributing to the system find themselves unable to get a pension due to the low density of contributions (Novoa, 2006). These workers will also benefit from a new unemployment insurance proposed by the commission which would pay the social security tax during the time the worker is unemployed. Other interesting suggestions are to create a state fund to subsidize the first two years of social security tax in order to encourage fulltime hiring of new young employees and the early payment of the monthly contribution.

A large section of the report is dedicated to gender issues, and the goal of the recommendations is to increase women's pensions, equalizing the value of male and female pensions, and arguing that as citizens women are entitled to the same pension benefits as men, and that the state is obligated to correct the inequities generated by the market and the society. In order to achieve these goals the commission proposed a number of interesting measures including the following among others: to make infant and child care a worker's right, to create a system through which the state will pay for up to a year of contributions per child in order to sustain the level of female contributions during the child rearing years and to allow women to access the universal pension at age 60 but calculating the benefits as if the woman were 65 years old in order to benefit women in the lower-income groups. It is necessary to highlight the importance of these proposals, particularly the notion that as citizens women are entitled to a decent pension and a pension that is not different from the male citizens and that equalizing women's pensions constitutes a positive step towards the reduction of socioeconomic inequalities and economic development.

The members of the commission also spent a considerable amount of time analysing the way in which the AFPs function and devising mechanisms to improve performance, accountability and competitiveness and reduce costs without changing the basic nature of the industry. As argued above, although profits in the industry are very high, there is little competition as the insured appears to be insensible, or not aware of the costs, because of the legal obligation of charging the same commissions to all the affiliates within an AFP and because of the existence of several barriers of entry. Given the complexity of these issues, the goals here are to increase awareness among the insured about the impact that the administrative costs have on their pensions and allow the entrance of new actors in the system while maintaining financial stability and efficiency. In order to achieve these goals the commission proposed to create a system through which entrance of new workers to the system will be regulated by the state through a 'biding system', according to which every year the state will group the newcomers into 'packets' and the AFPs will have to offer formal bids regarding commissions and other administrative costs. The state after examining the bids will allocate the entire group to the selected AFP. Once an AFP obtains a 'packet' of insured, they will be obligated to maintain the value of the commissions for at least 18 months. The report also proposes to modify the form in which the commissions are calculated in order to increase transparency and awareness about the value and impact of the commissions (Informe Comisión Marcel, 2006).

Finally, the report deals with the investment of the funds proposing measures to rationalize and introduce more flexibility in the investment regulations, including expanding investments abroad from the current 30 per cent to 80 per cent within three years. This policy if approved will certainly affect the local stock market, but it has been applauded by Wall Street. By November of 2006, investment abroad by the AFPs amounted to $27.2 billion or 31.4 per cent of all the pension fund (Keller, 2006). The bill also calls for the formation of 'a committee of users' for the workers, pensioners and administrators in order to increase the transparency of the system and for allowing banks to enter into the business of administering and providing pensions.

Legislative proposals

On receiving the Commission's report, President Bachelet named a Ministerial Committee headed by the Minister of Labor, Osvaldo Andrade, and formed by the Minister of Finance, the Director of the Budget Office and a few other high level officials charged with quickly drafting the necessary legislation on the basis of the Commission's report. The Inter-ministerial Committee finalized its work in mid-December 2006, and a bill was submitted to Congress soon after. However, renewed fear of political maneuvering and gridlock also began to appear even before the proposal was made public. Although the Bachelet administration has given high priority to this project, and the project is expected to have a solid majority in Congress, nobody expects an easy or quick legislative process. According to most analysts, discussion in Congress will take at the very least a year.

By and large, the proposals made by the Marcel Commission were well received by politicians. Antonio Leal, president of the Chamber of Deputies called it 'one of the most important social initiatives in the history of Chile and asked his colleagues to support the project in its entirety without getting stacked in the details' (Muñoz, 2006). Other members of Congress called for initiating the universal pension system in 2008, instead of 2009 as suggested by the Marcel Commission. Even El Mercurio, Chile's most conservative newspaper, editorialized that the proposals made by the Marcel Commission were an improvement over the current system of minimum and welfare pensions. El Mercurio was quick to praise the fact that no new taxes will be established to pay for the new benefits; however, it highlighted the fact that the PBU could diminish the incentive to contribute to the private system and did not support the idea of increasing competitiveness through the bids. Administradoras de Fondos de Pensiones' representatives also opposed this proposal and have argued that it is actually unconstitutional and that they are willing to go to court to fight for their exclusive right to administer the pension funds. On the other hand, the AFP's representatives favour investment deregulation and expanding the opportunities for investment abroad (El Mercurio.com, 17 December, 2006).

The Chamber of Deputies' Labor Committee approved the 'legislative idea' in January of 2007 and was expected to begin detailed discussions of the bill in March of 2007. Members of the committee are expected to introduce modifications to the bill, including the idea of limiting the commissions charged by the AFPs and forcing the employers to contribute to the system. While both measures are unacceptable to the right wing opposition parties, both government and opposition agree that the PBU should be given to women at age 60 and not 65 as proposed by the bill because it discriminates against women, since women can now retire at 60 (Alvarez, 2007).

The proposed universal pension and economic development

The current economic model emphasizes the importance of the market and the country's integration into the world economy as critical engines of economic development. Throughout the world the process of globalization has increased inequality both within and among countries and the Chilean case fits this mould. From 1990 to 1998 the economy grew at a rate of about 7 per cent per year, and after a decline due to the Asian crisis the economy began to grow again in 2005. In 2005 economic growth rate was 5.2 per cent and for 2006 it was 4.2 per cent. Estimates for 2007 indicate that the economy will grow at more than 5 per cent. The high rates of growth have produced dramatic reductions in poverty from over 40 per cent in 1990 to 18 per cent in 2004, but inequality has actually increased. Chile's Gini coefficient is estimated to be between 0.56 and 0.58, depending on the analyst. This coefficient places Chile as one of the most unequal countries in the world and third worst in Latin America, which is the continent that exhibits the most pronounced inequalities. Thus, despite social commitments of the post-Pinochet administrations, inequality is slightly worse today than what it was in 1990 (Borzutzky and Hecht-Oppenheim, 2006).

If approved by Congress, the reforms proposed by the Marcel Commission should have a positive effect both on the retirees and on economic development. Since the major problems with the current system are lack of coverage and socioeconomic and gender inequities, the reforms proposed by the commission are geared to directly reduce these inequities and increase coverage. But for these policies to have a positive effect on economic development the universal pension has to reflect a real increase in the income of the lower-income groups that it is expected to serve. The value of the universal pension is expected to increase from $160 to $330 per month between 2009 and 2012. At $160 per month, the PBU is not a real improvement over the $130 currently received by those who can only get a minimum pension, but it will be a real gain for those who are not getting a pension at all. If and when it reaches $330, the effects should be clearly beneficial. Another form of assessing the impact of the universal pension is by looking at the number of people receiving this benefit. Current estimates are that as soon as the new law is approved 510,000 people will receive some fiscal contribution and that by 2017 the number of beneficiaries will reach 1,600,000. Politicians from the right and the government coalition are asking for a faster implementation of the new provisions beginning not in 2009 but in 2008 (Alvarez, 2007).

The proposals regarding the creation of a pension insurance for the unemployed, and mechanisms to supplement women's pensions should also have beneficial effects on those specific groups as well as on the overall distribution of retirement income. Bringing in the banks into the system has the potential of increasing competitiveness and reducing administrative costs; assuming the government is determined to regulate the commissions charged by the industry.

Chile today has a strong economy and a large fiscal surplus. If all the Commission's proposals are implemented, new social security expenditure will amount to 1 per cent of GDP by 2025, which is double of what the state will spend in minimum and welfare pensions if the system were to remain as it is now. Most of the new spending (0.8 per cent of GDP) will go to financing the proposed PUB (Rojas, 2006). The country's economy generated a $22.2 billion surplus in 2006, and it is estimated that for 2007 the surplus will be between $13.2 and $18.6 billion depending on the price of copper and the amount of copper exported mostly to China and India (Castañeda, 2007a). However economic policymakers have designed the so called 1 per cent rule according to which only 1 per cent of the surplus can be invested in the country in order to avoid inflation and pressures on the exchange rate. Although foreign and national experts argue that a larger portion of the surplus could be brought to the country, Finance Minister Velasco has consistently argued that a larger investment in social programmes is likely to destabilize economic performance.

Poverty in the midst of plenty: challenge for the future

As indicated in the introduction to this book, economic development is a concept that involves some tangible improvements in the living standards of the majority of the society. This chapter has examined the connections between social security and economic development in Chile under two different systems and the potential effects of the Bachelet administration's proposed reforms.

Chile's economy is growing at healthy rates; there is low inflation and low debt, and trade is generating a sizeable surplus. At the same time, while social spending has grown since the beginning of the transition to democracy, it has not grown enough to offset the inequalities embedded in the market economic model. From our standpoint, reluctance to increase social spending will limit future growth and development. Existing research points to the fact that pro-growth market policies such as financial development, trade liberalization and reductions in social spending increase inequality and limit future economic growth. The same research also argues that only pro-poverty and pro-equality policies will have some redistributive effect and facilitate domestic economic growth and equality (Lopez, 2003). Among those policies social security occupies a critical place.

To the extent that inequality is limiting the possibilities of economic development in Chile, I would argue that the effects of the current social security system has been to deter and not foster development. As argued above, Chile exhibits one of the most unequal distribution of income in the world with a Gini coefficient of about 0.57, and 'the distribution of retirement income is much more unequal than the distribution of active life income for the same cohort. ... The same can be said for the level of minimum pension guaranteed by the state' (Reyes and Pino, 2005). In conclusion, the Marcel commission has designed a set of policies that have the potential to improve distribution and economic development if they are fully implemented and if spending on social security increases substantially. If the government fails to increase spending in social security and other social programmes, a large group of Chileans will in the future continue to live in poverty in the midst of plenty.

References

Acuña, R. and Iglesias, A. (2001). 'Chile's Pension Reform After 20 Years', Washington D.C.: World Bank, Working paper/0129.

Alvarez, I. (2007). 'Cambios en el sistema de pensiones: Los seis puntos que encenderán el debate sobre la reforma provisional desde Marzo' El Mercurio. com, 29 January, 2007.

Arenas de Mesa, A. (1999). 'Efectos fiscales del sistema de pensiones en Chile: Proyección del déficit previsional, 1999–2037', Presented to the Seminario sobre responsabilidades fiscales en el sistema de pensiones, Santiago, 2 and 3 September.

Arenas de Mesa A. and Montecinos, V. (1996). 'The Privatization of Social Security and Women's Welfare: Gender Effects of the Chilean Reform', *Latin American Research Review*, 34, 37 and 38.

Arenas de Mesa, A. and Hernández, H. (2001) 'Analísis, evolución y propuestas de ampliación de la cobertura del sistema civil de pensiones en Chile' en F. Bertranou (ed.) *Cobertura previsional en Argentina*. Brasil y Chile, Santiago: OIT.

Bertranou, F. and Arenas de Mesa, A. (2003). *Protección social y género en Argentina*. Brasil and Chile, Santiago: OIT.

Borzutzky, S. (2002) *Vital Connections: Politics, Social Security and Inequality in Chile*. Notre Dame, Indiana: University of Notre Dame Press, chapter 3.

Borzutzky, S. (2005). 'From Chicago to Santiago: Neoliberalism and Social Security Privatization in Chile', *Governance*, 18(4), October 2005.

Borzutzky, S. and Hecht-Oppenheim, L., eds (2006). *After Pinochet: The Chilean Road to Democracy and the Market*. Gainesville: University Press of Florida.

Castañeda, L. (2007a). 'Exportaciones e importaciones: Expertos prevén caída del superávit comercial por menor precio del cobre' El Mercurio.com, 10 April, 2007.

Castañeda, L. (2007b). 'Informe de OIT: Desempleo de chilenas llega a mínimo en 8 años, pero participación laboral aun es baja', El Mercurio.com, 8 March 2007.

Consejo Asesor Presidencial para la Reforma Previsional, or Comisión Marcel, Informe, El Mercurio.com, several issues, 16 November 2007.

Engel, E. (2005). 'El terror de las AP', *La Tercera*, 29 August, 2005.

Fermandois, J. (2006). 'Peace at Home, Turbulence Abroad: The Foreign Policy of the Lagos Administration'. In Borzutzky, S. and Hecht-Oppenheim, L. (ed.), *After Pinochet: The Chilean Road to Democracy and the Market*. Gainesville: University Press of Florida, pp. 118–171.

Frei, E. (1965). State of the Nation Speech.

García, D. (2006). 'Reforma previsional: Banco Mundial crítica falta de competencia y altos precios de las AFP', El Mercurio.com, 18 April, 2006. This World Bank report was presented to the Marcel Comisión.

García, D. (2007). 'Utilidades en 2006: Arthur defiende ganancias de las AFP ante las críticas', El Mercurio.com, 12 March, 2007.

Gill, I., Packard, T. and Yermo, J. (2004). *Keeping the Promise of Old Age Income Security in Latin America: A Regional Study of Social Security Reform*. Washington DC: World Bank.

Hecht-Oppenheim, L. (2006). 'Chilean Economic Policy under the Concertación: The Triumph of the Market?' In Borzutzky, S. and Hecht-Oppenheim (eds), *After Pinochet: The Chilean Road to Democracy and the Market*. Gainesville: University Press of Florida, pp. 93–117.

Holzmann, R. (1997). 'Pension Reform, Financial Market Development and Economic Growth: Preliminary Evidence from Chile', Washington DC: IMF Staff Papers No. 44.

Keller, N. (2006). 'Wall Street valida alza de límite de inversión de las AFP', El Mercurio.com, 26 December, 2006.

Lopez, H. (2003). 'Macroeconomics and Inequality', Washington DC: World Bank, (PRMPR). 25 September.

Mesa-Lago, C. (1976). *Social Security in Latin America: Pressure Groups, Stratification and Inequality*. Pittsburgh: University of Pittsburgh Press.

Mesa-Lago, C. (1998), 'Pension Reform Around the World: Comparative Features and Performance of Structural Pension Reforms in Latin America', *Brooklyn Law Review*, 64, 786.

Mesa-Lago, C. (2001). 'La reforma estructural de las pensiones en América Latina: Modelos, características, resultados y conclusiones', *Revista Internacional de la Seguridad Social*, 54(4), 67–92.

Mesa-Lago, C. (2004). 'Lecciones y desafíos de 23 años de reformas estructurales de pensiones en América Latina' in El Sistema de pensiones en Chile en el contexto mundial y de América Latina: Evaluación y desafíos: Ponencias del Seminario Internacional, Santiago 22 y 23 de Abril de 2004', Oficina Internacional del Trabajo.

Muñoz, D. (2006). 'PDC plantea adelantar beneficio de la pensión básica', El Mercurio.com, 12 December, 2006.

Novoa, S. (2006). 'Las definiciones pendientes de Bachelet', El Mercurio.com, 26 June, 2006.

Reyes, G. and Pino, F. (2006). 'Income Inequality in an Individual Capitalization Pension System: The Case of Chile' p. 1, Superintendencia de AFP, mimeo, safp.cl internet.

Rojas, M. (2006). 'Propuesta previsional de la Comisión Marcel: Eyzaguirre cuestiona la fórmula de financiamiento de la reforma', El Mercurio.com, 14 July, 2006.

Rother, L. 'Chile Proposes to Reform Pension System', *New York Times*, 27 January, 2005.

Superintendencia de Administradora de Pensiones (SAFP), Boletín Estadístico Mensual, Vols. 9 and 10, (148) Diciembre, 1998: 3 and 28.

SAFP (2001). Unpublished data.

SAFP (2003). Boletin Estadístico Mensual, No. 5.

Walker, E. and Leffort, F. (2002). 'Pension Reform and Capital Markets: Are There Any (Hard) Links?', Washington DC: World Bank Social Protection Paper No. 0201.

5
China: Social Security in the Context of Rapid Economic Growth

Kwong-leung Tang and Raymond Ngan Man-hung

China has experienced extraordinarily rapid economic growth in the past two decades. For the years 2002–2005, it registered a 9 per cent average annual growth rate. It is now predicted that China's economy will grow by 8.8 per cent for 2007, down only slightly from this year's expected 9.5 per cent (Asian Development Bank, 2006). The country's remarkable performance makes it the fastest growing of the world's major economies. By some measures, China accounts for an even bigger share of global growth than does the United States.

But this strong economic performance and the government's commitment to growth belies the fact that China has also been devoting attention to social development. Political and social stability is critical to maintaining its growth momentum, and the social security reforms it has undertaken in recent years has improved the livelihoods of poor, unemployed and elderly people. Former Premier Zhu Rongji declared that social security was a major issue for development which would positively affect economic and social stability (*China Daily*, 6 March, 2001). Social stability could be easily undermined by distorted development – a situation in which social development lags greatly behind economic development (Midgley, 1995, 1999).

Because China's social security reforms have implications for the rest of the world, this chapter describes the social security changes that have taken place and analyses them in the light of economic development of China. We argue that current economic reforms in China have been complemented by a wider social policy agenda involving old age, social assistance, health care and unemployment benefits that addresses the social consequences of economic development and ensures the investment in human capital necessary for economic growth. The main focus of our analysis is the old-age social insurance programme catering to retirement needs. This programme has the following advantages: it widens coverage, facilitates economic development, seeks a minimum entitlement, fosters social integration and enhances individual participation and responsibility.

China: history, politics and the challenge of development

Looking back, China (or 'Zhongguo' meaning the Central Kingdom) had a long and glorious history. Chinese officials and historians traditionally positioned the Emperor of China at the centre of the world, conceiving of concentric rings that extended from the cultural centre to barbaric borderlands. In the Ming/Qing Dynasties (fifteenth to nineteenth centuries), there was intensive trade between Europe and China, institutionalized under a system of ports of trade that kept the political economy of China intact.

In the nineteenth century, there was a marked transformation as Asia became the target of Western powers. Imperial China (the Qing dynasty under Manchu rule) was strong until the middle of the nineteenth century when it was defeated in a series of wars with various Western powers. After the downfall of Qing dynasty, the people in China suffered tremendously in the next fifty years under the rule of the Nationalist Government, which was not able resist the encroaching aggression of the imperialist powers.

Immediately after the end of Second World War, the Communists defeated the Nationalists after a bitter civil war and declared the establishment of the People's Republic of China on 1 October 1949. The Chinese Communist Party (CPP) under the leadership of charismatic Mao Zedong was in full control of the country and perceived itself as the embodiment of the general will of the Chinese society (Liu, 1996). During Mao's era (1949–1976), China witnessed a long period of political revolution in the 1950s, culminating in the disastrous Cultural Revolution in 1966–1967.

After Chairman Mao's death in 1976 came the era of Deng Xiaoping who made a number of significant political changes: de-collectivizing agriculture, dismantling communes, advocating commodification of land values, encouraging private investment and propagating the idea that it was good to have a few to get rich first (Davis, 1989). In addition to this social revolution, the CPP opened up China introducing the idea of 'socialism with Chinese characteristics' and initiating economic reforms. The goals of Deng's reforms could be summed up by the Four Modernizations: those of agriculture, industry, science and technology and the military. The strategy for achieving these aims of becoming a modern, industrial nation was the socialist market economy. On the welfare front, Deng's strategy was to drop the egalitarian ideals and collectivist solutions pursued by Mao, embracing instead an ideology that 'validates individual rather than group goals, and private rather than public solutions' (Davis, 1989, p. 578). There were signs that privatization of social welfare provision had gained ground (Tang, 1999; Wong, 1994).

Under Deng's leadership (1978–1992), China developed into one of the fastest growing economies in the world. The next generation of leadership under Jiang Zemin and Zhu Rongji carried on the economic reforms initiated by Deng. Economically, under Jiang's leadership (1992–2004), China secured an average of 8 per cent GDP growth annually. The economic success of China made it a model of development for many developing countries. Notably, President Jiang introduced the idea of 'Three Represents', legitimizing the entry of private business owners into the Communist party. In 2002, this doctrine was enshrined in China's Constitution.

However, after years of unfettered economic growth, social development clearly lagged behind economic growth. Moreover, the structural problems in the Chinese economy, linked with the legacy of Dengist reforms, became apparent. Besides the increasing regional disparity, new wealth generated continued to be massively concentrated in few hands (Fabre, 1999). There were other social problems: widening urban–rural gaps, peasant unrest, corruption, inadequate social services and environmental degradation.

These issues posed as serious social and political problems to the successors of President Jiang, threatening to undermine the political stability of the country. The plight of the 'losers' of economic reforms did receive attention from the current Chinese government (Hu-Wen Administration). Balancing social stability with economic development is the main development of the government. The idea of 'harmonious society' was first proposed by President Hu Jintao in 2005 as the guiding philosophy for his administration, which served as a corrective to the over-emphasis on economic development. He aimed at achieving an overall societal balance, reducing social tensions. In principle, a harmonious society would feature democracy, the rule of law, equity, justice, sincerity, amity and vitality (*People's Daily online*, 21 February, 2005).

Such a society would give full scope to people's talent and creativity, enable them to share the social wealth brought by economic reform and forge a closer relationship between the people and government.

Economically, President Hu's vision was to build moderately prosperous society in an all-round way that would benefit all the peoples, aiming at raising China's GDP to US$4 trillion by 2020, averaging US$3,000 per person. One important factor that could affect this economic target comes from China's growing population. Its population now exceeds 1.3 billion (compared to 0.583 billion in 1953). China is the world's most populous country, one out of every five people in the world lives in China. Admittedly, demographic transition has occurred more rapidly in China than in most developed countries. As the population ages, the growth rate of the working-age population has started to decline and the absolute quantity of the working-age population will begin to shrink after 2015, which would inevitably result in structural labour shortage (Cai and Wang, 2006).

As discussed, the central government has concentrated on the importance of building a harmonious society in the past two years. President Hu Jintao has instructed his senior officials to establish a fine-tuned management system and enhanced their capacity to deal with the problems facing the country. Additionally, he has stressed the importance of balancing the interests of different social groups and making sure that people live safe and happy lives in a politically stable community (*China Daily*, 20 February, 2005).

The building of a harmonious society has to be seen in the context of China's rising social inequities and social unrest. As noted in the *2006 Blue Book of Social Development*, published by the prestigious Chinese Academy of Social Sciences (2006), social stability has weakened since 1990 amid widening wealth disparities – between rich and poor, between urban and rural areas and between rich coastal cities and poorer inland provinces. A dramatic rise in land disputes and clashes between the public and government officials over environmental issues was noted, especially during the years 2003–2005 (*Financial Times*, 25 January, 2006). The rural–urban prosperity gap remains large. In 2005, per capita disposable income in urban areas rose by 9.6 per cent in real terms to 10,493 yuan (in December 2007, US$1 = 7.3 yuan). In the rural areas, where three-fifths of the population resides, there was a more modest growth rate of 6.2 per cent, taking average income to just 3,255 yuan (Chinese Academy of Social Sciences, 2006; *South China Morning Post*, 27 January, 2006).

In this socially divisive context, social security reforms – especially changes in social security protection schemes for vulnerable social groups such as the unemployed, the destitute and the old – carry added significance. The National People's Congress in March 2006 endorsed the 11th Five-Year Plan (2006–2010), which builds on a gradual shift in the government's emphasis since 2003 on policies of balanced, equitable and sustainable development. This plan gives attention to standards of living and the environment as well as to the economy (ADB, 2006). Eight of the twenty-two core goals of the 11th Five-Year Plan (2006–2010) touch on social development (years of education per capita, coverage of urban basic old-age pension, coverage of rural cooperative medical care, new jobs created for urban residents, number of rural labourers transferred to non-agricultural sector, urban registered unemployment rate, per capita disposable income of urban residents and per capita net income of rural residents), while another eight deal with the environment. As noted, one of these goals relates to the old-age pension system. In 2004, China published its first-ever White Paper on social security, detailing the current conditions of the country's social security programme and the government's policy on social security (Information Office of the State Council, 2004). The White Paper relates how China established and improved its socialist market economy system in the mid-1980s. It also describes the social security reforms that were introduced and outlines a basic framework of a comprehensive social security system under the market-economy system.

The new old-age insurance programme

According to the White Paper on Social Security (2004), China's social security system includes social insurance, social welfare, the special care and placement system, social relief and housing services. Social insurance is given prominence and includes old-age insurance, unemployment insurance, medical insurance, work-related injury insurance and maternity insurance.

Social security reform has been given the high priority by the Chinese leadership. Under Maoist socialism, urban workers received welfare services through the state-owned enterprises and collectives in which they worked. The state-owned enterprises were based primarily in urban areas and employed the minority of the population. The collectives were rural communal institutions. As a result of China's transition to a market economy, the traditional enterprise-based and collective-based welfare system has been gradually dismantled and replaced with a new and more market-oriented system to cope with an aging population and millions of laid-off state workers. Questions about the financing and delivery of pensions, unemployment benefits, social assistance and medical care to workers have come to the forefront (*China Daily*, 10 December, 1998).

It was soon after the Communist takeover when China, ahead of most other developing countries, introduced social security for its industrial workers largely in the urban areas. The social security programme in China can be traced back to 1951, when the first Labour Insurance Regulation was promulgated. The government introduced an elaborate social security programme covering health insurance, injured worker insurance and old-age insurance for its workers. This programme which was known as 'labour insurance' applied only to industrial workers in China's state-owned enterprises. While the benefits were generous, all the costs of the labour insurance programme were borne by these enterprises (Liu, 1996). The system was funded on a pay-as-you-go basis. The pensions were paid from the output of current workers and the profits of their enterprises. There was no contribution from the employees, since the worker's rights to labour insurance had been specifically written into the country's Constitution (Wong et al., 2004, Dixon, 1981).

Over time, social spending gradually became a heavy burden on most state-owned enterprises. More importantly, many state enterprises were inefficient, and they suffered heavy economic losses. Ever since the 1980s, the enterprise system has faced a financial crisis – indeed, one-third of state-owned enterprises were loss-making (Hu, 1998; Tang and Ngan, 2001). The central government poured in more than 80 per cent of its reserve financial assets into the state-owned enterprises to encourage growth in the mid-1990s and to maintain the loyalty of urban workers and local managerial elites. This is important, since some 70 per cent of urban households have workers employed in the state sector.

Since 1978, the Chinese government introduced a series of economic reforms which transformed the country into a 'socialist market economy'. More individual and private enterprises, joint ventures and foreign-owned enterprises have been set up, and the central government began to privatize many bankrupt state-owned enterprises. In this context, the state-owned enterprises faced a very competitive environment. They had to assume social responsibilities for their workers and at the same time had to survive intense competition from a new, dynamic private sector. In 1987, new labour standards were introduced, changing the system of 'iron-bowl' lifelong employment to one of employment by contract. The government realized that there was an urgent need to introduce fundamental changes in the old enterprise-based social security system to make it compatible with economic reforms and with the state's obligation to pay off its pension debt (Ngan and Tang, 2003).

There was also demographic pressure to reform the existing state-owned enterprise social security system. China's population of seniors has grown very rapidly. According to some estimates (World Bank, 1997a), the number of China's elderly will rise from about 76 million in 1995 to 300 million by 2050. Compounding this problem is the fact that the whole system of state-owned enterprise welfare has been inherently fragile and decentralized. The uneven sharing of financial responsibility for employees' social security among enterprises was problematic, and the financing and administration of the programmes was fragmented, with varying rates of pension payment. Its coverage was limited. Older enterprises with more retired people to support were disadvantaged when compared to newer enterprises (Tang and Ngan, 2001).

In the light of these developments, massive reforms were launched in the early 1990s to revamp the enterprise-based social security system into a national old-age insurance system administered at the provincial level by Social Insurance bureaus. All pension-related receipts and payments on pensions are now the responsibility of these bureaus (Tang and Ngan, 2001). Initially, the new system was tested in several provinces, but since 1997, with the promulgation of a national decree (*'A Decision on Establishing a Unified Basic Pension System for Enterprise Workers'*) it has been adopted nationally, creating a unified pension system.

The decree requires that each worker contribute regularly to a basic old-age pension funded through social insurance and also to an individual pension account. The basic pension is comprised of two parts: a flat rate pension and an income-related pension component. The individual account is a fully funded pension scheme and accumulated contributions can be withdrawn with interest when the worker retires. The decree also requires that the basic old-age insurance pension be set at 20 per cent of the average wage of the local area in which the pensioner resides. The pension will be adjusted in line with increases in the average wage to offset inflation. Contributions to the old-age insurance pension by employing enterprises should not exceed 20 per cent of the enterprises' total wage bills.

Starting from 1997, workers' contributions were set at no less than 4 per cent of their monthly salaries. This is to be raised by 1 per cent every two years from 1998, eventually reaching a ceiling of 8 per cent. Contributions to the individual funded pension account are matched by contribution from the employing enterprise. It is expected that contributions to these individual accounts will rise to 11 per cent of the worker's salary. In other words, when the mandatory worker contributions reach 8 per cent, it is anticipated that enterprises may be able to reduce their contribution to as low as 3 per cent.

A basket of other supportive social security programmes

The shift from a state-owned enterprise social security system to a national, provincially administered social security system has been necessitated by the privatization and breakdown of the state enterprises which employed the bulk of China's urban, industrial workers. In addition to covering the current and former workers of the state-owned enterprises, other urban workers in regular employment are also covered. However, in view of the dramatic changes which have taken place, the new insurance system is supplemented and augmented by other social security programmes. Because many inefficient enterprises have been forced to close due to the market reforms resulting in layoffs, the government has introduced an unemployment insurance programme which provides for the maintenance of income for those who are unemployed. It has also introduced a social assistance scheme and worker retraining programmes to soothe the transition of laid-off workers back into the job market.

Unemployment insurance was first introduced in 1986, covering workers in urban enterprises and based on contributions from enterprises and individual workers. An allowance equal to 50–75 per cent of the basic wage was available for a maximum of two years. In 1993, the allowance was revised to 120–150 per cent of the local social relief rate. In 1995, the total number of staff and workers receiving unemployment insurance reached 95 million. By the end of 2003, some 103.73 million people were participating in the unemployment insurance scheme, which provided unemployment insurance benefits of varying time limits to 7.42 million laid-off employees. The programme guaranteed the basic livelihood of unemployed workers and helped them find new jobs (White Paper on Social Security, 2004).

Between 1997 and 2000, a new three-tier basic income support system was introduced for unemployed workers. Under this system, redundant workers were referred to approach Labour Re-employment Service Centres established by their enterprises and their counties of residence where they participated in retraining and re-employment services. They were paid a monthly basic living subsidy for a maximum of three years. The hope was that workers with these living allowances would be able to be retrained and take advantage of re-employment services without worrying about making a living. After the three years of retraining, workers who are still unable to find a job can receive additional unemployment insurance benefits for a maximum of two more years. If they had not found employment by the end of this period, they were to be referred for consideration for social assistance.

Overall, the central government favours a multi-pronged approach that relies on job creation, re-employment and strengthening minimum protection to help laid-off workers. This approach has been supplemented by provincial and municipal governments. A case in point is the city of Shenyang which invested 20 million yuan in infrastructural projects to create jobs for the laid-off workers. Importantly, this endeavour was supplanted by an old-age insurance system and a minimum living standard allowance (Hurst and O'Brien, 2002).

In addition to the unemployment programme, a national social assistance programme has been put in place primarily to assist workers who have been made redundant by the breakdown of the state-owned enterprise social security system and who have exhausted their unemployment benefits. The social assistance system was first introduced in Shanghai in 1993 and is known as the Minimum Living Standard Guarantee System (MLSGS). It extended the coverage of an existing emergency relief system, raised the levels of benefits and obtained financial contributions from local governments. As of September 2002, the system had spread to almost all major cities in China. By then 19.63 million people were receiving benefits.

Of the recipients of the system, 79 per cent are known as the new urban poor. They are comprised of redundant workers whose unemployment insurance has expired and who are still awaiting employment. They have a per capita household income lower than the minimum living standard. The programme also serves pensioners receiving benefits under the old state-owned enterprise system which are too meagre to ensure a basic standard of living. Also included among the new urban poor are unemployed migrant workers who came from the rural areas in search of work (Shanghai Encyclopedia, 1999). The remaining 21 per cent of recipients are destitute people who have no family members to support them, no income and no earning capacity. These criteria are colloquially referred to as the 'three no's'. Although the programme provides cash for urban poor residents, it carries a certain degree of stigma. In addition, benefit levels are generally low (Leung, 2006).

The average benefit payment to beneficiaries under the scheme nationwide in 2004 was 65 to 70 yuan per month. However, at this time the average minimum income standard nationwide was 159 yuan per capita per month (Leung, 2006). The total spending on payments for social assistance system in the major cities was in the range of 18.5 to 20.5 billion yuan for the years 2004 and 2005 (Ministry of Civil Affairs, 2005). Moreover, the scheme has several problems. In addition to paying meagre benefits and stigmatizing claimants, it faces funding challenges. In terms of the source of financing, the costs are met by local counties and municipal governments which obtain revenues by taxing local firms including the state-owned and private enterprises. These enterprises thus face double taxes to meet the costs of social security at both the national and local levels.

Although the social assistance programme provides some relief to the unemployed and poor in the country's cities, the prospect of them escaping the poverty trap created by the system remains dim. Generally, many long-term unemployed people are unable to find jobs in the open market, often because their long record of unemployment works against them. Others are unable to find employment because of personal incapacities related to advancing age or disability. Nevertheless, social assistance plays a crucial role in China's social security system and also serves to maintain social stability during a time of rapid economic change and dislocation (Leung, 2006).

Challenges to the new old-age insurance programme

Overall, the old-age insurance programme has become more financially viable and pragmatic. The system is state managed and redistributive. After some years of implementation, however, a number of problems with the system have been identified. The scheme is not yet fully implemented throughout China. Payment transfers among different provinces, especially from provinces in the South to the poorer inner provinces in the West (as in the case of migrant workers), are still not done effectively. According to a study by the Chinese Academy of Social Sciences (2004), almost all provinces (except Fukien, Chejang and Shangdong) struggled to balance their annual receipts and pension claims in 2001. An accumulated annual deficit of 30 billion yuan was reported in the same period, especially in cities with older industries

(Chinese Academy of Social Sciences, 2004). There is still room for improvement in extending the unified pension system from local cities and provinces to the national level.

There is also the problem of under-reporting enterprise payments to the new old-age insurance system. This problem has been identified by local Ministries of Labour and Social Security. It is particularly acute among those private enterprises employing large number of migrant workers who have no registered household in the employing city.

There are other implementation problems as well. As the China Economic Research and Advisory Programme (2005), comprised of leading Chinese officials and overseas experts, notes

> Fragmented organization and limited coverage contributed to financing difficulties and to incompleteness of social insurance. The deficits contribute to the 'empty individual accounts' – empty because local governments often use the contributions made by workers to their individual accounts to finance deficits in the social pool. Moreover, a system has not been developed for organizing investments in capital investments. (p. 1)

The problem of contributions came to light when industrial workers were interviewed by the authors of this chapter who in 1999 conducted a focus group comprising six young (26–36 years old) to middle-aged (40–45 years old) workers from the Cadre Cultivation Department of the Guangzhou Workers' University (Ngan and Tang, 2003). Our informants expressed concern about paying higher contribution rates not only for their pensions but also for housing and medical insurance accounts. They had to contribute at least 5 per cent of their pay to their own housing units; another 3 per cent was set aside for the medical insurance scheme. The informants knew that a few bankrupt enterprises had failed to pay regular contributions to their old-age insurance funds for at least three years, and they were worried about the prospects of their own enterprises meeting their obligations.

Obviously, China's present old-age insurance system has room for improvement in terms of legislation, coverage, contributions, fund-pooling, management and risk resistance. At the same time, China has been exposed to various ideological forces that impinge on social security policy resulting in tensions and even confusion. Several scholars (Tang and Ngan, 2001; White, 1998; Wong et al., 2006) have identified potent forces at work: socialist, neoliberal and pragmatic. The socialist position emphasizes state responsibility and redistributive fairness as guiding principles for social security reform. Because China is still officially a socialist state, this position is popular among some groups (the Ministry of Labour, trade unions and civil servants). But it is hard to envisage China going back to its earlier enterprise-based socialist model of pension provision. It would impose a great financial burden on the country, and such an approach is not congruent with the dominant route of a socialist market system that emphasizes individual responsibility.

On the other hand, some people on the right of the political spectrum have suggested that the government of China must drop its socialist commitments and develop a market-based system for old age and health protection based on individual accounts and private investments. This form of market liberalism requires individuals to be fully responsible for their retirement with the state playing only a limited, residual role. For example, neoliberal analysts such as Song and Chu (1997) suggest that China develop a market-based system based on individual accounts and private investments to provide adequate old age and health protection. The crux of their argument is that a private system will increase economic growth and assist economic restructuring. In addition, the basic insurance-funded pension pillar has been heavily challenged by neoliberal critics. For instance, Feldstein (2004) has called for greater emphasis on funded benefits and a shift to a conditional defined (state) benefit guarantee.

Rising unemployment and expensive health-care costs have fuelled the call for a privatized system. Recommendations to the Chinese government to privatize these social services is backed by seemingly alarming cost estimates from international organizations that favour full privatization. The World Bank (1997a, 1997b) has estimated that China's implicit pension debt (benefits paid to today's pensioners and the pension rights of current workers) at 141 per cent of national income. The International Monetary Fund estimated that the minimal cost in 2003 of shifting to a viable pension system was 7 per cent of national income (approx. $160 billion).

On the other hand, some scholars such as Li and Li (2003) raise the issue of transition costs pointing out that China lacks a good transition plan to bridge the change from a pay–as–you–go pension scheme to a funded pension programme. The funds needed to meet current pension expenses while allowing a new funded system to be established would, they contend, be substantial. For this reason, they propose that a special debt fund (known as an earmarked pension debt) be introduced. They claimed that this initiative is socially equitable, since future generations who will probably be richer than the current one given the continual economic growth and human capital investment will have to shoulder the burden by paying more taxes to the government.

Clearly, the government needs to address the financial concerns raised by neoliberal critics. However, the central government is cautious and is reluctant to undertake radical solutions such as the neoliberal or notional defined contribution approach. If they did, they would seem to be losing sight of the social goals of the present system. On the one hand, the direction of change is affirmed by the central government. On the other hand, the fear of social instability has provided a strong and consistent incentive for the government not to forfeit its responsibility to urban workers. In terms of social development, the Chinese government is moving cautiously, maintaining a viable balance between social protection and economic development (Tang and Ngan, 2001).

Directions of change

The future development of social security in China will depend on incremental decisions taken by the central government in the light of domestic realities. But, as was shown already, the government is also influenced by international developments. Well respected international experts and multinational organizations such as the World Bank and International Monetary Fund have all influenced the formulation of social security policy. The government is also aware of changes taking place in other parts of the world, particularly in Latin America where a number of governments have privatized their insurance funded old-age retirement programmes in recent years. In a quantitative analysis of 57 countries, Brooks (2005) constructed a causal model to explain the likelihood and degree of pension privatization, based on the unique incentives and constraints created by domestic political and economic structures in each country. He finds that the likelihood and degree of structural pension reform is shaped by the cost of the existing pension system, political party structures, domestic investment and debt levels as well as geopolitical networks.

In China, it is clear that forces such as domestic political and social contexts, along with rapid economic development, have significantly influenced the central government's thinking on social security. At present, there is no indication that the Hu administration will adopt the neoliberal recipe for full privatization. The government is aware that if it goes in this direction, the problem of social inequality will inevitably worsen. In the context of rising social inequalities in both the cities and rural areas, the government will avoid exacerbating this existing situation. The government may also realize that increasing workers' contribution rates to their individual accounts is not a simple matter. In particular, workers in the state-owned enterprises are not able to do much with their individual accounts.

Even though China acceded to the World Trade Organization (WTO) in 2001 and has been the beneficiary of open and free trade, the government's stance towards neoliberal globalization is cautious and reveals a high degree of pragmatism. This cautious attitude does not come from its ideological socialist roots but rather from a pragmatic assessment of the situation. Facing rising income inequities and peasant unrest, it is increasingly aware of the harmful effects of free trade, competition and deregulation on its peoples (Oi, 1999). Faced with greater exposure to economic globalization, the current leadership under Hu Jintao and Wen Jiabao is becoming more sympathetic to the losers of the economic reforms. These include unemployed workers, landless farmers and others who have been affected by rapid economic change.

It is unlikely that the government will abandon its present support of a pragmatic social security model which incorporates the strengths of the social insurance old-age retirement programme supplemented by individual retirement accounts. In other words, it remains committed to the present model. However, it is also likely that changes will be forthcoming. As the White Paper on Social Security (2004) points out, 'To press ahead with the improvement of the social security system is an important task for the Chinese government in its efforts to build a moderately prosperous society in a comprehensive way.' Through a series of pilot projects in the country, the government will attempt to refine this evolving model. In fact, some modest reforms of the programmes have been completed. In 2001, China's State Council sanctioned an experiment in the north-eastern province of Liaoning to increase the use of 'social pooling' and to create a firewall between the pay-as-you-go pillar and individual accounts. A national social security fund was also established at about this time (Sin, 2005).

Recently, in the 11th Five-Year Plan (2006–2010), Premier Wen Jiabao pledged to proceed with old-age pension reforms to improve the low pension rates for those with low monthly salaries who retired before the 1993 pension reforms. He also promised to promote the implementation of individual workers' saving accounts with effective computerization throughout the country to allow mobility of workers among different provinces. He also indicated that the government would seek to maximize participation among all forms of enterprises and workers, with a view of including individual entrepreneurs and small business. Multiple sources of financing for the old-age retirement pension funds would also be identified in order to spread the contribution load among employing enterprises, workers and the government.

In addition, the central government has recently introduced two new measures. First, it increased the subsidy for basic old-age insurance funds from its general revenue budget. Second, it called upon the provincial governments to restructure their financial expenditures and increase their contribution to the old-age insurance funds. In 2003, contribution to the basic old-age insurance funds from the different levels of government amounted to 54.4 billion yuan, of which 47.4 billion yuan came from the central budget (White Paper on Social Security, 2004). Most importantly, the central government in 2000 established a national social security fund. A variety of funding sources for old-age insurance have now emerged. In addition to direct subsidies, the funds derive income from stock ownership assets, investment returns and income raised by other means approved by the State Council. The national social security fund is administered by the National Social Security Fund Executive Council and is operated on market principles. The national social security fund provides an important financial reserve for the implementation of old-age insurance and other social security programmes. By the end of 2003, it had accumulated to more than 130 billion yuan.

All these improvements are clearly relevant. While the government is clearly adopting a proactive hands-on approach, it continues to face administrative challenges. These challenges are, of course, not only confined to China but also affect the management of social insurance programmes in many other countries as well. Research on pension reform in developing and transition economies tends to take for granted the capacity of states to implement ambitious and complicated new schemes for the provision of old-age income to pensioners, when in fact the success of these programmes depends on administrative efficiency. In his study of China, Frazier (2004) identifies the fragmented, decentralized pattern of pension administration in China as an unintended consequence of pension reform. Policy legacies from the command-economy period, principal–agent problems during the reform period and the threat of pension protests left urban governments largely in control of pension administration. He believes that while the central government succeeded in its policy goal of introducing a new old-age pension system, it has not been able to fully gain administrative control over the pension funds.

Administratively, China's central government needs to do more to address these problems. Some pertinent recommendations proposed by scholars and research institutes should be considered. For example, some have recommended the reorganization of the mandatory pension into a single national system with a single national pool and greater national control over the individual retirement account system. This they believe will improve the programme's administrative effectiveness and increase its economic efficiency (China Economic Research and Advisory Programme, 2005).

Social security and economic development in China

Since the late 1970s, China's urban enterprise-based welfare system has been gradually dismantled in the wake of economic reform and the country's transition to a market economy. The government's overarching goal was to set up a contributory old-age retirement programme based on a combination of social insurance and funded individual accounts. The use of retirement accounts signals a reduction in the state's financial responsibility and an emphasis on individual duty and family and community support. At the same time, the use of a universal insurance system reaffirms collective responsibility for social welfare. China's social security reform has also moved in the direction of welfare pluralism with reliance on the state for welfare provision, private sector and non-profits. Finally, China's approach in social security can be described as developmental – it seeks to ensure people's integration into society as productive citizens who contribute not only to their own well-being but also to the development of the community.

The reform of the old-age insurance system in China has generated much international interest. The government has largely dismantled the employer-based labour insurance programme operated by the state-owned enterprises and replaced it with a mixed social insurance and individual accounts programme. At a time when many governments around the world have begun to apportion greater responsibility for old-age income provision to individuals and market forces through the privatization of their pension systems (Brooks, 2005; Dorn, 2004),

China is bucking the trend by creating an old-age protection system that both meets the social objectives of integration, social protection and quality of life and at the same time fosters the goal of economic development (Tang and Ngan, 2001).

It is true that China's current old-age insurance programme faces a number of challenges. But one must not forget the many instances where developing countries kept unaffordable pension systems afloat by using continual budget transfers and ultimately facing rising budget deficits as well as economic crises. A case in point is Brazil (World Bank, 2005). In 1998, in the aftermath of the East Asian and Russian financial crises, a fiscal deficit of more than 6 per cent of GDP subsequently triggered a crisis. Two-thirds of this deficit, some 4 per cent of GDP, was due to the cost of pensions. Seen in this light, China's pension reform has clearly averted a potential fiscal crisis. The pension model that has emerged is not a market-based retirement system, and it does not endorse the privatization of social security. Rather, the continued involvement of the government in the system represents a pragmatic approach to the issue of old-age protection.

It is worth noting that the World Bank (2005) has recently recommended that a new multi-pillar framework for social security be adopted in both the developing and developed nations. Five pillars are introduced: (a) a non-contributory or 'zero pillar' (in the form of a demogrant or social pension) that provides a minimal level of protection; (b) a 'first-pillar' contributory system that is linked in varying degrees to earnings and seeks to replace some portion of income; (c) a mandatory 'second pillar' that is essentially an individual savings account; (d) a voluntary 'third-pillar' arrangement that can take many forms (individual, employer-sponsored, defined benefit, defined contribution) but are essentially flexible and discretionary in nature and (e) informal intra-family or inter-generational sources of both financial and non-financial support to the elderly, including access to health care and housing.

China's new old-age insurance scheme has incorporated three of the five pillars. The suggestion of having 'informal intra-family or intergenerational sources of support' is most pertinent to China, as access to other social security services is critical to elderly Chinese. However, the Chinese government needs to allocate more resources to other social insurance programmes, such as social assistance, to back up the pension scheme. The same is true for health care. Since 1998, China has also promoted a national reform of the basic medical insurance system for urban employees. By the end of 2003, some 109.02 million people around China had joined the basic medical insurance programme, including 79.75 million employees and 29.27 million retirees (White Paper on Social Security, 2004). But China's health care system's weakness emerges when the plight of the uninsured is considered. More importantly, demerits are added when the new programme is compared with those of other countries. Comparatively, China's government health budget as a share of the total spending has dwindled, declining from 36.2 per cent of the total spending in the early 1980s to 15 per cent in 2002 (Wong et al., 2006).

Inevitably, any discussion of old-age insurance reform in China should seek an appropriate and pragmatic answer to the neoliberal challenge while finding ways to restructure and strengthen the public social security programme to meet social needs. At the same time, the harmonization of social and economic objectives should not be emphasized. Although it is still too early to say that China's emerging old-age insurance programme has brought about a complete harmonization of social and economic goals, social values such as meeting basic need, solidarity, adequacy and redistribution have been upheld by the central government in China in the context of a strong commitment to economic development. In effect, the government has endorsed the use of social security, in particular, old-age insurance and social assistance to guarantee retirement income, alleviate poverty and contain social inequities. Interestingly, in the process, the introduction of an old-age insurance model and unemployment insurance (along with retraining of laid-off workers) is facilitating economic development of the country. Rather than merely responding in an ad hoc fashion to pressing social problems, it is using a pragmatic but proactive approach to promote social welfare. These policies are also intentionally investment oriented.

Since China is a gradually ageing society, providing for the elderly and guaranteeing them with a basic living standard is extremely important. China began its social security reform when the market-oriented economy was first promoted in the late 1970s. Despite many challenges, a great deal has been accomplished since then. For example, the government has been able to extend its old-age insurance programme to cover a wide section of the population. The number of people participating in the basic old-age insurance scheme across China has reached 155.06 million – of these, 116.46 million are employees (White Paper on Social Security, 2004).

Benefits levels have also improved. The new pension programme pays higher benefits than the old pension system administered by the state-owned enterprises. The basic insurance funded pension is set at a level of 20 per cent of the average annual wages of workers in the locality in which the pensioner resides. In 2003, the monthly basic pension for enterprise retirees covered by the new old-age insurance scheme was 621 yuan (about US $75) on average. By maintaining a minimum floor of protection, the provision of a basic pension demonstrates the state's commitment to maintain a basic level of living after retirement. The basic pension meets the basic subsistence needs of retirees, though those in the cities fare better.

In addition, funding for the programme is now quite impressive. In 2003, the basic old-age insurance premium paid by enterprises nation-wide totalled 259.5 billion yuan (or about US $31.3 billion). These trends reaffirm our earlier assessment of China's new old-age insurance initiative as a positive innovation based on a number of social and economic criteria (Tang and Ngan, 2001). It is likely that the future goal of extending social security coverage to every urban and rural worker will be achieved. This is obviously important since rural peasants have long been deprived of a effective state-sponsored old-age retirement programme.

The new old-age insurance programme also aims to promote individual responsibility. In addition to guaranteeing a basic minimum pension through social insurance, workers are able to save for their own future retirement needs by contributing to their own funded pension accounts. By combining an insurance and savings approach, pension-pooling and risk-sharing under the new system provides added security. These efforts are expected to achieve provincial-level pooling of funds, unify the contribution rate as a proportion of payrolls and implement full payment of benefits and collection of contributions. The main benefit of this policy is that social security expenses are shared equitably among enterprises. The new insurance system is able to solve the bankruptcy problems that faced the old labour insurance funds owned by the state-owned enterprises.

More importantly, the new initiative contributes to economic development by fostering productivist or developmental welfare. The reform of social security supports the government's wider economic development policies and initiatives and particularly the viability of the state-owned enterprises (Tang and Ngan, 2001). One of the key goals in the restructuring of these enterprises is to lower the costs of operations so that they become more competitive and are not overburdened by social spending. The mayor of Shanghai remarked that the new pension plan, one of the main directives of Shanghai's Five Year Development Plan, has served an important function in the city's restructuring process (Ngan et al., 2004). The creation of individual accounts helped the state-owned enterprises to reduce their heavy commitments to social security spending.

It is expected that as the contributions from enterprises and workers accumulate, there will be sizeable funds for local governments and social security authorities to invest in local infrastructural and economic projects, thus harmonizing the twin goals of social and economic developments. Academics have described such efforts as 'developmental statist' (White, 1998). It is also compatible with the notion of developmental welfare, as defined by Midgley (1995, 1997, 1999). This orientation puts emphasis on rapid economic growth along with the pragmatic redesign of the pension programme. The accumulation of funds from the pension programme is encouraged, and these resources will be channelled into the economic sphere to help stimulate the local economy.

Last but not least, the synergy between the old-age insurance initiative with other social policies and programmes such as social assistance, medical insurance and unemployment insurance ought to be acknowledged. Combining the reformed old-age insurance programme with these other social protection programmes can help people with low incomes and special needs to engage in productive employment and self-employment by ensuring that their basic social needs are met. The experience of China shows that social programmes such as old-age insurance can be investment oriented, promoting economic participation and generating positive rates of return for the economy. Overall, China's social security initiatives can be seen in the light of a developmental approach to social welfare, which seeks to ensure people's integration into society as productive citizens who contribute not only to their own well-being but also to the development of the community (Midgley, 1997). The Chinese government's approach to social security avoids the perpetuation of welfare dependence and links social and economic development policies. It deems economic development to be a desirable and essential element in social welfare, and it also promotes the idea that social programmes should support economic development imperatives. The state's role is active, promoting economic development, raising standards of living and simultaneously meeting social needs.

References

Asian Development Bank (ADB) (2006). *Asian Development Outlook 2006.* Available online at http://www.adb.org/documents/books/ado/2006/prc.asp. Accessed 16 November 2007.

Brooks, S. M. (2005). 'Social Protection and Economic Integration: The Politics of Pension Reform in an Era of Capital Mobility', *Comparative Political Studies*, 35(5), 491–523.

Cai, F. and Wang, M. Y. (2006). 'Challenge Facing China's Economic Growth in Its Aging but Not Affluent Era', *China & World Economy*, 14 (5), 20–31, September–October.

China Daily (1998). 'Pension Reform Aims at Sound System'. December 10.

China Daily (2001). 'Nation Drafts Five-Year Blueprint'. March 6.

China Daily (2005). 'Building Harmonious Society CPC's Top Task'. February 20.

Chinese Academy of Social Sciences (2004). *Green Book of China Social Security System, 2001-2004.* Beijing: China Social Sciences Academic Press.

China Economic Research and Advisory Programme (2005). *Social Security Reform in China: Issues and Options.* Singapore: The Author

Davis, D. (1989). 'Chinese Social Welfare: Policies and Outcomes', *China Quarterly*, 199, 577–597.

Dixon, J. (1981). *The Chinese Welfare System 1949–1979.* New York: Praeger.

Dorn, J. A. (2004). 'Pension Reform in China: A Question of Property Rights', *Cato Journal*, 23(3), Winter, 433–446.

Fabre, G. (1999). 'China in the East Asian Crisis', *Economic and Political Weekly*, 34 (45): 3191–3194, 6 November, 1999.

Feinstein, M. (2004). 'Social Security Pension Reform in China.' In A. M. Chen, G. Liu, and K. H. Chang (2004) (ed.), *Urbanization and Social Welfare in China.* London: Ashgate Publishing, pp. 11–22.

Financial Times (2006). 'Data Show Social Unrest on the Rise in China', January 25.

Frazier, M. W. (2004). 'After Pension Reform: Navigating the "Third Rail" in China', *Studies in Comparative International Development*, 39(2), 45–70.

Hu, A. D. (1997). 'Reforming China's Social Security System: Facts and Perspectives', *International Social Security Review*, 50(3), 45–65.

Hu, Z. L. (1998). 'Social Protection and Enterprise Reform.' In M. Rein, B. Friedman and A. Worgotter (eds), *Enterprise and Social Benefits from Communism.* Cambridge, Cambridge University Press, pp. 284–304.

Hurst, W. and O'Brien, K. J. (2002). 'China's Contentious Pensioners,' *China Quarterly*, 170, 345–360.

Information Office of the State Council, PRC (2004). White Paper on Social Security. Available at http://www.china.org.cn/e-white/20040907/index.htm. Accessed 16 November 2007.

Leung, J. C. B. (2006). 'The Emergence of Social Assistance in China', *International Journal of Social Welfare*, 15(3), 188–198.

Li, D. D. and Li, L. (2003). 'A Simple Solution to China' s Pension Crisis', *Cato Journal*, 23(2), Fall, 281–289.

Liu, Alan P. L. (1996). *Mass Politics in the People's Republic: State and Society in Contemporary China*. Boulder, CO: Westview Press.

Midgley, J. (1995). *Social Development*. Thousand Oaks, CA: Sage Publications.

Midgley, J. (1997). *Social Welfare in Global Context*. Thousand Oaks, CA: Sage Publications.

Midgley, J. (1999). 'Growth, Redistribution and Welfare: Towards Social Investment', *Social Service Review*, 77(1), March: 3–21.

Ministry of Civil Affairs Statistical Bulletin (2005). Statistical Bulletin. Available at http://www1.mca.gov.cn/artical/content/WGJ_TJBG/2006518170321.html. Accessed on 24 December, 2007.

Ngan, R. and Tang, K. L. (2003). 'Social Security Reforms and Prospects in the Twenty-first Century.' In Joseph Cheng (ed.), *China's Challenges in the Twenty-first Century*. Hong Kong: City University of Hong Kong Press, pp. 597–626.

Ngan, R., Yip, N. M. and Wu, D. (2004). 'Poverty and Social Security.' In L. Wong, L. White, and S. X. Gui (2004) (eds), *Social Policy Reform in Hong Kong and Shanghai. A Tale of Two Cities*. New York: M. E. Sharpe, pp. 159–182.

Oi, J. C. (1999). 'Two Decades of Rural Reform in China: An Overview and Assessment', *The China Quarterly*, 159: 616–628.

People's Daily Online (21 February, 2005). Building harmonious society important task for CPC: President Hu. Available online at: http://english.people.com.cn/200502/20/eng20050220_174036.html.

Shanghai Encyclopedia (1999). Shanghai: Shanghai Scientific Press.

Sin, Y. (2005). *China: Pension Liabilities and Reform Options for Old Age Insurance*. May, Working Paper 25-01. Washington DC: World Bank.

Song S. F. and Chu G. S. F. (1997). 'Social Security Reform in China: The Case of Old-Age Insurance', *Contemporary Economic Policy*, 15(2), 85–93.

South China Morning Post (1998). 'Greying Population Set to Strain Economy', October 13.

South China Morning Post (1998). 'Foreign Firms Eye Foot in Door of Lucrative Pension Sector', November 13.

South China Morning Post (1998). 'China Rises to Old Challenge', November 19.

Tang, K. L. (1999). 'Social Development in China: Progress and Problems', *Journal of Contemporary Asia*, 29(1), 95–109.

Tang, K. L. and Ngan, R. (2001). 'China: Developmentalism and Social Security', *International Journal of Social Welfare*, 10 (4), 250–257.

White, G. (1998). 'China: Social Security Reforms.' In R. Goodman, G. White, H. J. Kwon (eds), *East Asian Welfare Model*. New York: Routledge, pp. 175–198.

Wong, C. K., Lo, V. I. and Tang, K. L. (2006). *China's Urban Health Care Reform: From State Protection to Individual Responsibility*. Lanham,MD: Lexington Books.

Wong, L. (1994). 'Privatization of Social Welfare in China', *Asian Survey*, 34(4), 307–325.

Wong, L., White, L. and Gui, S. X. (2004) (eds). *Social Policy Reform in Hong Kong and Shanghai. A Tale of Two Cities*. New York: M. E. Sharpe.

World Bank (2005). *Old-Age Income Support in the Twenty-First Century: An International Perspective on Pensions and Reform.* Washington DC: World Bank.

World Bank (1997a). *China 2020: Development Challenges in the New Century.* Washington DC: World Bank.

World Bank (1997b). *Old Age Security: Pension Reform in China.* Washington DC: World Bank.

6
The United States: Social Security Policy Innovations and Economic Development

James Midgley

Debates about the relationship between social security and economic development have flourished in the United States in recent decades. These debates have also inspired much international discourse on this topic. Indeed, the vigorous advocacy of market liberalism by American social scientists has exerted considerable global influence. These social scientists have argued persuasively that government income protection programmes have a negative impact on economic development and should be replaced with market-based provisions which, they believe, are economically preferable to statutory programmes. Of course, arguments against income protection programmes in the United States have been generalized to all forms of government welfare intervention. All government social programmes, it is frequently claimed, have negative economic consequences.

In the United States, these debates have focused narrowly on the federal government's Old Age, Survivors, Disability Insurance (OASDI) programme, which is referred to as Social Security, and on means-tested social assistance programmes that are jointly administered by the federal and state governments. The most widely criticized of these was the Aid to Families with Dependent Children (AFDC) which, as is well known, was replaced by a new welfare-to-work programme known as Temporary Assistance for Needy Families (TANF) in 1996. Market liberal critics allege that these and similar programmes dampen work incentives, create a large dependent and economically unproductive group of people, incur high and economically harmful public costs which require punitive levels of taxation, distort labour markets, promote consumption at the expense of much needed capital formation and have other harmful economic effects. Of course, these programmes have also been attacked on social grounds. They allegedly undermine moral values, foster dependency and weaken traditional forms of social support.

Although these and other criticisms have been adequately debated and need not be repeated here, it should be noted that disagreements about the relationship between social security and economic development have been constrained by a framework that has narrowly limited analysis to conventional social insurance and means-tested programmes. Social security policy innovations that do not rely on social insurance or social assistance approaches have been largely disregarded, and their potential to contribute positively to economic development has not been properly assessed.

This chapter considers the issue with reference to three social security policy innovations in the United States. The first is the TANF welfare-to-work programme mentioned earlier. Although this programme has been hailed as a major success, it has not met its stated goal of facilitating the transfer of needy people from social assistance to adequately remunerated employment with sound opportunities for upward mobility. Nevertheless, it has the potential to contribute to this goal. The second is the Earned Income Tax Credit (EITC), which is not actually a recent innovation, but which has expanded significantly and now supplements the incomes of many low-paid workers. The third is the individual savings account approach by which retirement savings are subsidized through tax revenues or by which the savings of people with low incomes are matched by government and other sources. The most popular of the former is the Individual Retirement Account (IRA) while the latter matched savings accounts are known as Individual Development Accounts (IDA). Although these programmes vary in the extent to which they are state managed and funded, all require significant state intervention. Also, in different ways, they all contribute positively to economic development. Their contribution will be assessed with reference to a number of economic impact but first, a brief overview of social security in the United States and some demographic and economic facts about the country is provided.

The United States and its social security system

The United States of America is a federal republic situated on the North American continent. It is the third largest country in the world in terms of land mass after China and Russia and among the world's most populous nations. Its population was 281 million at the time of the last census in 2000 and is now estimated to have reached 300 million. However, this excludes an estimated 12 million undocumented immigrants who have come to the country illegally but who contribute significantly to its economic prosperity. Population growth is just under 1 per cent per annum. The proportion of the population over the age of 65 years is approximately 13 per cent which is significantly lower than in many other Western countries.

The United States is comprised of 50 states of which the most populous are California, Texas and New York. Its population is concentrated along its coastal regions and particularly along the Atlantic coastal region. The country is predominantly urban with almost 80 per cent of the population living in towns and cities. The largest urban areas are around New York with approximately 19 million people, the Los Angles metropolitan area with approximately 13 million people, and the urban area around Chicago with approximately 9.5 million people.

The country's population is ethnically and culturally diverse being comprised of Native American people and people of European, African, Asian and Latino descent. The Indigenous Native American people, who settled the North American continent approximately 35,000 years ago, now only form a small proportion of the population having been displaced by European colonists who populated the territory from the fifteenth to the twentieth centuries. The descendents of the European settlers currently comprise about 60 per cent to 65 per cent population. Those who came to the United States from Latin America currently comprise about 15 per cent of the population. The African American population amounts to approximately 12 per cent of the population while Asian Americans account for almost 5 per cent. Despite the country's population diversity, 94 per cent of American speak English.

The United States has the largest economy in the world with a gross domestic product of about $13 trillion. The country's per capita income of approximately $37,000 is also among the highest in the world. It is the second-largest exporter and the largest importer of goods in the world. Its major trading partners include Canada, China, Mexico, Japan and Germany. The proportion of the labour force engaged in agriculture and industry has declined steadily over the last century and more than 75 per cent of workers are currently employed in the service sector. Despite short recessionary spells, the economy has grown steadily over the past 15 years. During the 1990s and early years of the twentieth century, the average annual economic growth rate was 2.1 per cent. Unemployment is currently just below 5 per cent. Although incomes among highly skilled and educated workers have risen steadily, the incomes of low paid and middle income workers have stagnated resulting in a marked increase in income inequality. The top 10 per cent of income earners receive approximately 30 per cent of income which is higher than in other Western countries. Income inequality between those in the top and lowest percentiles is particularly marked. The salaries of corporate executives are the highest in the world. Wealth is also highly concentrated.

Although the country's aggregate social indicators compare favourably with the other member states of the Organization for Economic Cooperation and Development (OECD), many social policy scholars believe that social conditions among ethnic minorities and lower paid families leave much to be desired. The country ranks tenth in the world on the United Nations Development Programme's Human Development Index (HDI) and infant mortality is significantly higher than that of many other Western countries. Life expectancy is also lower. Significant differences in access to quality health care and education also exist among different income and ethnic groups. The country's poverty rate is also high in comparison with other Western countries with approximately 17 per cent of the population living below a poverty line defined as 50 per cent of the median income. Government spending on education and health is comparable with that of other Western countries but private spending on health far exceeds that of these countries. Military expenditures are also higher than in other Western countries.

The social security system

As noted earlier in this book, the term social security is used in the United States to refer to the country's old-age retirement system and, unlike many other parts of the world, it is not used generically to connote all income maintenance and support programmes. To complicate matters further, the country's many other income maintenance and support programmes are known by a variety of other terms. Generally, these programmes can be classified into means-tested social assistance and contributory social insurance programmes but even here, they differ significantly from those that have been established in Europe and elsewhere.

Social security programmes in the United States are administered by different levels of government. For example, the old-age retirement, survivors and disability insurance (OASDI) programme mentioned earlier is administered by the federal government while the country's unemployment insurance programme is jointly managed by the federal and state government. Since the replacement of the means-tested Aid to

Families with Dependent Children (AFDC) programme with the Temporary Assistance for Needy Families (TANF) programme, the states have exercised considerable latitude in setting eligibility standards and imposing work and other conditions.

As in other Anglophone countries, social security in the United States is rooted in the English poor law. When the early colonial settlements became established and constitutionally formalized, a number adopted the Elizabethan statute. The first was the Plymouth Colony which enacted its own version of this statute in 1642 followed by Virginia in 1646 (Trattner, 1999). As in England, the law was administered by a government appointed overseer working with the local parish authorities who often showed a measure of compassion for the indigent elderly, orphans and disabled but dealt harshly with the able-bodied and particularly with beggars and vagrants. Similar approaches were adopted by the other European powers that settled the North American continent such as the Dutch in New York who enacted legislation in 1661 to permit the whipping and the deportation of paupers who had apparently become a growing nuisance. In the French and Spanish settlements, the authorities generally left the care of needy people to the church, monasteries and fraternities. However, by the late nineteenth century, income support programmes in the United States had acquired a greater degree of uniformity and the poor law approach was widely used to provide limited and meagre 'outdoor' benefits as they were known. It was also used to incarcerate needy people in a variety of residential institutions.

By the end of the nineteenth century, the efforts of progressive reformers to expand income support and other social services gathered pace. Among these was the campaign to introduce workers' compensation. After constitutional wrangles and initial opposition from business interests, non-contributory employment injury insurance programmes were established in several states beginning with Maryland in 1904. Although this statute was struck down as unconstitutional, a number of Northern states including Wisconsin, Minnesota and New York had established programmes by 1909 and by 1920, 43 states had followed suit. Today, approximately 126 million employees are covered by the workers' compensation programme operated by the state governments and in excess of $54 billion is paid in benefits. In the great majority of states, firms utilize commercial insurers to protect their workers and only a few operate through publicly managed insurance carriers.

The campaign for workers' compensation reflected a growing awareness of income protection innovations in Europe and elsewhere, and soon the social insurance approach was activity promoted by reform-minded individuals, academics and the labour movement. On the other hand, some mostly women reformers urged the introduction of more generous and expansive social assistance programmes known as mothers' or widows' pensions. These were established in several states in the early decades of the twentieth century. These programmes emerged out of growing concern about child neglect and abandonment and the rising costs of maintaining children in orphanages. By providing benefits to enable low-income, lone mothers to care for their children, reformers believed that these problems would be addressed. By 1920, forty states had established mothers' pensions and by 1935 only two states had failed to do so. However, implementation was haphazard particularly in rural areas and many eligible families were excluded.

In addition to the mothers' pensions, a number of states also introduced means-tested old age pensions as well as cash payments to disabled and blind people. In 1914, Arizona became the first state to establish a separate, old-age pension but this programme also encountered constitutional difficulties and was limited in scope and had stringent eligibility requirements. Nevertheless, other states followed and a number of states, including Pennsylvania, Montana and Nevada introduced means-tested old age pension programmes in 1923 followed by Wisconsin in 1924 and Kentucky in 1926 (Leiby, 1978). The expansion of state funded social assistance old age pensions accelerated rapidly so that by 1934, 28 states had established old-age pension statutes paying benefits to approximately 180,000 indigent elderly people (Douglas, 1936).

The question of income protection in old age did not feature prominently in debates about how the economic problems of the Great Depression should be addressed. During the drafting of the 1935 Social Security Act, which formed an integral part of President Roosevelt's New Deal, the president himself initially questioned the need for a federally administered old-age insurance programme. Unemployment was the overriding challenge of the time and the need to introduce a comprehensive unemployment insurance programme was given top priority. Nevertheless, faced with political pressures to expand income protection to the elderly, the legislation made provision for the introduction of a new, federal old-age insurance programme. The existing state administered old-age assistance programmes were retained but their costs were subsidized by the federal government. In 1974, these state programmes were replaced with a federal means-tested programme known as Supplemental Security Income. The states retained their old

Poor Law programmes which subsequently became known as General Assistance. However, since the 1980s many states have abolished these programmes. Currently 35 states maintain General Assistance programmes but the number of recipients, who are usually homeless people, are generally small and may number less than one million people. The annual cost is estimated to be approximately $3.50 billion.

On the other hand, mothers' pensions were immediately replaced with a joint federal and state programme known initially as Aid to Dependent Children and subsequently as Aid to Families with Dependent Children or AFDC. The states set eligibility and benefit levels but the costs were matched by the federal government which also established national policy requirements and guidelines. In 1939, the Social Security Act was amended to permit the payment of survivors benefits and in 1956, disability benefits were added. The OASDI programme is currently the largest income protection programme in the United States providing pension benefits to almost 40 million retirees and disability benefits to another seven million people. These programmes cost about $460 billion per annum. The Supplemental Security Income programme pays benefits to approximately 6.5 million people at an annual cost of about $38 billion.

Unlike these programmes, the unemployment insurance programme established in terms of the 1935 Social Security Act is jointly administered by the federal and state governments through a complicated formula by which each state imposes a payroll tax supplemented by federal resources. Revenues are banked by the federal government but each state sets its own eligibility and benefit levels. The programme currently costs about $53 billion dollars but these costs vary depending on prevailing economic conditions. Similarly, the number of recipients of unemployment benefits also varies depending on these conditions.

Several social policy innovations were introduced during the Johnson administration's War on Poverty in the 1906s. These included Medicare, the nation's first health-insurance programme for retirees, and a means-tested health programme known as Medicaid. Both have subsequently expanded considerably and now consume a significant proportion of the federal budget. The AFDC programme also began to expand during this time resulting, by the 1980s, in the widespread criticism that its growth had fostered welfare dependency, illegitimacy, crime and other social ills associated with the 'underclass'. By the end of the decade, these criticisms resulted in the intensification of job training and placement services for welfare recipients and eventually with the replacement of the AFCD programme with the 'work first' TANF programme in

1996. Despite a 60 per cent decline in the case load since the introduction of the TANF programme, about five million people are currently in receipt of benefits at an annual cost of approximately $13 billion.

One War on Poverty innovation that did not attract much criticism is a food voucher or food stamps programme for people with low incomes. Although piloted during the Kennedy administration, it was expanded at the national level by the Johnson administration in 1964. Today, the programme provides benefits to approximately 20 million people at an annual cost of about $25 billion.

Both the New Deal and the War on Poverty are regarded by social historians as pivotal developments in the evolution of social policy and income protection in the United States. The income protection programmes initially introduced in terms of the Social Security Act as well as those subsequently added in terms of various amendments to this legislation, now comprise the core of the American social security system. Although some programmes such as food stamps and housing subsidies are governed by different statutes, they are often regarded as a part of the social security system. On the other hand, the use of the tax code to provide income support has not been widely recognized as forming an integral part of this system. It will be shown that tax funded benefits play an increasingly important role in income protection in the United States with significant implications for economic development.

Social security policy innovations and economic development

Despite their importance, these income protection programmes have been widely criticized for impeding the country's economic development efforts. They have also been condemned for their allegedly deleterious social effects. These criticisms were particularly cogent in the 1970s when the United States and many other Western countries experienced slow rates of economic growth, high unemployment and high levels of wage inflation which appeared to be resistant to Keynesian policy remedies. Stagflation, as this situation was known, was attributed to various causes but allegedly generous social programmes were often singled out for blame. Social welfare, it was argued, was the primary cause of economic stagnation.

These ideas were articulated by numerous academics, right-wing activists, politicians and others who presented an increasingly plausible image of the negative social and economic effects of government income protection programmes. Academic critics made an especially effective contribution to undermining the consensus which had emerged around social policy in the years following the Second World War. Some, such as the Harvard economics professor Martin Feldstein (1974), focused on social insurance attacking the OASDI programme for encouraging consumption at the expense of much needed capital investments. Using sophisticated econometric models, he demonstrated that the expansion of social insurance had been accompanied by a steady decline in the savings rate. Because people were no longer required to save for their retirement, savings and investments had dwindled and the capital needed to replenish and modernize the economy had dangerously declined. Others, such as Roger Freeman (1981) of the Hoover Institution in California, paid particular attention to AFDC and related means-tested programmes. Spending on these programmes, he pointed out, had increased faster than the rate of economic growth with disastrous consequences. As many more people had stopped working and become reliant on income transfers, a declining number of producers were compelled to support a growing number of welfare dependents resulting in economic stagnation. Although Charles Murray (1984) and Lawrence Mead (1986) focused largely on the social consequences of government welfare programmes, both emphasized their harmful effects on work incentives and economic progress. Similarly, Nobel Laureate Milton Friedman (1980) and his wife Rose Friedman launched a scathing attack on welfare programmes on both economic and social grounds. In addition to undermining the social and moral fabric of society, they generated huge amounts of waste, required increased public spending and taxation, reduced incentives to work and save and impeded the accumulation of capital needed for economic success.

The evidence mustered in support of the view that income protection programmes harm economic development was often presented within a wider, more comprehensive attack on government intervention. President Reagan was a particularly effective communicator of this idea. In his 1988 State of Union address, he ridiculed the Johnson administration's War on Poverty by announcing that it had resulted in a victory for poverty. Government, he often declaimed, is not the solution but the primary cause of economic and social problems. Republican House Speaker Newt Gingrich (1995) also generalized the evidence by arguing that the vast majority of Americans had rejected the claim that government welfare programmes can improve the lot of the poor and bring about social improvements. They recognize that these programmes have undermined the work ethic and that many poor people are trapped in a world where 'income maintenance' has replaced individual responsibility. The 'welfare state', he insisted, must be replaced with an economically vibrant opportunity society in which the bureaucratized state is downsized and local communities, non-profit institutions and individual citizens assume responsibility for their own welfare.

However, claims about the allegedly negative economic effects of social security and means-tested welfare and, indeed of all forms of government intervention, do not provide sufficient evidence to support the anti-welfarist case. Indeed, these claims can be challenged by examining the way that some statutory income protection programmes – other than social insurance and social assistance – contribute to economic development. As will be shown, these programmes have a demonstrably positive impact on economic development. They not only promote economic development but also foster the social well-being of millions of American citizens today.

Welfare-to-work and the TANF programme

Most Western countries have adopted policies designed to maximize participation in the productive economy and raise people's standards of living through remunerative employment. Indeed, the success of the so-called Western 'welfare states' has been largely dependent on maximizing wage employment among both men and women. These policies have not only been concerned with job creation and the introduction of labour market regulations that benefit workers but also with the provision of childcare and a variety of employment supports. Social programmes have featured prominently in this approach, and social insurance and social assistance have both been widely used to complement these policies.

However, in the 1970s and 1980s, as many Western countries faced serious economic difficulties, the payment of unemployment, disability and other social benefits increased rapidly. The adoption of employment activation or welfare-to-work programmes by the governments of many Western countries was designed to address this issue, and today these programmes have become an increasingly important social policy tool. Typically welfare-to-work programmes include job counselling, referral and placement, training and the provision of employment supports. In many countries, these programmes are based on the premise that most welfare recipients prefer to work than receive benefits and that they will utilize employment services and training to achieve this goal. By facilitating employment, welfare-to-work programmes are widely commended for contributing to economic development.

Job training, counselling and referral services have been employed in the United States since the 1960s. Following the enactment of the Family Support Act in 1988, which created the Job Opportunity and Basic Skills (or JOBS) programme, AFDC recipients were prompted to participate in employment training programmes in the hope that they would acquire educational qualifications and skills which would prepare them for regular employment. However, like the AFDC programme, the JOBS programme was heavily criticized. Critics claimed that many welfare recipients had not only failed to obtain the required skills and qualifications but also had failed to find steady employment. Some studies also revealed that the incomes of those who participated in the JOBS programme were actually lower than those who were placed in employment without prior job training (Handler, 1995). Although the difference was marginal, it was widely used to support claims about the ineffectiveness of the JOBS programme. The answer, critics argued, lay in requiring welfare recipients to engage in work irrespective of whether they had educational qualifications or job skills. 'Work first' became the new mantra of welfare reform and the TANF programme.

The TANF programme is a major social security policy innovation in the United States. It replaced both the AFDC and JOBS programmes with the more aggressive work-first approach which required welfare recipients to engage immediately in employment as a condition for the continued receipt of benefits. Sanctions, which result in the reduction or termination of benefits, have been used to ensure that participants comply with this requirement. In addition, the programme imposed lifetime time limits on the receipt of benefits. The programme's work-first philosophy is designed to promote economic participation, regular work and the inculcation of appropriate work habits among welfare recipients who, it is often claimed, lack the motivation and self-discipline to hold down steady jobs. By requiring recipients to engage in regular work, they would not only acquire desirable work habits but also earn regular wages which would lift them out of poverty and ensure long-term economic success. Although the programme was established at the federal level, states were given considerable flexibility in the way they designed and managed their own programmes. This resulted in wide variations between the different state programmes (Rowe and Giannarelli, 2006).

Today, politicians of quite different ideological persuasion claim that the TANF programme is a huge success. Republicans contend that their emphasis on work first produced the desired results while Democrats insist that it was their president, Bill Clinton, who initiated welfare reform and signed the TANF legislation into law. All point to the dramatic decline in the welfare caseload since the programme's inception as evidence of its success. By 2003, the case load was approximately 60 per cent lower than in 1996 and by 2005, had fallen even further. Although the number of families receiving cash welfare benefits actually began to decline before the TANF law was passed, politicians have used the data to argue that large numbers of allegedly idle welfare recipients who previously lived on cash benefits have now been compelled to engage in regular employment and, by implication, are on their way to self-sufficiency and success. The twin problems of indolence and welfare dependency have, it appears, been solved.

Although the welfare rolls have declined dramatically, this does not necessarily mean that people who previously received benefits are now working regularly in well-paid jobs and that they are self-sufficient and successful. Indeed, numerous studies show that very few 'welfare leavers', as they are known, are working regularly for decent salaries and living the American Dream (Acs and Loprest, 2004; Besharov and Germanis, 2000; Brauner and Loprest, 1999). On the contrary, many are working in low-paid jobs with limited opportunities for upward mobility. Many are also working intermittently or on a part-time basis (often because of the demands of caring for small children), and many experience crises which compel them to apply for benefits again. It also appears that some are not working at all. Studies of those who continue to receive TANF benefits and are required to work show a similar pattern of irregular, low-paid employment and of struggling to make ends meet in the face of numerous challenges (Burtless, 1999; General Accounting Office, 1999). These challenges are particularly severe for those with few educational qualifications or technical job skills and for those suffering from mental illnesses, developmental disabilities or other psychological problems (Danzinger and Seefeldt, 2003; Pavetti, 1997). These findings are consistent with the findings of studies of low-wage employment in the United States which show that workers who lack job skills and educational qualifications face enormous challenges in competing successfully particularly in a dynamic and volatile employment market in which technical abilities and knowledge qualifications are highly prized (Appelbaum et al., 2003; Shipler, 2004; Shulman, 2003).

Despite widespread claims about the TANF programme's success, many scholars recognize that it has not propelled former welfare recipients into a world of remunerative employment and success and that its contribution to poverty alleviation has been minimal. Some also believe that its failure to address the problem of poverty, and particularly of child poverty in the United States, is a matter for grave concern. The unabashed use of the programme to reduce welfare case loads through the intimidating use of work requirements, sanctions and ultimately time limits may have reduced the case load significantly, but it has not reduced the incidence of poverty and deprivation. Even proponents of welfare reform recognize that its promise as an effective welfare-to-work programme has not been fulfilled (Besharov, 2006).

These findings have fostered dissatisfaction with the work-first approach and a recognition of the need for appropriate education qualifications and job skills among those transitioning into regular work. Although many states permit TANF recipients to receive benefits while enrolled in educational institutions or to combine work with job training, a recent study (Shaw et al., 2006) revealed that education and training is not given much priority and that many states place more emphasis on caseload reduction. Most adhere to the work-first approach and only a small number recognize the need for postsecondary educational credentials as a way of transitioning recipients off welfare and into successful, long-term employment. The study found that the number of welfare recipients enrolled in postsecondary educational institutions, and particularly community colleges, has declined significantly since the TANF programme began. This short-sighted strategy has eroded college access for welfare recipients and impeded their prospects of securing regular employment with decent wages and good opportunities for upward mobility.

On the other hand, because the states are able to develop their own welfare-to-work programme, some states have effectively promoted job training and educational qualifications. One example is Minnesota which began in the mid-1990s to pursue a multi-pronged strategy of employment counselling, job referral and training and education even though job training was being heavily criticized at the time. The state also implemented a demonstration work incentive programme, known as the Minnesota Family Investment Programme, by which welfare recipients who engaged in regular employment were allowed to retain a significant proportion of their benefits. These were phased out gradually as incomes rose. This mitigated the disincentive or 'poverty trap' problems that many welfare-to-work programmes have encountered. An evaluation of this programme yielded very positive results (Knox, Miller and Gennetian, 2000). Despite reducing the programme's work incentive allowance, the state government expanded the programme on a state-wide basis. Also relevant are Minnesota's extensive system of work supports. These include the provision of childcare, the use of Headstart, support for schooling, health care, and support for accessing food stamps and both the federal and Minnesota's own earned income tax credits (Burke, Green and Duke, 1998). It also helps that Minnesota's welfare-to-work programme operates in the wider context of sound economic and social policies and a progressive system of income taxation and social spending, which has ensured that the economy grows steadily and that the state's people have high levels of education and a generally good standard of living.

The neglect of education and training, and particularly of opportunities for welfare recipients to secure postsecondary credentials, is a major reason why the TANF programme has not succeeded in promoting employment participation with opportunities for upward mobility. Although there is evidence to show that steady employment in low-wage jobs does result in improvements in income over a long-term period, there is even more evidence to show that many low-paid American workers are trapped in a low-wage economy with limited opportunities. To be successful, many scholars believe that welfare recipients require postsecondary qualifications and credentials. Many studies have shown that there are enormous advantages in acquiring postsecondary credentials. In 2005, the average annual income for adults without a high school diploma was $19,915. For those with a high school diploma, the average annual income was $29,448. On the other hand, those holding an associate degree from a community college earned an average of $37,990 while those with a bachelor's degree earned $54,689 (Manpower Development Research Corporation, 2007).

These data clearly reveal the importance of appropriate qualifications and skills in a dynamic and competitive economy. By refusing to invest in the human capital of welfare recipients, most welfare-to-work programmes in the United States have failed to prepare clients to participate effectively in this economy. On the other hand, states that have combined the employment placement and human capital development approach in their welfare-to-work programmes (within the wider context of employment supports and effective social policies) have shown that welfare-to-work is an effective social policy tool that governments can use to attain both economic development and social welfare objectives. Hopefully, as the long-term outcomes of welfare-to-work programmes are evaluated, their potential to contribute more effectively to economic development and the well-being of clients will be recognized.

Subsidizing wages through the
Earned Income Tax Credit

Although low wages may be good for corporate profits, and have the added advantage of suppressing inflation, they are not good for economic development and particularly for economic development strategies that seek to be inclusive, maximize participation in the productive economy and bring about widespread prosperity. Despite the popularity of market liberal ideas which posit a trickle-down growth effect, many development scholars and policy makers believe that economic growth must be accompanied by steady increases in incomes among all sections of the population if the idea of development is to be meaningful.

It is widely, although not universally, accepted that the presence of a significant numbers of low-wage workers in the economy who struggle to make ends meet and have limited opportunities for upward mobility has negative economic consequences. Persistent low incomes among sizable groups of people lowers the demand for consumer goods and dampens economic growth. Productivity is also impeded because low-wage workers lack the skills needed to contribute positively to a dynamic, growing economy. Widespread deprivation is also associated with high social costs, such as crime, which has a negative impact on economic development. Similarly, the children of low-wage workers are less likely to acquire the educational qualifications and skills that will permit them to participate effectively in the competitive, knowledge economy. The entrepreneurial skills required to propel this economy are hardly likely to flourish if human capital formation lags.

These problems have been widely recognized and different policy tools have been adopted over the years in the Western countries in an attempt to resist the downward pressures on wages that characterize capitalist economies. Among these policy tools are minimum and living wage mandates and the provision of health care, medical and family leave, childcare, unemployment and work injury insurance. Because these programmes supplement the incomes of low-wage earners, they are sometimes said to comprise a 'social wage'. Efforts to secure decent wages through collective bargaining have also been supported and indeed mandated by many Western governments. Finally, some governments have used the tax system to subsidize the wages of those in regular employment. This approach has become more popular in recent times and is currently used by the government of the United States in the form of the Earned Income Tax Credit (EITC).

The problem of stagnating wages in the United States has attracted a good deal of attention in recent times. Although the virtuous economic growth trajectory of the post-Second World War years was accompanied by steady increases in household incomes, even among low-income earners, the trend has since been reversed, and since the mid-1970s, income growth has been sluggish and the wages of low-income workers has actually declined in real terms (Appelbaum et al., 2003; Bluestone and Harrison, 2000; Mangum et al., 2003). This trend has been attributed to a variety of causes such as the stagflation of the 1970s, persistent unemployment, falling productivity levels, international economic competition, declining demand for non-skilled labour and the outsourcing of manufacturing jobs to other countries. Attention has also been drawn to the way government policy has favoured corporate interests and those with higher incomes and neglected the interests of low-income workers (Blau, 1999; Rank, 2006). Tax relief and exemptions have increasingly benefited the rich, while retrenchments in social programmes, deregulation, deteriorating educational opportunities, concerted efforts to enervate the negotiating powers of the unions and weakened minimum-wage mandates have all contributed to wage stagnation. Although market liberals have long argued that steady economic growth and the rising tide of income and wealth will lift all incomes, this argument has little credence today and there is growing support for the idea that those who work hard and engage in regular, steady employment should be adequately compensated. But while the rhetoric of 'making work pay' has resonance, the pressure to produce ever higher corporate profits has continued to squeeze wages. It is in this context that the policy of subsidizing the wages of low-income workers through the tax system has secured significant political support.

Although the tax system in the United States is used to provide a variety of subsidies to individual households as well as commercial firms, these subsidies overwhelmingly benefit higher income and middle-class workers. Many in low-paid occupations who have low tax liabilities are not able to take advantage of these benefits by, for example, deducting health care and retirement contributions or mortgage interest. The EITC is specifically designed to extend income benefits to these workers.

The EITC provides a cash benefit to low-income families in the form of a tax credit. The credit is refundable in that it is not only set against household tax liability but households receive an actual cash payment in excess of any taxes they owe. The programme is administered by the Inland Revenue Service. Households with earned income below a specified level are eligible. The value of the credit increases as earnings increase, but as earnings rise further, it is gradually phased out. The value of the credit is higher for two-child than one-child households.

Households without children are also eligible but the benefit paid is comparatively small. Of course, the EITC is only available to those who apply for a refund. There is evidence to show that knowledge of the EITC has increased significantly over the years and that the majority of eligible low-paid workers do apply. Those receiving the credit prefer a lump sum annual payment rather than regular payments through their pay cheques (Phillips, 2001; Smeeding et al., 2001).

The EITC was introduced in 1975 in the midst of acrimonious congressional debates about the negative effects of social assistance and proposals to introduce a negative income tax. Dennis Ventry (2001) reports that both President Nixon's Family Assistance Plan, which proposed to replace AFDC with a welfare-to-work programme, and Milton Friedman's negative income tax floundered for lack of support. But Senator Russell Long (D-LA), chairman of the powerful Finance Committee and son of legendary Louisiana governor Huey Long, thought there was merit in paying what he described as a 'work bonus' to low-income workers who were not in receipt of welfare benefits and who were, he believed, treated badly by the regressivity of the tax system. He was particularly concerned about the regressive nature of social security payroll taxes which unfairly burdened low-paid workers.

Long was able to secure passage through the Senate of a modest work bonus proposal on more than one occasion, but it was rejected by the House and it was only with the passing of the Tax Reduction Act in 1975 that the EITC, as the work bonus became known, was enacted into law. One reason for its success was the sharp recession which followed the first oil shock of 1973. Although there were no hearings or much debate on the proposed EITC, there was sympathy for Long's argument that it would mitigate the negative effects of the recession by stimulating employment and reducing the welfare rolls. The credit was initially modest amounting to 10 per cent or $400 of the first $4,000 of annual earned income. Above this level, it phased out gradually reaching zero at $8,000. In 1978, the EITC became a permanent feature of the Internal Revenue Code. Initially, the credit was calculated and paid as an annual lump sum, but in 1979 the rules were changed to permit monthly payments in advance of the annual refundable lump sum.

Although there were some criticisms of the EITC on grounds of fraud and abuse and purported work disincentives at the phase out level, it attracted relatively little attention or debate and the numbers claiming refunds were generally small. However, with the enactment of President Reagan's major tax reform overhaul in 1986, the need to ease the tax burden on low-income workers was widely recognized. Although corporate taxes had declined, the tax burden on paid workers had increased. In addition to raising the standard deduction and personal exemption, Congress also endorsed the expansion of the EITC recognizing that it would create work incentives and subsidize both employers and employees. The maximum credit was raised and also indexed to inflation, and more than six million low-paid workers benefited from these changes.

Two significant additional expansions took place in the 1990s. President Bush signed an amendment to the tax code in 1990 which further raised the value of the credit, and in 1993 President Clinton signed legislation which raised the maximum credit for a family with two or more children to $3,556. Also families with no children were now for the first time permitted to claim the credit. These two increases raised the total cost of the EITC from about $7.5 billion in 1990 to $28 billion in 1996 (Hoffman and Seidman, 2003). Clearly, many more low-paid workers had become aware of the EITC and many more were now claiming refunds.

By the year 2000, the EITC was being claimed by more than 20 million households – an increase of more than 70 per cent since 1990. The costs of the programme now exceeded $30 billion per annum. Families with two children and an income of less than approximately $32,100 per annum were eligible to apply while the eligibility level for a family with one child was approximately $28,200 per annum. The maximum credit for a family with two children was approximately $4,000 and for a family with one child, approximately $2,400. The average payment was about $1,625. It is estimated that the credit lifted more than four million people above the poverty line at about this time (Hoffman and Seidman, 2003). In addition, 13 states have introduced their own EITC programmes which offer an additional credit based on the value of the federal credit. Of these states, nine provide a refundable credit while the remaining states limit the value of the credit to the household's tax liability.

The EITC has positive economic effects. One reason for its acceptance by conservative politicians is its subsidization of labour costs, which currently comprises a major share of the production costs of many enterprises. By subsidizing labour costs, firms are able to remain competitive. The EITC also subsidizes the incomes of low-paid workers, lifting many above the poverty line. By increasing disposable incomes, the EITC also creates work incentives and encourages employment participation. As people realize that they can receive extra cash benefits in addition to regular wages, they are more likely to seek employment. Several studies have shown that the programme's incentive effects are quite powerful and may be a major factor in promoting regular employment among welfare recipients (Meyer and Rosenbaum, 2001). Although there has been some controversy about whether the phase out of the credit has a disincentive effect which discourages workers from seeking jobs paying higher wages, research reveals that the credit's only serious disincentive effect concerns two-couple households with moderate incomes. In these households, it appears, the phase out of the credit may discourage both couples from working (Hoffman and Seidman, 2003).

A good deal of evidence has been collected to show that the EITC fosters consumption contributing to the demand for goods and services which is especially important in low-income neighbourhoods. Although only a few studies of EITC recipients have been undertaken, a survey by Timothy Smeeding and his colleagues (2001) of low-income taxpayers in Chicago found that the credit was used first to pay bills and meet routine household expenses and second to acquire consumer durables such as furniture, household appliances or a motor car. Indeed, the lump sum payment was largely perceived as a means of acquiring sufficient funds to purchase consumer durables. The study also found that a significant proportion of those surveyed intended to use the credit for what were described as household mobility purposes. These included the purchase of a car to improve transportation to work, the purchase of a home in a better neighbourhood and educational expenses. Only a small proportion of those interviewed (20 per cent), indicated that they had no plans for using the credit and would spend it as needs and opportunities arose.

Smeeding and his colleagues also believe that the EITC has a strong investment effect. Approximately a third of households in the study at the higher phase out levels reported that they saved most or all of the credit. Even those at the lower phase in level reported that they use the credit for savings. Of particular significance is the use of these funds for educational and transportation purposes which, they believe, is indicative of a strong desire among low-income workers to improve their situation and secure better opportunities for their children. Far from having negative economic effects, as critics of government social programmes contend, the EITC promotes employment, consumption and savings. It also supports the efforts of low-income families to invest in the human capital of their children with positive implications not only for their own welfare but also for the economy as a whole.

Savings accounts, public expenditures and capital mobilization

Of the different types of capital required by modern economies to achieve sustained economic development, the role of financial capital is usually emphasized. This is understandable since it plays a vital role in securing the facilities, equipment, technologies and other resources that enterprises need to be competitive and successful. Financial capital is primarily obtained from banks and other financial institutions and is dependent on readily available resources made available by individual savers and corporate investors.

It is well known that the United States has a comparatively low-savings rate and, as was noted earlier in this chapter, this has often been blamed on the country's social insurance retirement system. Instead of encouraging savings, it is claimed that the system transfers a huge volume of resources to pensioners and other beneficiaries who immediately use these funds for consumption purposes. Critics point out that if the programme had not been established, workers would have been compelled to save for their retirement with the result that substantial investment resources would be available to entrepreneurs. The ready availability of these funds would have obvious beneficial effects on economic development.

Although there is controversy about the extent to which the social insurance retirement system impedes capital formation in the United States, the government has adopted various policies and incentives to promote savings including insuring bank deposits and providing safeguards that minimize savings risks. In addition, income protection measures designed primarily to meet social rather than economic objectives have also been used. These include retirement savings account and matched savings accounts. Of the former, the Individual Retirement Account or IRA is the best known. Matched savings accounts are known as Individual Development Accounts or IDAs. Both are subsidized through public revenues and subject to statutory regulation.

Individual Retirement Accounts were first introduced in 1974 as a little noticed part of the Employee Retirement Income Security Act (ERISA). The Act itself was the result of more than a decade of congressional deliberations about the sustainability and security of occupational pensions. Although the statute was primarily intended to regulate corporate pension funds and also, with the creation of the Pension Guarantee Corporation, to ensure that corporate bankruptcies did not result in the total loss of workers' pension accumulations, it also included a provision which created a tax advantaged savings account known as the IRA. The IRA was initially intended to address the problem of portability which, at the time, was thought to apply largely to higher paid professional employees who regularly changed jobs. By permitting them to invest in a tax free retirement savings account, they would accumulate sufficient funds to offset any pension losses they might incur through frequent job changes.

Although the rules have changed over the years, and several different types of IRAs have been developed, the IRA is a popular tax advantaged retirement savings account which earns tax free interest and into which pretax or income deductible deposits are made. Withdrawals are permitted but incur a heavy penalty. Retirement accumulations may be withdrawn without penalty when the saver reaches the age of 59 and a half years. At this time, withdrawals are treated as taxable income. Savers are required to begin withdrawing their accumulations on reaching the age of 70 and a half years. Originally, all income earners were permitted to establish an IRA but high-income earners have since been excluded. However, the Roth IRA, as it is known, permits non-deductible contributions from higher-income earners into tax free interest accounts.

IRAs attracted relatively little attention until the 1980s, when they were promoted by the Reagan administration. Having declared its opposition to social security, the administration sought to popularize alternative ways of accumulating retirement funds. In addition to the IRA, it expanded a little-known provision of the tax code which had been introduced in 1978 to resolve tax complications associated with profit sharing. In 1981, this provision, which is governed by section 401(k) of the code, was amended to permit employees to make contributions into a retirement savings account established at their place of employment and usually matched by employers. The 401(k) pension plan has since been widely used and has emerged as a popular alternative to traditional defined-benefit plans based on earnings at the time of retirement. Although the 401(k) account is established by the employer, it is normally participant directed in that the employee selects from a number of investment options including mutual funds, stocks, bonds and other instruments. Some plans, notably the one established by the now insolvent energy firm, Enron, encourage employees to invest in the firm's own stock. Often, commercial carriers are used to manage the plan. Like the IRA, the 401(k) permits pretax deposits and earns tax free interest. Accumulations may be withdrawn when the employee retires, and at this time withdrawals are treated as taxable income. Like the

IRA, employees are required to begin withdrawing their accumulations on reaching the age of 70 and a half years. The 401(k) pension plan has since been augmented by other tax advantaged retirement savings plans such as the 403(b) plan for employees in the non-profit, educational and governmental sectors and by a variety of other tax advantaged savings accounts which can be used for educational and health-care purposes.

These savings accounts have been widely used, particularly by higher-income earners. Laurence Seidman (2001) reports that as many as three quarters of eligible higher-income earners contribute to IRAs while the proportion of low-paid workers who contribute is less than 15 per cent. He also estimates that the tax subsidy to IRAs was approximately $11 billion in 1999. Although he does not provide data on the cost of excluding contributions to 401(k) plans, he estimates that the total tax subsidy to all pension funds, including the 401(k) plan, was about $72 billion. This amount was the second highest income tax subsidy after deductions for medical insurance premiums.

The regressive nature of these provisions are not always recognized or publicized, but it is clear that they disproportionately benefit higher-income earners. This is in keeping with the way a variety of subsidies and tax incentives operate in the United States. For example, mortgage tax relief which is estimated to cost $54 billion annually in public revenues is primarily used by the middle class (Seidman, 2001). Agricultural and commercial subsidies, which are estimated to cost in the region of $100 billion annually (Zepezauer, 2004), have the same effect. While direct cash transfers to the poor are readily criticized for harming economic development, corporate welfare and the 'middle class welfare state' is seldom subjected to attack.

In an important book published in 1991, Michael Sherraden drew attention to the way the government subsidized the asset accumulations of the middle class and wealthy but neglected to support asset accumulation among the poor. To remedy this situation, he proposed that public revenues be used to establish matched savings accounts, to be known as IDAs, which would promote savings among those with low incomes. Although based on earlier proposals, the idea that the deposits of low-income savers be matched with public revenues was highly original. He originally proposed that IDA savings accounts be established for all citizens at birth, but that matches be used only to supplement the deposits of low-income earners with a phase out for those with higher incomes. Deposits could be matched on a one-to-one basis, but depending on the availability of resources a higher factor could also be used.

The IDA could be single or multipurpose: for example, it could be used to accumulate savings to meet the costs of postsecondary education, a deposit on a house purchase, start-up capital for a small business, funds for retirement or a combination of these and other purposes.

Sherraden's proposal attracted widespread attention from politicians, foundation executives and non-profit organizations, and in the early 1990s, several IDA projects were established by local community and social service organizations. Although his recommendation that IDAs be established for citizens at birth has not been implemented, by the end of the 1990s, at least 200 IDA projects providing opportunities for short- and medium-term savings were operating in different parts of the country. Since then, the number has exceeded 500 (Edwards and Mason, 2003). A nation-wide demonstration project managed by a non-profit organization, the Corporation for Enterprise Development, and funded by foundations, non-profit organizations and public funds was initiated in 1997 at 14 sites around the country with a total of 2,353 participant low-income savers. The demonstration project ended in 2003 and has been positively evaluated by Sherraden (2001) and his co-workers (Schreiner, Clancey and Sherraden, 2002). By 2004, 34 states, the District of Columbia and Peurto Rico had established IDA projects. Although not all of them are functional, having floundered for a lack of funds or because of implementation difficulties, 22 states had opera-tional IDA programmes in 2005 (Warren and Edwards, 2005). With the enactment of the Assets for Independence Act in 1998, federal funds were made available to non-profit organizations, credit unions and state and local public agencies to fund IDA projects. The average award is approximately $350,000 for a five-year period. Federal legislation that would potentially fund many more IDA accounts has also been debated but not enacted by the Congress. This legislation builds on earlier pro-posals by President Clinton to establish what he called Universal Savings Accounts or USAs which would allocate in excess of $33 billion to match the savings of low-income families. President Bush has also endorsed the idea, promising to support the programme through a federal tax credit to banks that offer IDAs to low-income savers.

However, publicly funded IDA projects operate primarily at the state level. Karen Edwards and Lisa Mason (2003) report that Iowa was the first state to introduce an IDA programme in 1993 as part of its welfare reform initiative and Tennessee and Texas followed in 1996. Many of these IDA programmes were established at the behest of community and non-profit activists and many were initially operated as demonstra-tion projects. These are usually managed through contracts with community and social service organizations. Most of the states use funds allocated under the TANF programme to finance their IDAs, which has the disadvantage of linking them specifically to welfare efforts, but ten fund their programmes out of general revenues. A few such as Minnesota, North Carolina and Pennsylvania have recognized the wider potential of IDAs as an economic development tool and state revenues have been allocated to support their expansion. Nevertheless, as Edwards and Mason report, substantial state funding has yet to become a policy trend, and the potential of IDAs to contribute significantly to asset accumulation among the poor has yet to be recognized. They note that several states that operated IDA demonstration projects have not taken a decision to implement a state-wide IDA programme. However, they are optimistic that many more state managed IDAs will be established in the future and that their role in asset accumulation and economic development will be fully appreciated.

Conclusion: social security, the state and economic development

As noted earlier, claims about the allegedly negative economic effects of government income protection programmes in the United States have been largely concerned with social insurance and social assistance. Although these claims have been challenged, they are now more widely accepted. They have also been generalized by academics, activists and political leaders on the political right to all forms of government welfare intervention. However, as has been shown, government income protection programmes such as welfare-to-work, the EITC and statutory savings accounts are seldom accused of harming economic development. This is not because they have escaped scrutiny but because their positive economic impact is generally recognized. These programmes have been shown to promote employment, foster educational opportunities and skills development, increase disposable incomes with positive implications for consumption and productivity, and promote savings.

These positive economic effects challenge the anti-statist argument that government spending on income protection inevitably harms economic development. They also demonstrate the need for social policy scholars to more clearly identify and articulate the positive contribution that social security programmes make to economic development. In addition, those programmes that have a demonstrably positive impact on economic development should be given greater prominence in debates about social security and economic development. Greater efforts need to be made to challenge claims about the inevitable trade-off between social and economic objectives. The social security policy innovations described in this chapter demonstrate that government income protection programmes can ensure the well-being of all while simultaneously promoting economic development and prosperity.

References

Acs, G. and Loprest, P. (2004). *Leaving Welfare*. Kalamazoo, MI. UpJohn Institute.

Appelbaum, E., Bernhardt, A. and Murnane, R. (eds) (2003). *Low-Wage America: How Employers are Reshaping Opportunity in the Workplace*. New York: Russell Sage Foundation.

Besharov, D., (2006). *Two Cheers for Welfare Reform*. Washington DC: American Enterprise Institute.

Besharov, D. J., Germanis, P. (2000). 'Welfare Reform: Four Years Later', *The Public Interest*, 140, 17–35.

Blau, J. (1999). *Illusions of Prosperity: America's Working Families in an Age of Economic Insecurity*. New York: Oxford University Press.

Bluestone, B. and Harrison, B. (2000). *Growing Prosperity: The Battle for Growth with Equity in the 21st Century*. New York: Houghton Mifflin.

Brauner, S. and Loprest, P. (1999). *Where Are They Now? What State Studies of People Who Left Welfare Tell Us*. Washington, DC: The Urban Institute.

Burke, M. R., Green, R. and Duke, A. E. (1998). *Income Support and Social Services for Low-Income People in Minnesota*. Washington, DC: Urban Institute.

Burtless, G. (1999). 'The Employment Experiences and Potential Earnings of Welfare Recipients.' In J. E. Hansen and R. Morris (eds), *Welfare Reform, 1996–2000*. Westport, CT: Auburn House, 51–74.

Danzinger, S. and Seefelt, K. S. (2003). 'Barriers to the Employment of the "Hard to Serve": Implications for Services sanctions and Time Limits', *Social Policy and Society*, 2 (2), 151–160.

Douglas, P. (1936). *Social Security in the United States: An Analysis and Appraisal of the Federal Social Security Act*. Washington DC: Beard Books.

Edwards, K. and Mason, L. M. (2003). *State Policy Trends for Individual Development Accounts in the United States, 1993–2003*. St. Louis, MO: Center for Social Development, Washington University.

Feldstein, M. B. (1974). 'Social Security, Induced Retirement and Aggregate Capital Accumulation', *Journal of Political Economy*, 83 (4), 447–475.

Freeman, R. A. (1981). *The Wayward Welfare State*. Stanford, CA: Hoover Institution Press.

Friedman, M. (with Friedman, R.) (1980). *Free to Choose*. New York: Harcourt.

General Accounting Office (1999). Welfare Reform: Information on Former Recipients' Status. Washington DC.

Gingrich, N. (1995). *To Renew America*. New York: Harper.

Handler, J. (1995). *The Poverty of Welfare Reform*. New Haven, CT: Yale University Press.

Hoffman, S. D. and Seidman, L. S. (2003). *Helping Working Families: the Earned Income Tax Credit*. Kalamazoo, MI: W.E. Upjohn Institute for Employment Research.

Knox, V., Miller, C. and Gennetian, L. (2000). *Reforming Welfare and Rewarding Work: A Summary of the Final Report of the Minnesota Family Investment Plan*. New York: Manpower Research Demonstration Corporation.

Leiby, J. (1978). *A History of Social Welfare and Social Work in the United States*. New York: Columbia University Press.

Mangum, G. L., Mangum, S. L. and Sum, A. (2003). *The Persistence of Poverty in the United States*. Baltimore, MD: Johns Hopkins University Press.

Manpower Development Research Corporation (2007). *How Much is a College Degree Worth?* New York.

Mead, L. M. (1986). *Beyond Entitlement: The Social Obligations of Citizenship*. New York: Free Press.

Meyer, B. D. and Rosenbaum, D. T. (2001). 'Making Single Mothers Work: Recent Tax and Welfare Policy and its Effects.' In B. D. Meyer and D. Holtz-Eakin (eds), *Making Work Pay: The Earned Income Tax Credit and Its Impact on American Families*. New York: Russell Sage Foundation, pp. 69–115.

Murray, C. (1984). *Losing Ground: American Social Policy, 1950–1980*. New York: Basic Books.

Pavetti, D. L. (1997). *Against the Odds: Steady Employment among Low Skilled Women*. Washington, DC: The Urban Institute.

Phillips, K. R. (2001). *Who Knows about the Earned Income Tax Credit?* Washington, DC: Urban Institute.

Rank, M. (2006). *One Nation Underprivileged: Why American Poverty Affects Us All*. New York: Oxford University Press.

Rowe, G. and Giannarelli, L. (2006). *Getting on, Staying on and Getting off Welfare: The Complexities of State-by-State Policy Choices*. Washington, DC: Urban Institute.

Schreiner, M., Clancey, M. and Sherraden, M. (2002). *Final Report: Savings Performance in the American Dream Demonstration*. St. Louis, MO: Washington University Center for Social Development.

Shaw, K. M., Goldrick-Rab, S., Mazzeo, C. and Jacobs, J. A. (2006). *Putting the Poor to Work: How the Work-First Idea Eroded College Access for the Poor*. New York: Russell Sage.

Siedman, L. (2001). 'Assets and the Tax Code.' In T. M. Shapiro and E. N. Wolff (eds), *Assets for the Poor*. New York: Russell Sage Foundation, pp. 324–356.

Sherraden, M. (1991) *Assets and the Poor: a New American Welfare Policy*. Armonk, NY: M. E. Sharpe.

Sherraden, M. (2001). 'Asset Building Policy and Programmes for the Poor.' In T. M. Shapiro and E. N. Wolff (eds), *Assets for the Poor*. New York: Russell Sage Foundation, pp. 302–323.

Shipler, D. K. (2004). *The Working Poor: Invisible America*. New York: Knopf.

Shulman, B. (2003). *How Low-Wage Jobs Fail 30 Million Americans*. New York: New Press.

Smeeding, T. M., Phillips, K. R. and O'Conner, M. A. (2001). ' The Earned Income Tax Credit: Knowledge, Use, and Economic and Social Mobility.' In B. D. Meyer and D. Holtz-Eakin (eds), *Making Work Pay: The Earned Income Tax Credit and Its Impact on American Families*. New York: Russell Sage Foundation, pp. 301–329.

Trattner, W. (1999). *From Poor Law to Welfare State. A History of Social Welfare in America*. 6th Ed. New York: The Free Press.

Ventry, D. (2001). 'The Political History of the Earned Income Tax Credit.' In B. D. Meyer and D. Holtz-Eakin (eds), *Making Work Pay: The Earned Income Tax Credit and Its Impact on American Families*. New York: Russell Sage Foundation, pp. 15–66.

Warren, N. and Edwards, K. (2005). *Status of State Supported IDA Programmes in 2005*. St. Louis, MO: Center for Social Development, Washington University.

Zepezauer, M. (2004). *Take the Rich off Welfare*. Boston, MA: South End Press.

7
Korea: Economic Development, Social Security and Productive Welfare

Joon Yong Jo

Korea is one of Asia's Newly Industrialized Countries (NIC). It emerged from the devastation after the Korean War in the early 1950s to become the world's 11th largest economy and a member of the Organization for Economic Cooperation and Development (OECD). Between the early 1960s and the 1990s, Korea's authoritarian military governments placed top priority on economic development and export-oriented industrialization. In those days, social security was subordinated to the country's pro-growth economic policy. Government spending on social security was minimal and welfare depended on economic growth, full employment and traditional family ties.

However, when the Korean economy was affected by the East Asian financial crisis in 1997, the gains of previous decades were suddenly reversed. In 1998, GDP growth fell by 6.7 per cent and unemployment reached an unprecedented rate of 6.8 per cent. Many families were plunged into poverty and homelessness increased. Korea's welfare system was shaken at its roots. Without a comprehensive social security programme, the rate of poverty doubled (Kim and Son, 2002; Moon et al., 1999). This situation called for an immediate response from the government. The rise in the number of the unemployed and low-income families also triggered the idea that social security should be expanded. However, some argued that social welfare should be associated with human capital investment and economic development rather than adopting a subsidization or entitlement approach characteristic of welfare policy in the European countries.

It was in this context that President Kim Dae-Jung formally adopted the productive welfare approach as one of the three pillars of his administrative philosophy. The others were democratic politics and a market economy. In terms of the pillar of productive welfare, social security was viewed as an 'investment for improved productivity, rather than as a simple transfer of income' (Office of the President, 2000). The concept of productive welfare had been formulated by President Kim Young Sam, who was President Kim Dae-Jung's predecessor, but it was not given as much priority during the Kim Young Sam administration and had a rather different connotation focusing on self-reliance and the market in social welfare. Although it was not rigorously defined in theoretical terms, the concept was used by President Kim Dae-Jung in a more proactive way and required much more state intervention. The concept was influenced by both indigenous and external ideas. Much of the policy work associated with the productive welfare concept was vague and had limited practical application. It also lacked policy impact. However, for the first time in Korea's history, the productive welfare approach laid a framework for a positive relationship between social security and economic development.

This chapter traces the emergence of the productive welfare approach during the Kim Dae-Jung administration and examines its impacts on Korea's economic development. It pays special attention to the government's self-support programme, which is a welfare-to-work programme introduced by the government under the National Basic Livelihood Security System (NBLSS) in 2000. The self-support programme is designed to help welfare recipients and the borderline poor to find jobs and to establish micro-enterprises. It provides work experience which the government believes will help them achieve self-sufficiency. In this way, it is hoped that welfare recipients will enhance their capacity to function in the productive economy, become self-reliant and improve their standard of living. By facilitating economic participation through productive employment and self-employment, the programme also contributes to economic development. This chapter describes the programme and considers evidence relating to its effectiveness. But first, it begins by providing some information about Korea and its people, and the history and features of the country's social security programme.

Korea: the Land of Morning Calm

Korea, officially known as the Republic of Korea, is a country in northeastern Asia occupying the southern portion of the Korea Peninsula. Korea is bounded on the north by North Korea; on the east by the East Sea; on the south by the Korea Strait, which separates it from Japan; and on the west by the Yellow Sea. In 2005, the country's population was approximately 47 million and Gross National Income (GNI) was US $16,413 per capita. Korea has a democratic government, while the Democratic People's Republic of North Korea is ruled by a Communist regime. The capital city of Korea is Seoul. Korea is one of the most ethnically homogeneous countries in the world.

Korea's history dates back to 2333 BCE, when King Tan-gun established the first kingdom of Ancient Chosun. After the fall of Ancient Chosun, Korea was divided into a number of small patriarchal states, which were gradually unified into the Three Kingdoms, namely, Koguryo (37 BCE–678 CE), Baekje (18 BCE–676 CE) and Shilla (57 BCE–935 CE). Ever since the Shilla dynasty unified the peninsula in 668 CE, Korea has been ruled by a single government and has maintained its political autonomy and cultural and ethnic identity despite frequent foreign invasions. The name 'Korea' derives from the Koryo dynasty (918–1392 CE), and its nickname 'the Land of Morning Calm' comes from the translation of the Chinese character representing the Chosun dynasty (1392–1910 CE). Both the Koryo and Chosun dynasties exercised centralized government power and flourished culturally. However, in the late nineteenth century, imperialist nations such as China, Russia and Japan all sought to dominate the country. In 1910, Japan annexed Chosun and instituted colonial rule, bringing the Chosun dynasty to an end and with it the end of traditional Korea. Korea's liberation from colonial rule coincided with the official ending of the Second World War on 15th August 1945. The statehood of modern day Korea was established in 1948 following the partitioning of the peninsula between the occupying forces of the United States in the south and the USSR in the north.

The first president of Korea, Rhee Syng Man (1948–1960), adopted a vigorous anti-communism ideology as the main goal of his government, and the North Korean leader, Kim Il Sung, sought to unify the entire Korean Peninsula under his Communist regime. To this end, Kim Il Sung launched a full-scale military attack on the South in June 1950, which began the 1950–1953 Korean War. As is well known, the Korean War was bloody and devastated the country.

Politics and economic development

After the Korean War, the country's economy was critically dependent on relief funds from the United States and international aid. President Rhee adhered to a strong anticommunist ideology, which was used as an excuse against the introduction of liberal democracy (Kwon, 1999).

In 1960, a blatant manipulation of the national election by the Rhee administration led to a nationwide student revolution which culminated in the President's forced resignation.

In 1961, a military coup led by Major General Park Chung Hee overthrew the government of Chang Myon, who assumed office after Rhee's resignation. Three months later, Park became the president. Park's era (1961–1979) was marked by extraordinary economic growth based on export-oriented industrialization. Park made economic growth the top priority of his government and in this way sought to legitimize his military rule (Amsden, 1989). A series of Five-Year Economic Plans was launched in 1962. The Economic Planning Board, which was established in 1963, played a crucial role in the country's rapid development. It drafted a series of economic development plans and ensured that economic policy was effectively implemented. The primary focus of these plans was the development of the manufacturing sector and the export of manufactured goods. Contrary to the claim that Korea embraced a free market economy, Park's military government deliberately intervened in the market and regulated the economy by imposing strict performance standards on private industries (Amsden, 1989; Cho, 1994). To finance investment, the government adopted policies that attracted foreign capital. To repay foreign debt, the government promoted exports even further by providing preferential credits to exporters (Cho, 1994). The consequence was a dramatic spurt of industrialization and export growth which resulted in a 13.8 per cent GNP growth in 1969.

Such extraordinary economic growth and industrialization did not, however, lead to the development of democratic institutions. On the contrary, an even more 'bureaucratic-authoritarian regime' of concentrated power emerged (Im, 1987). In 1972, in the face of widespread protests, President Park declared martial law. He also introduced the Yusin (revitalizing) constitution, securing for himself a life-long presidential tenure. During the Third Five-Year Economic Plan (1972–1976), the Yusin government concentrated its energy on developing heavy industries in an attempt to promote an even higher rate of economic growth and exports. The Yusin government also established general trading companies by selecting a few large firms which took over the export business to achieve the export goal set by the government. The selected firms were provided with special benefits and government allowances, and they soon evolved into giant, family-owned conglomerates. It was at this time that the formation of these close government–business relationships prompted the popular expression 'Korea-Inc'

(Cho, 1994). But the government's authoritarian rule continued to provoke opposition and numerous emergency measures were implemented to restrict civil liberties and remove political opponents. Amidst growing dissatisfaction with the Yusin regime, President Park was assassinated in October 1979.

In December 1979, General Chun Do Hwan and his military colleagues staged a coup, removing the Korean Army's chief of staff and seizing control of the government. Chun expanded the provisions of the Park government's martial law provisions and brutally suppressed opposition. Chun was elected president by a puppet electoral college in 1980. He instituted a new constitution which retained many of the Yusin-type policies. The Chun Do Hwan government, which was in power until 1988, also promoted continued economic growth. The balance of imports and exports continued to favour Korean firms, which brought in pressures from abroad for import liberalization (Cho, 1994). Chun's authoritarian government, however, was challenged by the general election of 1985 which contrary to its expectation favoured the opposition. Despite suppressing the opposition, the election results encouraged the strengthening of the democratization movement. Following a series of mass protests in 1987, President Chun promised democratic reforms including direct presidential elections. Voters adopted a new democratic constitution in a referendum, and Roh Tae Woo, the presidential candidate from Chun's political party, was elected president in December 1987.

Despite his links with the military regime, Roh's government (1988–1993) was considered to be more democratic than its predecessor. Over his five-year term, President Roh was given credit for additional democratic reforms and improved relationship with North Korea. In September 1991, South Korea and North Korea were simultaneously admitted to the United Nations as separate countries. In addition, Roh's government introduced a number of economic liberalization reforms. During the Sixth Five-Year Economic Plan (1987–1991), government intervention in the market was considerably reduced and the Korean economy became increasingly liberalized.

In December 1992, Kim Young Sam, the former opposition leader who had joined Roh's ruling party, became Korea's first civilian president in more than three decades. President Kim adopted a New Economy Plan which resonated with the neoliberalistic globalization scheme. The New Economy Plan emphasized a further reduction of state intervention and the liberalization of the capital market. By 1996, Korea's GNI per capita reached US $12,000, almost 100 times the 1966 level. At this time, Korea became the world's 11th largest economy and was admitted to the OECD. However, premature liberalization of the capital market rendered the country vulnerable to the volatility of speculative international capital flows. Moreover, an exorbitant amount of debt accumulated by the country's family-owned conglomerates led to a serious liquidity problem when foreign creditors collectively demanded repayment of short-term loans. These conglomerates were also recognized to have very inefficient management structures which exacerbated the problem of credit worthiness. These factors, together with East Asia's financial crisis of 1997, led to the collapse of Korea's foreign investor credibility, triggering a massive flight of capital. The government sought help from the International Monetary Fund (IMF) in the form of an emergency loan in November 1997 and engaged in rigorous structural reforms of the financial and corporate sectors. The loan was repaid in August 2001.

The Kim Dae-Jung government, which came into office in 1998, had to confront the serious economic and social consequences of the financial crisis. Growth plunged by 6.7 per cent in 1998, and GNI per capita fell from about US $11,100 in 1997 to US $7,355 in 1998 (Bank of Korea, 2007). By the end of 1998, real wage had dropped by 10.7 per cent, and the unemployment rate, which had been hovering around 2.6 per cent until 1997, shot up to 8.7 per cent in February 1999. In addition to dealing with the crisis, President Kim adopted a number of new economic, social and diplomatic policies. In addition to pursuing closer links with North Korea, his government promoted further democratization and many believe that the country became a full-fledged democracy. The government also introduced rigorous structural market reforms and expanded social programmes.

By August 2001 when Korea completed the repayment of the IMF loan, the unemployment rate had decreased to 3.4 per cent. President Kim was awarded the Nobel Peace Prize in 2000. The government's neoliberal economic reforms, which were prescribed by the IMF, were accompanied by social programmes conducive to country's macroeconomic performance, especially job creation. It was in this context that President Kim introduced the concept of productive welfare which will be discussed in more detail later in this chapter.

Kim Dae-Jung was succeeded by President Roh Moo Hyun in 2003. Roh was Kim's political heir and protégé. The Roh Moo Hyun government has continued and sought to further develop many of the policies introduced by its predecessor (Lee, 2004). With regard to social security policies, Roh's government is currently exploring the possibility of using tax credits and matched savings accounts for low-income families.

Korean social policy scholars have produced several analytical accounts of the development of the country's social security system. Some have viewed the expansion of social security as a key element in the process of legitimizing Korea's authoritarian governments (Kwon, 1999) but others view the development of social security as an adjunct to the nation's pro-growth economic policies (Hwang, 2006). Several scholars have pointed out that during the political democratization period of the late 1980s, the government expanded social security significantly in an attempt to garner political support from civil society and the working class (Ahn and Lee, 2005; Kwon, 1998; Woo, 2004). However, until the mid-1990s, economic development remained at the top of government priorities with social security playing only a subsidiary role to economic development. The notion of productive welfare which was promoted by President Kim Dae-Jung has also been documented by Korean scholars, but there are different points of view about the goals and social impact of this policy and whether it functioned effectively as a social investment measure. The issue will be considered later in this chapter.

Korea's social security system

Korea's social security system is comprised of four social insurance programmes and a social assistance programme. The social insurance programmes include the National Pension Scheme (NPS), the Industrial Accidents Compensation Insurance scheme (IACI), the National Health Insurance scheme (NHI) and finally the Employment Insurance (EI). In addition, the social assistance programme, known as the National Basic Livelihood Security System (NBLSS), is designed to cover all eligible low-income people regardless of their work ability.

The National Pension Scheme (NPS)

The National Pension Scheme (NPS) provides old-age retirement, disability and survivor's benefits. It covers the entire population from the ages of 18 to 60, except civil servants, military personnel and private-school teachers who are covered by a special pension scheme. It is financed by 9 per cent of payroll taxes levied equally on the insured (4.5 per cent) and their employers (4.5 per cent). For farmers and fishermen, the government provides a subsidy which is equal to their own contributions. The National Pension Corporation established by the government under the Ministry of Health and Welfare is responsible for the administration and management of the scheme.

The NPS was introduced under President Park's military government in 1973 with the enactment of the National Welfare Pension Act. The real motive behind the Act, however, was to support the government's economic development policies. At that time, the Park government was eager to obtain investment funds to develop heavy industries. In this context, the Korean Development Institute (KDI), which is a research institute under the Economic Planning Board (EPB), designed the pension scheme as a means of mobilizing domestic capital (Hwang, 2006; Kim, 2006). However, President Park postponed implementing the scheme because of economic concerns following the first oil crisis of 1973.

In 1986, the Chun Do Hwan government enacted the National Pension Act, which was, in essence, a revision of the 1973 National Welfare Pension Act. The purpose of the National Pension Act was to secure electoral support and to legitimatize the authoritarian government (Aspalter, 2001; Kim, 2006). The NPS was finally implemented in 1988 with compulsory coverage for employees in firms with ten or more employees. The coverage expanded to firms with five or more employees in 1992 and was then expanded to cover the rural population in 1995. Finally, in 1999, the coverage of the scheme expanded to cover the entire population as the Kim Dae-Jung government aggressively expanded social programmes to respond to the financial crisis and deal with its economic and social consequences. By 2005, the number of those insured under the scheme exceeded 17 million, and about 1.7 million people were receiving benefits from the scheme (National Pension Service, 2006).

Industrial Accidents Compensation Insurance (IACI)

The IACI provides medical care, wage replacement, disability, injury-disease compensation, nursing, funeral and survivor's benefits to injured workers and their families on a no-fault principle. Participation is compulsory for all workers and employers. Through the scheme, the government assumes responsibility for compensating workers for accidents and injuries they sustain at work. It is administered by the Korea Labor Welfare Corporation, which was established by the government under the Ministry of Labor.

The scheme is governed by the Industrial Accidents Compensation Insurance Act which was enacted in 1963 and became effective in 1964. Originally, it covered firms with 500 or more workers. The scheme was the first social insurance programme established for the general public in Korea's history. While pensions for civil servants, which were introduced in 1960, are often said to be the first social insurance programme in Korea, its coverage was limited to government employees (Lee, 1999). The Industrial Accidents scheme was introduced to protect workers from industrial accidents. This was obviously important during the rapid industrialization that took place under President Park's military government. However, in the early phase of the scheme, the military government limited its coverage to firms with 500 or more workers in order to minimize the economic burden on businesses (Nam, 2000). Coverage has been gradually expanded to firms with a minimum of 100 workers in 1967, with five workers in 1988 and finally in 2000 to all firms with at least one worker. As of 2005, the scheme covered more than 12 million workers in 1.1 million enterprises (Ministry of Labor, 2006).

National Health Insurance scheme (NHI)

The NHI is a comprehensive medical insurance programme that covers Korea's entire population. It provides both in-kind benefits, such as health care and health check-ups, as well as cash benefits such as reimbursement, maternity allowances and funeral expenses. The scheme is financed by contributions from insured workers, employers and the government. Equal contributions are made by insured workers and employers. For the self-employed, contribution are made by the insured and the government. The scheme is managed by the Ministry of Health and Welfare through the National Health Insurance Corporation.

The idea of national health insurance was first introduced in 1963 when President Park's government passed the Medical Insurance Act. However, to avoid placing a financial burden on business, the Act did not require compulsory coverage. Take-up was low and it was hardly an effective health social insurance programme. The Medical Insurance Act was then revised in 1976 and implemented in 1977 to provide compulsory coverage for employees in firms with 500 or more workers. In 1979, coverage was expanded to firms with 300 or more workers. At the same time, civil servants and private-school teachers were covered by health insurance. However, the scheme did not cover farmers, the self-employed and the unemployed. In addition, the government did not make any financial contribution to the scheme and only regulated the scheme (Kwon, 1997, 2001). It was only during the 1989 that health insurance expanded to cover the entire population.

Although the original scheme provided universal coverage, unresolved issues of inefficiency and inequality within the system hampered its effectiveness. The scheme was also administratively complex having multiple numbers of insurers based on different types of insured workers. To resolve these problems, the Kim Dae-Jung government passed the National Health Insurance Act in 1999 and all workers were integrated into one single insurer, the National Health Insurance Corporation. The Act became effective in 2000, and the country's new NHI now provides comprehensive medical benefits including prevention and rehabilitation. The government's contribution was also increased to subsidize the self-employed. In 2005, the scheme covered 47.3 million beneficiaries or 96.4 per cent of the total population. The remaining 3.6 per cent or 1.7 million people are covered by medical aid, which is a part of the country's social assistance programme (HIRA and NHIC, 2006).

Employment Insurance (EI)

Employment Insurance (EI) is designed to provide unemployment benefits to workers, employment security subsidies to employers as an incentive to hire and retain workers, and vocational training subsidies to both workers and employers. Unlike traditional unemployment insurance in Western counties, which only provide unemployment benefits, Korea's Employment Insurance scheme is a compound of unemployment benefits and active labour market policy. The scheme is funded primarily by employer contributions, except that unemployment benefits are funded by both workers and employers who make equal contributions. The scheme is administered by the Ministry of Labor. Since 1999, the Korea Labor Welfare Corporation has been entrusted with setting and collecting contributions.

Like many other social security programmes in Korea, unemployment insurance originated with President Park's government in the early 1960s, but proposals to introduce unemployment insurance was discarded because of cost to the business community and the fear that it might harm the economy by undermining work incentives (Hwang, 2006; Kim and Kim, 2003). It then resurfaced in the early 1980s under President Chun's government but again no action was taken. However, in the late 1980s changing economic circumstances required greater restructuring and labour market flexibility, and despite the government's reluctance, there was growing realization that unemployment insurance would serve economic policy interests.

It was in this context that the Korea Labor Institute proposed that unemployment insurance be linked with active labour market policy in a comprehensive programme and this proposal was generally accepted (Hwang, 2006). The Employment Insurance Act was legislated in 1993 under the Kim Young Sam government and finally implemented in 1995, covering firms with 30 or more workers. By implementing the programme, Korea's social insurance system became quite comprehensive, and the country was regarded as a leader in social security development among the newly industrializing developing countries. The financial crisis of 1997 and the ensuing problem of mass unemployment further reinforced the need for a programme of this kind and resulted in its rapid expansion. In 1998, coverage of the scheme was expanded to all enterprises. During President Kim Dae-Jung's administration, the eligibility criteria for unemployment benefits were relaxed and the amount of unemployment benefits was increased. In addition, the duration of unemployment benefits was extended, and maternity protection allowances were introduced. Together with its active labour market policy, the scheme now plays an important role in the country's economic development strategy. In December 2005, the scheme covered 8 million workers in 1.1 million enterprises (Human Resources Development Service of Korea, 2006).

The National Basic Livelihood Security System (NBLSS)

Korea's social assistance programme is known as the National Basic Livelihood Security System (NBLSS). It provides cash benefits and medical, housing, education, childbirth, funeral and self-support benefits. The NBLSS is a non-contributory welfare provision funded by the state from general revenues. Eligibility for the scheme is determined through a means test of the recipients and their immediate families. The NBLSS is managed by the Ministry of Health and Welfare.

The first modern social assistance programme in Korea was the Chosun Relief Decree of 1944, established under Japanese colonial rule. However, this programme covered only a small proportion of the country's impoverished population. When Korea was devastated by the Korean War in the 1950s, the poor received relief and aid primarily from international relief agencies and Voluntary organizations. At this time, social assistance was non-functional due to a lack of economic sources. To provide limited support for destitute families, the Livelihood Protection Act was enacted under President Park's government in 1961. The Act established the Livelihood Protection Programme (LPP) to provide cash benefits, medical aid (1978) and educational support (1979) to the poor who were unable to work and without any family member able to assist them. Under this programme, those between the ages of 18 and 65 were categorically excluded from receiving benefits. The poverty line was determined by the government and the benefit level was unrealistically low. By introducing and applying the notion of the 'deserving poor' and 'less-eligibility' from the English Poor Law, the scheme sought to compel the poor to work and thus effectively supplied cheap labour for the government's industrialization policy (Kim and Sung, 1993).

However, as was noted earlier, the rate of unemployment increased rapidly during East Asian financial crisis of 1997, and this was accompanied by a sharp increase in the numbers of people in absolute poverty. Demands for a more effective public social assistance programme increased, and this was supported by many academics and politicians. The international agencies also recommended that the social safety net be strengthened as a condition for providing structural adjustment loans. Consequently, in 1999, President Kim Dae-Jung's government replaced the 38-year-old Livelihood Protection Act of 1961 with the National Basic Livelihood Security Act.

The new NBLSS, which was implemented in October 2000, abolished the eligibility age categories of the previous scheme, which excluded those between the ages of 18 and 65 from receiving benefits. Coverage was extended to those in need regardless of their work ability. The official poverty line was redefined in terms of the minimum cost of living and it became more generous. The scheme also introduced a welfare-to-work self-support programme to help recipients become self-sufficient through economic participation. As will be discussed in the next section, the NBLSS comprised the core of President Kim's productive welfare policy, an idea that relates welfare provision with human capital investment and economic development. In 2005, the scheme provided benefits to 1.5 million individuals in approximately 809,000 households, or about 3.2 per cent of total population (Ministry of Health and Welfare, 2006).

Productive welfare and economic development

As noted previously, successive Korean governments have prioritized economic development over social security relying on full employment and family supports to meet income-protection needs. This practice was particularly noticeable during the period of rapid industrialization when the Park government adopted policies designed to promote economic growth through export-led development strategies. President Park was clear about his government's economic priorities pointing out that growth was a precondition for improvements in welfare and standards of living. As he put it in 1962,

> The economic, social and political goals we set after the revolution are the promotion of the public welfare, freedom from exploitation and the fair distribution of an income among the people. ... Before these goals can be achieved ... we must take a great leap forward toward economic growth. (quoted from Amsden, 1989, p. 49)

It was in this context that the Korean government used social security as an adjunct to the nation's pro-growth economic policy. The subsequent but still limited introduction of social security by the country's authoritarian governments was popular with the public and served the additional goal of legitimizing the authoritarian military governments that ruled the country for many years. In addition, it is clear that social security was regarded by these governments as an integral part of its plan to stimulate industrialization and economic growth. For example, the NPS was introduced to mobilize domestic capital for industrialization. The IACI was introduced to minimize the economic costs to the corporate sector in the event that workers who were injured at work successfully litigated against their employers. This is not to deny that the scheme also protected workers against the contingency of industrial injury and thus served a welfare function. But it is clear that the scheme served to support economic development goals. The government was mindful of the costs that social programmes would impose on employers, and it sought to avoid placing additional burdens on them. For example, in order to lessen the financial burden of business, the Medical Insurance scheme of the 1960s did not require compulsory coverage. Finally, social assistance was used to supply cheap labour for industries. As such, Korea's social security policies during the period of rapid industrialization were subordinated to economic growth, served economic goals and supported the government's economic development plans. Although there was a notable expansion of social security during the political democratization period of the 1990s, the government continued to function as a regulator rather than a provider of welfare. Government expenditure on social security never exceeded 1 per cent of GDP until 1997, and social security continued to play an adjunct role to economic development.

Because Korea's pro-growth development model was sustained by vigorous economic growth, full employment and strong family ties, the need for extensive government welfare programmes was limited. However, after the financial crisis of 1997, it became obvious that Korea's state-led pro-growth policy could not secure welfare for its people in the market globalization with its economic vicissitudes and risks. The serious economic and social consequences of the financial crisis, together with inadequate social security programmes, called for a more effective response from the state. In particular, a rise in the unemployment and poverty rates supported calls for more extensive state welfare and social security programmes. In particular, the idea that the government should adopt social security policies that promote human capital investments and economic development gained popularity. It was in this context that President Kim Dae-Jung adopted the idea of productive welfare as a key element of his government's administrative philosophy.

The productive welfare model

Productive welfare is Korea's new normative approach to social policy. It was formally adopted by the Kim Dae-Jung administration when, in a public speech in August 1999, President Kim announced that the concept of productive welfare would serve as a basis for social security and social welfare services. This was followed by the publication of *DJ Welfarism: A New Paradigm for Productive Welfare in Korea* in 2000. The document which is the official manifestation of President Kim's productive welfare policy was produced by the Presidential Committee for the Quality of Life in the Office of President. The document begins with the recognition that the constitutional right to social welfare has never been realized in Korea due to a distorted development process that favoured economic development over welfare. In this regard, productive welfare represents a proactive role for social policy and social security. It is based on the notion that welfare provisions should be integrated with economic development and that welfare expenditures can be an economic investment.

> Productive welfare begins with the recognition of human rights ... and ends with the principle of welfare through work. ... welfare through work addresses the need for a balance between the too often conflicting principles of the market and of welfare. ... welfare policies can be viewed as an investment for improved productivity, rather than as a simple transfer of income through administrative procedures. (Office of the President, 2000, pp. 9–10)

It was noted in the introduction to this chapter that the term 'productive welfare' had been coined earlier during the presidency of Kim Young Sam (1993–1998), when he announced that his government would pursue a Korean style welfare model designed to meet the country's unique economic and social circumstances. The concept was outlined in rather general terms in a document entitled *The Welfare Plan for the Globalization of the Quality of Life*, which drew extensively on the deliberations of the 1995 United Nations World Summit for Social Development. However, the notion of productive welfare was used at the time to emphasize the role of the traditional family and market participation by the poor as a way to minimize the government involvement in social welfare (Kim, 1997). On the other hand, President Kim Dae-Jung's notion of productive welfare emphasized a much more active role for government in promoting social development. As his administration noted,

[Productive welfare is] an ideology, as well as policy, that seeks to secure minimum living standards for all people, while expanding opportunities for self-support in socio-economic activities. ... As such, productive welfare endeavors to improve the quality of life for all citizens by promoting social development and a fair distribution of wealth. (Office of the President, 2000, p. 18)

President Kim Dae-Jung was actively involved in articulating the concept of productive welfare. The term in fact reflects President Kim's own beliefs and his views on Korea's unique social and economic situation and the need for an indigenous welfare philosophy. President Kim was a 30-year-long veteran opposition leader who had long been concerned about social issues. He had frequently criticized the government's reliance on family-owned corporations to achieve its economic growth targets, and he had attacked the way economic policy had created inequalities and produced a process of distorted development (Kim, 1985). However, the productive welfare concept was also greatly influenced by the British Third Way approach articulated by Anthony Giddens (Han, 2002; Kim, 2003; Sung, 1999). It appears that President Kim was inspired by his meeting with Anthony Giddens (Sung, 1999) and the notions of positive welfare and the social investment state which Giddens had formulated (2000). It is clear that the productive welfare approach shares many components of the Third Way approach. The Office of the President (2000, p. 69) also stated that productive welfare promoted a 'Third Way' type of approach to training and educational opportunities. It is for this reason that the concept of productive welfare has often been touted as Korea's Third Way (Han, 2002).

Productive welfare and welfare reform

Since the financial crisis in late 1997, the most urgent task facing the Kim Dae-Jung government was to cope with the problem of mass unemployment. Soon after the government came into office in 1998, coverage of the Employment Insurance scheme was extended to all enterprises. However, many unemployed people were casual and part-time workers who did not qualify for unemployment benefits because of their short contribution history. Few were eligible for social assistance due to age exclusion and the strict means test of the Livelihood Protection Programme. To deal with this problem, the Kim Dae-Jung government launched a sizable public works project which provided temporary jobs for unemployed people who were not covered by the unemployment insurance scheme or the Livelihood Protection Programme. Examples of these public works projects included forestry work, repairing public facilities, street cleaning and community services. These public works projects were quite effective and reduced the unemployment rate in the short term. In 1999, public works projects created an average of 400,000 jobs in each quarter, which reduced the overall unemployment rate by 2 per cent (Kwon, 2002). However, despite these successes, the long-term effects of unemployment caused great concern. In addition, the nature of public works projects were perceived by many in a negative way and many regarded them as a form of 'workfare' which provided benefits to the participants in return for easy labour (Kwon, 2002). For these reasons, the Kim Dae-Jung government realized that economic policy and the whole welfare system needed to be redesigned so that social programmes were more closely linked to economic policy and that long-term productivity as well as income security be ensured. It was this realization that led the President and his advisors to rethink the philosophical basis for the country's welfare system and to adopt the concept of productive welfare as a basis for welfare reform.

The most distinctive application of the notion of productive welfare was in social assistance. In 2000, the four-decade-old Livelihood Protection Programme was replaced with the NBLSS. The new scheme was implemented to provide eligible low-income people with cash income subsidies and to ensure that they achieved a minimum standard of living regardless of work ability. The age exclusion as well as the work ability requirement of the old Livelihood Protection Programme was abolished, and the Poor Law notion of serving only the 'deserving poor' was abandoned. The new scheme also established a new self-support programme, which is Korea's unique welfare-to-work programme. It is designed to enhance the capacity of social assistance recipients to achieve self-sufficiency through labour market participation. Recipients of social assistance benefits who are able to participate in welfare-to-work activities are referred to a local self-support agency where they receive training and job placement. These self-support agencies are non-profit organizations that contract with the government to provide services. In addition, they may be referred to a local municipal government to be placed in a public workfare-type programme. Placement with a local government agency or with a self-support agency is based on the client's work experience and job skills. A unique feature of the self-support agencies is that they target those clients who seek employment in the open job market or otherwise wish to establish their own businesses. They also provide marketable job training and education opportunities.

In 2005, 242 self-support agencies had contracted with the government to provide welfare-to-work services and they served about 16,000 clients. Each self-support agency had an average of 6.3 welfare-to-work projects and each of these projects had an average of 9.4 clients (Social Enterprise Development Agency, 2006). Examples of the welfare-to-work projects provided by the self-support agencies include housing repairs, lunch box preparation, cleaning, recycling and nursing aid services. Clients participating in welfare-to-work activities learn skills through specific training programmes and, of course, through work experience in these projects. The self-support agencies work with the clients until they are ready to find employment in the open job market or are able to establish small businesses. Many self-support agencies have a preference for cooperative business ventures and have encouraged their clients who are ready to establish a business to do so cooperatively with other clients. In 2005, about 340 cooperative micro-enterprises employing 1,762 clients had been established under the auspices of the self-support agencies.

Self-support agency clients receive social assistance benefits from the NBLSS while they are in the welfare-to-work programme. However, once they find a stable source of income either from regular employment or participation in cooperative micro-enterprises, they no longer receive cash benefits provided that their incomes do not fall below the poverty line. In this case, the scheme provides supplementary benefits to ensure that they reach the minimum income guaranteed by the government. However, it is hoped that clients who have participated in the welfare-to-work programme will attain self-sufficiency and enjoy a reasonably good improvement in their standard of living. However, as will be shown later, this goal has not always been reached by the self-support agencies.

While the NBLSS has incorporated the productive welfare notions of human capital investment and active labour market participation, changes to the country's social insurance system have focused on administrative reform, the extension of coverage and other wider goals. The Kim Dae-Jung government expanded the NPS to cover the vast majority of workers including the self-employed in 1999. It also unified the system so that different funds were combined into a single national system. By creating an integrated funding system, the government hoped to improve the efficiency of the pension system.

Although there was some resistance to this policy largely from the unemployed who often under-reported their income in order to avoid paying the full contribution, the government resolutely proceeded with its reform proposals and established what it called an 'integrated redistributive pension model' (Lee, 2004). This model, it explained, would not only be more efficient in administrative terms but also promote social solidarity by requiring all workers to participate in a single, unified pension system.

The health insurance scheme, which had also been operated by multiple insurers according to the type of enterprise and the community in which the worker resided, was unified in 2000 into one system. It was renamed as the National Health Insurance scheme (NHI) in 2000. The IACI was also extended to all enterprises in 2000. The Employment Insurance scheme, which was extended to all enterprises in 1998, continued to expand its benefit coverage. In particular, maternity benefits and child-care leave were extended. Maternity allowances were introduced in 2001. In sum, the social insurance system became more integrated through administrative reforms under the umbrella of productive welfare and continued to expand towards the goal of providing universal coverage for all.

The economic impact of productive welfare

Productive welfare is based on a positive relationship between social security and economic development. From a theoretical perspective, productive welfare promotes a 'social investment state' model described by Giddens (1998), where expenditures on welfare are regarded as investments that improve productivity and economic development performance. Despite this theoretical commitment, many aspects of the productive welfare concept in Korea were vaguely formulated and lacked specificity. Despite claims that productive welfare would have a major impact on economic development, it has in fact been applied in a limited way and has had a limited impact on the economic development process.

First of all, the public works projects, which were introduced as a major countermeasure against unemployment, did not have a long-term impact on the country's economic development. While the public works contributed to short-term macroeconomic performance by increasing public sector employment and reducing the unemployment rate, most jobs created under the public work project turned out to be ad hoc and temporary in nature. As noted previously, the public works projects were widely regarded as 'workfare' rather than real employment conducive to economic development.

Second, the changes introduced by the Kim Dae-Jung government to Korea's social insurance system have also had a limited impact on economic development. Although the expansion of the Employment Insurance scheme was intended to promote workforce security, and thus was highly relevant to economic development, other insurance programmes had little direct effect on development. The policy changes to the pension programme were not focused on economic development but were concerned with enhancing the efficiency of the system through administrative reform. These changes also sought to promote social solidarity through integrating the system. Current debates about social insurance, and particularly pensions, are not related to economic issues but rather with questions of financial sustainability and with benefit levels. Accordingly, the notion of productive welfare is seldom invoked in these debates.

On the other hand, as noted earlier, the NBLSS is most closely associated with the concept of productive welfare and indeed is regarded by social policy scholars in Korea as the primary vehicle for expressing its ideals. The issue of whether the system does in fact promote economic participation among people with low incomes and thus comprises a productivist form of social security that contributes positively to economic development needs to be considered. The question is particularly apposite to the self-support programme operated in terms of the NBLSS, which is specifically designed to promote productive employment and self-employment among the poor.

Unfortunately, official data published by the Ministry of Health and Welfare in 2007 show that the programme has only partially met this goal. These data show that in 2005 only 5.5 per cent of those who were in receipt of social assistance benefits had successfully obtained employment or engaged in self-employment and were no longer receiving benefits. Research undertaken by the author of this chapter found that the programme's comparatively low rate of success is largely due to the large proportion of unprofitable micro-enterprises that were established. Since 2001, 580 micro-enterprises were established through the self-support programme, but by 2005, 40.3 per cent of them had gone out of business (Social Enterprise Development Agency, 2006). This raises the question of whether the self-support agencies are pursuing the correct marketing research strategies when seeking to identify opportunities for new small businesses. It also raises the question of whether clients are being adequately trained and prepared to operate small businesses in a competitive commercial environment. It is clear that these implementation difficulties need to be addressed if the programme is to be successful. It also raises the wider question of whether the government should place as much emphasis on micro-enterprise as a mechanism for promoting economic self-sufficiency or whether more traditional employment placement strategies should be used.

A related problem is the all-or-nothing benefit structure of the NBLSS which does not allow the incremental phase out of benefits but instead reduces benefits to zero once a specified income level from employment or self-employment is reached. This all-or-nothing type of benefit structure discourages many self-support programme clients from actively participating in the economy for fear of suddenly losing all their benefits. Research undertaken by the author also reveals that many self-support programme clients prefer not to venture into the real world of market competition but seek to remain in the programme for as long as possible. This problem is currently being reviewed by the government of President Roh Moo Hyun ,which is exploring the possibility of introducing a new benefit structure that gradually phases out benefits and thus maintains incentives to work. It is also exploring the possibility of introducing an Earned Income Tax Credit as well as Individual Development Accounts (IDAs) which will match the savings of low-income people. It is hoped that these policy innovations will more effectively address the needs of low-income people in Korea and also more effectively complement the self-support programme.

Korea's productive welfare model seeks to foster a positive role for social security in economic development. However, as has been shown, it has not had a significant impact on economic development. Despite claims that the productive welfare model would reshape the country's social security system so that it will contribute positively to development, its effects so far have been confined to one social assistance programme and its success has been relatively limited. As the government seeks to make strategic amendments to social security in an attempt to more effectively link welfare provision with economic development, Korea's productive welfare model continues to reshape and evolve further. It is also hoped that the Korean government will consider the experience of other countries that have adopted welfare developmentalist strategies or sought to introduce forms of social security that contribute to economic development. In this way, the government may enhance its current commitment to fostering productive forms of social security that link economic and social policies and increase the well-being of the country's citizens in the context of the country's impressive record of economic progress.

References

Ahn, S.-H. and Lee, S.-C. (2005). 'The Development of the South Korean Welfare Regime.' In A. Walker and C.-K. Wong (eds), *East Asian Welfare Regimes in Transition*. Bristol: The Policy Press, pp. 165–186.

Amsden, A. H. (1989). *Asia's Next Giant: South Korea and Late Industrialization*. New York, NY: Oxford University Press.

Aspalter, C. (2001). *Conservative Welfare State Systems in East Asia*. Westport, Connecticut: Praeger.

Bank of Korea. (2007). *Economic Statistics System*. Retrieved May 12, 2007, from http://ecos.bok.or.kr.

Cho, S. (1994). *The Dynamics of Korean Economic Development*. Washington, DC: Institute for International Economics.

Giddens, A. (1998). *The Third Way: The Renewal of Social Democracy*. Oxford: Polity press.

Han, S.-J. (2002). 'The Third Way of Korea' (Hankookhyung je sam ui gil ul saengakhanda). *Policy Forum*, Spring, 4–19.

HIRA and NHIC (Health Insurance Review Agency and National Health Insurance Corporation). (2006). *2005 National Health Insurance Statistical Yearbook*. Seoul, Korea: Health Insurance Review Agency and National Health Insurance Corporation.

Human Resources Development Service of Korea. (2006). *2005 The Monthly Statistics of Employment Insurance*. Seoul, Korea: Kukje Munhwasa.

Hwang, G.-J. (2006). *Pathways to State Welfare in Korea: Interests, Ideas and Institutions*. Burlington, VT: Ashgate Publishing Company.

Im, H. B. (1987). 'The Rise of Bureaucratic Authoritarianism in South Korea', *World Politics*, 39(2), 231–257.

Kim, D. J. (1985). *Mass Participatory Economy: A Democratic Alternative for Korea*. Cambridge, MA: Harvard University/University Press of America.

Kim, J.-H. (1997). 'An Evaluation on the Planning on the Globalization of the Quality of Life ("Salmuijil" seagehwarl uihan gukminbokjiui gibongusange daehan pyungga).' *Situation and Welfare (Sanghwangwa bokji)*, 2, 111–120.

Kim, S. (2006). 'Towards A Better Understanding of Welfare Policy Development in Developing Nations: A Case Study of South Korea's Pension System.' *International Journal of Social Welfare*, 15, 75–83.

Kim, T. S., and Kim, J. S. (2003). *A Study on the Social Security (Sahoe Bojangron)*. Seoul, Korea: Chongmok.

Kim, T. S., and Son, B. D. (2002). *Poverty and Social Policy (Bingongwa Sahoebokji Jungchaek)*. Seoul, Korea: Chungmok.

Kim, T. S., and Sung, K. R. (1993). *A Study on the Welfare State (Bokjigukgaron)*. Seoul, Korea: Nanam.

Kim, Y.-H. (2003). 'Productive Welfare: Korea's Third Way?', *International Journal of Social Welfare*, 12, 61–67.

Kwon, H.-J. (1997). 'Beyond European Welfare Regimes: Comparative Perspectives on East Asian Welfare Systems', *Journal of Social Policy*, 26(4), 467–484.

Kwon, H.-J. (1998). 'Democracy and The Politics of Social Welfare: A Comparative Analysis of Welfare Systems in East Asia.' In R. Goodman, G. White and H.-J. Kwon (eds), *The East Asian Welfare Model*. New York, NY: Routledge, pp. 25–74.

Kwon, H.-J. (1999). *The Welfare State in Korea: The Politics of Legitimation*. New York: St. Martin's Press, Inc.

Kwon, H.-J. (2001). 'Globalization, Unemployment and Policy Responses in Korea: Repositioning the State?' *Global Social Policy*, 1(2), 213–234.

Kwon, H.-J. (2002). *Unemployment and Public Work Projects in Korea, 1998–2000*. Reference materials for the Asian Development Bank (ADB) Seminar on Social Protection for the poor in Asia and Latin America, 21–15 October 2002, Manila.

Lee, H. K. (1999). 'Globalization and the Emerging Welfare State-the Experience of South Korea', *International Journal of Social Welfare*, 8, 23–37.

Lee, H. K. (2004). 'Welfare Reforms in Post-crisis Korea: Dilemmas and Choices.' *Social Policy and Society*, 3(3), 291–299.

Ministry of Health and Welfare. (2006). *2005 The NBLSS Yearbook (2005 Gookmin Gicho Saenghwal Bojang Ahne)*. Ministry of Health and Welfare.

Ministry of Health and Welfare. (2007). *2007 Self-Support Program Plan (2007 Jahwal Saup Ahne)*. Ministry of Health and Welfare.

Ministry of Labor. (2006). *2005 The Industrial Accidents Compensation Insurance Statistical Yearbook*. Ministry of Labor.

Moon, H., Lee, H., and Yoo, G. (1999). *Economic Crisis and Its Social Consequences*. KDI Research Monograph 9901. Seoul, Korea: Korean Development Institute.

Nam, C. S. (2000). 'The History of the Korean Welfare System and Its Characteristics (Hanguk bokjijaedoui jungaegwajungwa sungkyuck).' In KSSI (ed.), *The Situation and the Issues on the Korean Welfare System (Hanguk Sahoibokjiui Hyunhwangwa Jaengjum)*. Seoul, Korea: Human and Welfare, pp. 17–47.

National Pension Service. (2006). *2005 National Pension Statistical Yearbook*. Seoul, Korea: National Pension Research Institute.

Office of the President. (2000). *DJ Welfarism: A New Paradigm for Productive Welfare in Korea*. Seoul, Korea: Tae Sul Dang.

Social Enterprise Development Agency (SEDA). (2006). *A White Book on the Self-Support Agency (Jahwal Hoogyunkikwan Saup Baeksuh)*. Seoul, Korea: SEDA.

Sung, H.-Y. (1999). 'A Nature of DJ's Mid way Line (DJ shin jungdonosun ui jungchae).' *Shindonga*.(June, 1999) Available at http://donga.com/docs/magazine/new_donga/9906/nd99060010.html.

Woo, M. (2004). *The Politics of Social Welfare Policy in South Korea*. Oxford: University Press of America, Inc.

8
Norway: Social Security, Active Labour Market Policies and Economic Progress

Espen Dahl and Thomas Lorentzen

In 1990 Esping-Andersen distinguished among three ideal-types of welfare state *regimes*, defined according to two dimensions; degree of decommodification and stratification and labour market participation. The former refers to the extent to which social policies make individuals independent of the market, while the latter concerns the extent to which the welfare state differentiates in the treatment of different groups. He claimed that it is not possible to understand welfare state variations linearly; rather, there are qualitative differences in the way social provision is provided and that welfare states tend to cluster into three different regimes forming interconnected configurations of state and market, and later, the family. Echoing Titmuss, Esping-Andersen identified three 'worlds of welfare states', which he labelled 'conservative-corporatist', 'liberal' and 'social-democratic' (or Nordic) regimes. The first is characterized by strong emphasis on the role of social partners, on the principle of subsidiarity, on an underdeveloped service sector and on the existence of labour market 'insiders' and 'outsiders'. Empirically it is illustrated, for example, by France and Germany. The second is characterized by minimal and targeted assistance measures, re-enforcement of job-seeking behaviour and promotion of systems of private welfare provision, and it is illustrated by the United Kingdom and the United States. The third idealized type, the 'social-democratic' regime, exemplified by Norway and the other Nordic or Scandinavian countries, is characterized by institutionalized redistribution, where the welfare state provides universal social rights (Esping-Andersen, 1990).

Because universal social rights are expensive, the social-democratic model is based on the premise of 'full employment', since its sustainability depends on a broad tax base. Thus, pertaining to this model are features like relatively high employment rates also among women and the elderly and active labour market policies (Huber and Stephens, 2001). Moreover, to a larger degree social services are financed and provided by public institutions than elsewhere; Among the Organisation for Economic Co-operation and Development (OECD) countries, Norway has the highest percentage of employed in the public sector, and public consumption and transfers are comparatively high (NOU 2000: 21: 118).

Neoliberal economic theory would argue that an economic system with these characteristics, in other words with a high degree of state regulation, a large public sector and comprehensive and expensive social security programmes, will hamper economic growth and would not be viable and sustainable in the long run (for a fuller account of these arguments, see Chapter 3 in this book). Societies with these characteristics will perform poorly in economic terms, it is claimed, because they transfer resources out of the productive economy as the state expropriates a large proportion of national resources and directs these resources into unproductive activities, for example, by transferring resources from productive workers to 'unproductive' benefit recipients who do not contribute to economic development. As a smaller proportion of the working population supports a growing number of unproductive people, economic output will be further restricted. By transferring resources from those engaged in productive activities to those who are unproductive, consumption increases and exerts inflationary pressures on prices. By reducing disposable income, high taxation will contribute to workers demanding higher wages and hence leading to inflation in wages. It is further contended that social security programmes have the perverse effect of fostering worklessness, dependency cultures and of undermining the work moral in the society at large. It is also argued that social insurance engenders low savings rate, because it fuels the public expectation that governments will meet their income needs in the future. Social security is accused of distorting labour markets, by limiting the supply of labour, and also the lack of mobility and flexibility of labour. This is because generous benefits deter workers from seeking new and better jobs and hence they fail to achieve full productive potential for themselves and for the economy.

This chapter will address this view and challenge some of these arguments by providing empirical evidence indicating that it is possible to combine a comprehensive welfare state with a dynamic, efficient, prospering and sustainable economy. The case studied will be Norway, but many of the arguments will also apply to the other Nordic countries, Denmark, Finland and Sweden as well.

The chapter begins by providing a broad account of some key parameters of the Norwegian society and economy focusing on economic performance, social quality, social inequality and labour market conditions over the past 10–15 years. Then it presents the major institutional features of the welfare system with an emphasis on the social security institutions and the reforms that have been brought about over the examined period. A short account of reforms in benefits and welfare organizations that are in the melting pot will also be given. Next, it focuses on one specific and rather unique characteristic of the Norwegian (and Nordic) welfare system, namely the active labour market programmes and the activation schemes targeted at different groups of unemployed. Finally, the relationship between economic performance and the Norwegian social security system and their mutual and systemic interdependencies will be examined.

The Norwegian context

In the early 1990s, all the Scandinavian welfare states experienced financial difficulties (Kautto et al., 2001). Representatives of trade and industry stated that the Nordic model was not competitive in a global economy. Hence, during the 1990s there was a widespread belief that the Nordic model would slowly be transformed into less extensive, leaner and less regulated and market oriented welfare model. Although the policy responses to the slump were somewhat different in each of the Nordic countries, no country reformed its welfare state arrangements in a radical way (Kautto et al., 2001).

As compared with the gloomy situation in the 1990s, the state of the nation today looks different and much brighter. Norway is now among the most competitive and financially sound economies in the world and, is together with the other Nordic countries, on the world's top ten list in competitiveness, technology and creativity according to the World Competitiveness Index 2004 (see Dølvik, 2007). According to the latest figures from the OECD, all four Nordic countries are clearly above the OECD average. Economic growth in the Nordic countries has been above the average OECD level (OECD Factbook 2007. Online www. sourceoecd.org/factbook). Moreover, Norway, like its Nordic peers, have a high quality of life – also known as 'social quality'. Norway is also for the fifth year in a row topping the United Nations Human Development Index (St.meld.nr. 1 (2005–2006), National Budget). The three other Nordic countries rank among the top 14 on the Human Development Index.

These are not the sole favourable social outcomes of a model characterized by social citizenship and a regulated market economy. For example, Norway is the only OECD country where child poverty is described as 'very low and continuing to fall' (UNICEF, 2005). It has been a central aim of the Norwegian social democratic policy in the post-Second World War period to contribute to a just distribution of public goods and services. Moreover, the post-war policy has explicitly aimed at cutting the tie between social background and life chances of the citizens (Hansen and Vibe, 2005).

The political emphasis on equality is visible in the way incomes are distributed nationally. Norway, together with the other Scandinavian countries, has a relatively compressed income distribution compared to other Western nations, as indicated by Table 8.1.

Table 8.1 presents the Gini index of income inequalities in selected countries. The table illustrates that all the Scandinavian countries have a rather compressed income distribution. When compared to United Kingdom and the United States, Norway comes out with substantially smaller income inequalities than the two former countries. This means that there are major differences between those with the highest and the lowest incomes in the United States and United Kingdom. Conversely, all the Scandinavian countries show a remarkably strong similarity in that they all have a low dispersion of incomes. Low income inequality goes hand in hand with low poverty: poverty rates among people in their working ages, as well as poverty rates among vulnerable groups such as aged and single mothers, are low compared to nations in the other welfare regimes (Atkinson, 1995; Fritzell, 2001; Huber and Stephens, 2001; Smeeding, 2002).

As mentioned, high male and female labour force participation is one of the hallmarks of the Nordic countries. While most welfare systems

Table 8.1 Income inequalities in selected countries as measured by the Gini index

Denmark	24.7
Sweden	25.0
Finland	25.6
Norway	25.8
United Kingdom	36.0
United States	40.8

Source: Adapted from UNDP (2003).

have been designed on the basis of traditional views of gender roles – male breadwinner, female carer (Barnes et al., 2002) – the Scandinavian countries have made efforts to adjust the welfare state arrangements to the relatively new situation of rising labour force participation among women. Such labour force participation has been systematically stimulated by welfare state arrangements. According to Esping-Andersen (1999), the Scandinavian countries are the only welfare states that meaningfully have committed themselves to a de-familialization of service burdens. De-familialization here is interpreted as the level at which households' welfare and caring responsibilities are taken care of by state provision (Esping-Andersen, 1999).

In Norway, the expansion of female labour force participation did not take off before the early 1970s. By the end of the 1980s, Norway was still lagging behind Denmark and Sweden in terms of female employment rates. In the course of the 1990s, however, Norway finally appears to have caught up with and even surpassed its Nordic neighbours in terms of female labour force participation and (in particular) employment rates. Women still have lower employment rates than men, but the difference has shrunk to less than 10 percentage points (see Table 8.2).

Over all, Norway has one of the highest rates of labour market participation in the Western world. To a large degree this is due to the extraordinary high level of employment among women (St. meld. nr 9 2006–2007, p. 149). Also, the employment rate among the elderly people between 55 and 64 years is comparatively high in Norway and is only surpassed by Sweden and Iceland (St.meld. nr. 6 2006–2007).

The convergence in employment rates between males and females shown in Table 8.2 coexists, however, with significant gender differences in the nature of employment. In 2000, women constituted only about 25 per cent of the employees in manufacturing and were also clearly under-represented in private businesses like finance. On the other hand, 83 per cent of employees in health and social services are women, and these jobs are mainly in the public sector. To a larger degree

Table 8.2 Male and female employment, as percentage of population aged 16–74, 1980–2005

	1980	1985	1990	1995	2000	2005 (2006)
Men	78.3	76.4	71.8	71.3	75.1	72.5 (73.0)
Women	53.8	57.7	59.4	61.1	66.6	65.6 (66.0)

Source: Adapted from Statistics Norway, Bank of Statistics 2007.

than elsewhere, the social services in Norway are financed and provided by public institutions. This is indicated by the fact that Norway is among the OECD countries with the highest percentage of workers employed in the public sector. It is twice as high as that in the United States of America, and about the same level as that in Sweden and Denmark, just above 30 per cent (NOU, 2000: 21: 117). Public consumption and transfers which are measured as a percentage of Gross National Product are clearly higher in Norway (about 24 per cent) than in the United States of America, but lower than in Denmark and Sweden (NOU, 2000: 21: 118). This large public sector has served as a dynamic 'employment machine' for women in Norway (Birkelund and Petersen, 2003; Kolberg and Esping-Andersen, 1992).

Social security in Norway: programmes, organization and reforms

The main architecture of the social security system in Norway was established during the first three decades after the Second World War. In this 'Golden Age', new benefits were introduced and integrated, coverage expanded and benefit levels raised. In the early 1990s, the 'Work Approach' was introduced to supplement but not to replace the 'Social Security Approach'. Since that time, a number of reforms have been launched in the benefit system with the purpose of 'making work the first choice'; in other words, to increase labour force participation among able-bodied people. Also, organizational reforms have been and are being implemented to promote this goal. The slogan capturing this policy is expressed in government documents that exclaim, 'Fewer on benefit, more in work'.

One might ask why Norwegian politicians and policy makers are so preoccupied with labour market participation since Norway has long had the highest rates of labour market participation in the Western world. Figure 8.1 provides a clue. It shows the growth in number of recipients of different benefits over the past 10 years. Today, almost 800,000 people, or about 25 per cent of the population of working age, receives a welfare benefit on any day. Some, such as disability pensioners, are permanent recipients, while others are on short-term benefits such as sickness pay. Although few of these recipients will remain on benefits for the rest of their lives, 'full employment' and a broad tax base are fundamental to the viability of a welfare state of the Nordic type. Hence, the trend portrayed by Figure 8.1 is a source of deep concern for most politicians and policy makers in Norway. This concern has both short-term and long-term consequences. The long-term

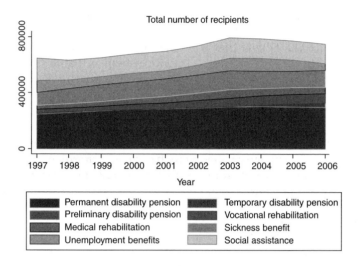

Figure 8.1 Trends in receipt of benefits over the past 10 years. Absolute numbers

Source: Adapted from SSB/NAV.

consequences are related to the ageing population, shrinking population in working age (in relative terms) and the forecasted decline in the oil revenues. Short-term consequences are related to the fact that some sectors of industry suffer from labour shortage. These factors are relevant to understanding current reforms proposals in social security.

It is a paradox that employment rates have increased at the same time as more and more people are receiving benefits. The solution to this conundrum is that women who previously were supported by their family/husband have become increasingly independent of family support through their own paid work. In turn paid work gives right to and easier access to work-related benefits such as sickness pay, unemployment benefit, rehabilitation benefits and disability pensions. Thus, an important reason for both employment rates and 'benefit rates' having increased simultaneously is of the increased involvement in paid work by women.

This section describes the major social security programmes in Norway and highlights the most important reforms that have been carried out over past 15 years. The benefits that make up the core of Norwegian social security, namely sickness benefits, unemployment benefits, rehabilitation benefits, transitional benefit for lone parents, disability benefit and old-age pension will be described. Although not part of the central government's social security system, social assistance, which is the responsibility of the municipalities, will be discussed not least because this programme has undergone profound changes over the past decade and now has a prominent position in policies to alleviate poverty.

On an analytical level, reforms in the benefit structure may take many forms. The most important reforms in Norway may be subsumed under the following categories: change in benefit levels and economic incentives, eligibility criteria, behavioural conditions, benefit duration/time limits and measures to enhance transition from benefit to work. Several organizational reforms that have taken place will be discussed and some innovations that have been, or are about to be, introduced will be examined. Despite the reform activity, the fundamental features of social security have been maintained. The state remains responsible for the programme; it has universal coverage and a relatively high level of minimum protection is provided. It is also worth noting that, compared with most other countries, more social risks are still covered (Hatland, 2001).

Sickness benefits. Since 1970 all employees have had the right to receive sickness benefit from the first day of sickness up to one year. The compensation rate is 100 per cent for all who earn less than a certain amount. The sickness benefit is the only benefit in Norway where the insured carries no own risk. High sickness rates have been a concern for the authorities since the 1970s, especially during periods when they have been increasing. Thus, several reforms have been launched to curb the sickness absence rates without, however, changing the compensation level. In 1988 Medical Certificate II was introduced. This made eligibility for sick pay exceeding eight weeks dependent on reassessment. The National Insurance Administration took over the formal authority to make this reassessment. In 1991 two other modifications were introduced. The first was that the benefit level for the unemployed was reduced to match the compensation level of the unemployment benefit. The second change was that the advisory role of medical doctors was strengthened to enable them to set more accurate medical diagnoses and to contribute to drawing up rehabilitation plans at an early stage of a person's sick leave. A second check was introduced in 1993 requiring that sick leave exceeding 12 weeks be subject to confirmation by the social insurance authorities. The same year marked the introduction of active sick leave. The purpose of this remedy was to enable sick employees to continue to work part-time and to maintain contact with the work place during this time. In 2004, stricter requirements were imposed on the employee, the employer and the physician: after eight weeks on sick pay, the employee was required to comply with activity demands; the employer was required to assess how the work place could be accommodated to the abilities of the sick person; and the physician was required to provide a thorough assessment of the patient's functional capacity. In short, the remedies introduced were designed to reduce sickness absence rates and control expenditures. These are characterized by behavioural requirements directed towards the key players involved in this programme.

Unemployment benefit. The compensation rate of the unemployment benefit is on average two-thirds of former wage. In principle it covers all employees residing in Norway. There is, however, an income-floor and an income-ceiling beyond which loss of income is not compensated. Certain behavioural conditions apply: to be eligible for benefit, claimants must have lost their job involuntarily; must accept the job offered; must be willing to move to another location if required to do so; and must participate in an active labour market programme if required. Non-compliance results in a loss of benefit for a period of time. Over the past few years these behavioural requirements have been tightened and are being enforced more energetically. In 1997, maximum duration of benefit was shortened somewhat and income requirements were raised. In 2003, during a period of high unemployment in Norway, somewhat more stringent changes were introduced. The requirement of loss of working time was increased; the minimum income amount to be counted as eligible was raised; activity requirements were made stricter, and maximum benefit period was reduced from 156 to 104 weeks. Hence, the reforms in unemployment benefits are characterized by a number of measures available to promote work and hinder benefit receipt: less eligibility, shorter benefit periods and stricter behavioural requirements. However, actual benefit levels have not been reduced.

Disability pension. Disability pension is granted to people who are certified by a medical doctor as being at least 50 per cent permanently occupationally disabled. Loss of work capacity must be caused by a medical problem. The vast majority of surviving disabled people receive their pension until they retire on old-age pension at the age of 67. As shown in Figure 8.1, the number and percentage of disabled pensioners have increased steadily since the introduction of the programme causing concern. In the early 1990s, this resulted in a tightening of the eligibility criteria and a stronger emphasis was placed on the claimants having a serious medical condition. This resulted in a slight reduction in numbers of pensioners, but the decline had actually started prior to the new policy, so the effect of more restrictive eligibility rules is hard to ascertain. A major change was introduced in 2004 when a temporary disability pension scheme was created. The purpose of this new scheme was to prevent the life-long receipt of disability benefit and to enhance work activity. Benefit is granted for a limited period of time for those who are considered to have 'residual' work capacity and who are expected to recover. To provide work incentives, the benefit level in this programme is lower than in the permanent scheme. The past 15 years of disability benefit reform thus include stricter eligibility criteria, and for certain groups of disabled, lower benefit levels and time limits (St. meld. 9 2006–2007).

Rehabilitation benefit. Rehabilitation benefit comes in two forms: medical rehabilitation and vocational rehabilitation. Both measures are designed to prevent people ending up on disability pension. Since the disability and rehabilitation schemes were both established in 1961, claimants are now carefully appraised before they are granted a disability pension. However, one criticism raised against the programme is that transfer to rehabilitation services occurs too seldom and often too late. Medical rehabilitation benefit is granted to people who are in need of health services. The aim is to improve their ability to work and to function better in every day life. To a certain extent, medical rehabilitation serves as an extended sickness benefit but is limited to maximum two years. The vocational rehabilitation benefit provides income protection for those who participate in programmes that aim to improve their employability. These programmes may include regular schooling as well as job training. In the early 1990s, stricter activation requirements were implemented, and the eligibility criteria were tightened in line with those of the disability pension. Also, a shorter duration time was imposed for medical rehabilitation. Several less significant reforms were introduced in the 1990s and the early 2000s to improve vocational rehabilitation services, but some restrictions were also imposed. The qualifying age limit was raised to 18 years in 1998 and, in 2002, the rules for calculating the benefit level were altered. The result is that most recipients received higher benefits (St. meld. 9 2006–2007). In 2004 the minimum level was again increased slightly. In the same year, the maximum years of schooling was set to 3, the age limit raised from 22 to 26 years of age and the programmes administration was transferred from the social security to labour market authorities (St. meld. 9 2006–2007, p. 262).

Old age pension. The official retirement age in Norway is 67 years. The actual retirement age is, however, close to 61 years of age mainly because many claimants receive disability pension before they reach retirement age. The retirement pension has two components, a basic and an earnings-related component. The system produces a redistribution of income from higher to lower earner partly because the basic pension goes to those who have little, if any, earnings and partly because earnings above a certain ceiling are not fully compensated. The basic retirement pension is a pay-as-you-go system. 'The best years principle' requires that the employee's 20 years of highest earnings are counted when the retirement pension is calculated. However, these features of the system are about to change. After six years of deliberation, the Parliament recently agreed on a new old-age pension system (St. meld nr. 5 2006–2007). It is claimed that the new system will be both economically and socially sustainable and fairer. To justify the need for the reform, the Government argues that the current system faces long-term economic challenges because of falling population growth, more elderly people, higher pension levels and rising life expectancy (Hansen, Minister of Work and Inclusion, speech 12.02.2007). In the new pension programme, all years of remunerated economic activity will count, not just the 20 best years. Pension levels will be adjusted in line with increases in life expectancy. One year increase in longevity will require eight months additional work activity in order to achieve the same benefit. People can still choose to retire from 62 years to 67 years, which is today's retirement age, but those who choose to retire before they turn 67 will be financially penalized with lower benefits. Unpaid care work for children also provides pension rights. The new retirement pension will come into effect in 2010 (St. meld nr. 5 2006–2007).

Transitional benefit for lone parents. Transitional benefit for single parents is an integral part of social security in Norway. Single mothers and fathers are both eligible. Until 1998, a single parent had the right to receive transitional benefit until the youngest child was ten years old. In 1998, the rules were changed to require that the parent be in work-related activity in order to maintain benefit eligibility after the youngest child in the family reached the age of three years. Work-related activity includes formal job-seeking or working or studying at least part-time. If the single parent is studying, the eligibility period may be extended to five and a half years. When this time limit was introduced, the annual benefit was raised by about NOK 10,000. Moreover, social security provides childcare benefit and education benefit for single parents. Childcare benefit is granted until the child is ten years old. In addition, the Social Security Administration set up a system of 'user-contacts' in all municipalities to assist and counsel single parents with regard to work activation including pursuing study and job training. This arrangement is intended to provide a social network in order to provide support, practical help, assistance and counselling to help recipients achieve self-sufficiency. Although the transition benefit is characterized by a reduction in the duration of the benefit period, benefit level was actually increased. In addition, a new organization was established in order to enhance single parents' transition from benefit to meaningful activation and self-sufficiency (Dahl and Drøpping, 2001).

Social assistance. Social assistance in Norway is the final safety net. As in other European nations, the provision of social assistance is a local responsibility and the benefits are means-tested (Gough et al., 1997; Seip, 1994). Individual caseworkers enjoy a great deal of autonomy in deciding who are entitled and in determining the benefits and the provision of services (Gough et al., 1997; Lødemel and Trickey, 2001). The central government and many municipalities have worked out guidelines for calculating benefit levels. Since the orthodox view is that 'work should pay', benefit levels are set quite low and have not kept up with the consumer price index. In a comparative perspective, however, benefits are rather generous – although not as generous as in the other Scandinavian countries (Gough et al., 1997). The minimum qualifying age is 18 years. Entitlement is based on the principle of domicile, and therefore foreigners who are legal residents are entitled to aid. Although the benefit is meant to provide temporary economic relief, no time limits are imposed, so entitlement remains for as long as the claimant meets eligibility conditions. In the early 1990s, the Law of Social Services was enacted which explicitly requires that entitlement to benefit could be based on work activities such as employment for the municipalities. Since then, many municipalities have increased the use of these activation measures and conditions are now more frequently used (Lødemel and Johannesen, 2005). Beneficiaries may be required to participate in the work activities offered by the labour market authorities or the municipalities (Lødemel and Trickey, 2001). This turn towards an activation oriented social assistance regime will be discussed in more detail below.

New Labour and Welfare Administration (NAV). In July 2006, a new labour and welfare administration was established. It has been dubbed the largest reform since the social security reforms of 1967. The new work and welfare bureaucracy is a merger of three formerly separate administrative bodies: the Labour Market Administration, the Social Security

Administration and the local Social Assistance administrations in the municipalities. It is expected that this new organization will provide a framework for the pursuit of the following goal: fewer on benefit, more in work. The reform is thus seen as a move to realize the ideas behind the work activation approach. In addition, it is intended that the new administration will pay more attention to the needs of clients and respond quicker to them. The aim is to provide 'holistic' and coordinated services to the public and particularly to the most vulnerable clients who often have multiple needs. The implementation of the reform will be accomplished by 2010 when a NAV administration will have been be set up in each municipality. A large evaluation research project has also been launched to assess outcomes and different aspects of this reform.

Inclusive Working Life (IA). In 2001, an agreement was struck between the three social partners, namely the unions, the employer organizations and the central government. The overarching goals of this agreement is to reduce sickness absentee rates, to raise the pension age and to include more people with disabilities in the labour market. An army of counsellors have been employed in the new Working Life Centres, of which there is one in each county. Individual companies may join the collaboration by signing up at their local centre. These participant companies enjoy some privileges, such as a subsidised company health service, an appointed counsellor at the centre, the right to use 'active' sick leave and subsidies for modifying the work place for those employees with occupational disabilities. In return, the employers are obliged to carefully monitor employees on sick leave and to adapt the work place to employees with disabilities (Øverbye and Hammer, 2006).

To sum up, over the past 15 years the work activation approach has been the major principle underpinning reforms in social security benefits and in the administration of welfare. Recently, this policy has been further reinforced (St. meld. 9 2006–2007). Social security reform in Norway has a number of distinctive features. The laws, rules and regulations governing the system have been frequently changed, but most of these changes have been fairly modest. Yet, their purpose is to promote work and limit benefit receipt. This reform reflects a commitment to change the social security programmes in a 'work friendly' direction. There is a distinct ethos of work and activity underpinning all reform initiatives. The organizational reforms which have accompanied this policy change have the same goal and reflect the same ethos. A more thorough discussion of the nature of these reforms and of their implications for social welfare in Norway now need to be offered.

Active labour market programmes and activation

Active labour market policies refer to a broad range of policies and measures targeted at people who have been or are at risk of becoming excluded from the labour market (Drøpping et al., 1999). Norway, along with the other Nordic countries, has a long tradition for active labour market policies (Drøpping et al., 1999; Lindquist and Marklund, 1995; Wilensky, 1992). Since the 1980s, Norway has together with Sweden been one of the OECD countries with the highest spending on work activation measures (Dale-Olsen et al., 2006; Hvinden et al., 2001). Historically, Norwegian active labour market policies have rested on two sets of justifications, the first relating to the individual and the second to society. Individual-based justifications centre on the importance of work to prevent negative personal experiences connected with joblessness. Societal-based justifications focus on the importance of everyone being integrated into society and reducing pressure on public budgets (Lødemel and Trickey, 2001).

Active labour market programmes can roughly be classified into four categories: work training, wage subsidies, theoretical courses and sheltered workshops for people with disabilities. These programmes are different in scope, design and content and vary significantly. Some offer short courses on how to search jobs, while others include a full college education. In principle, this menu of programmes is open for all unemployed people in need. Street level bureaucrats do, however, seek to match programmes and participants based on their needs and labour market resources. These vary for three different groups of participants in the labour market including the ordinary unemployed, the disabled and people with reduced work capabilities, and youth and social assistance recipients.

Programmes targeted at the ordinary unemployed who receive benefits are anti-cyclical, meaning that they are scaled up during recessions and back during economic upturns (Dahl and Drøpping, 2001). A number of effect evaluations of these programmes have been carried out. These have often demonstrated a positive effect on labour market participation (Raaum and Røed, 2002; Raaum et al., 2002a, 2002b; Roed and Raaum, 2006; Zhang, 2003). Programmes intended for disabled and persons with reduced work capabilities have grown considerably over the past years in response to the soaring number of vocationally impaired applicants (A-etat, 2005). However, evaluations of these programmes show less favourable results or otherwise have mixed results with different effects for different groups of participants (Aakvik, 2001,

2003; Aakvik and Risa, 1994; Børing, 2004; Hardoy, Røed and Zhang, 2006).

A new policy in Norway is that labour activation programmes are directed at groups that are more detached from the labour market. These include the long-term poor and long-term social assistance recipients. People receiving social assistance are a heterogeneous group, but have a common problem in that they have no right to social security benefits. Another common feature of long-term social assistance recipients is that they have multiple problems and are less able to participate in the labour market. A number of Norwegian studies of these groups involved in both compulsory and voluntary programmes has been undertaken. Recent evaluations of these programmes indicate that young people may benefit from participation but that the effects are moderate (Hardoy, Røed, and Zhang, 2006). Evaluations of programmes offered to social assistance recipients indicate that positive effects on earnings and labour market participation can be achieved if a 'creaming' recruitment strategy is used, but otherwise these programmes do not seem to be very effective (Dahl, 2003; Dahl and Lorentzen, 2005; Lorentzen and Dahl, 2005). This finding is consistent with the latest evaluation of a large-scale initiative launched by the government to bring long-term social assistance recipients into remunerative work and self-sufficiency (St.meld.nr 6 2002–2003). Rønsen and Skarðhamar (2006) found that programmes that excluded people with behavioural or medical problems had a weak but significant effect on labour market participation.

Depending on the programme's target group and the services it provides, the empirical evidence shows both positive and negative effects. For this reason, the political focus has moved from focusing on the scope of labour market activation policies to the question of how these policies should be designed and organized (Dale-Olsen et al., 2006). Despite the mixed results of studies into their effectiveness, and especially the lack of evidence of significant positive effects for very disadvantaged groups, policy makers strongly back these labour market activation programmes. Thus, these programmes are likely to continue to be an integral part of welfare policy in the future.

Economic aspects of social security

The political economy of work and welfare of the Norwegian society over the past ten to fifteen years is being examined in this section. It focuses on economic performance, the quality of life of Norwegian society, income and income distribution, the structure and reforms in social security and particularly the current emphasis on labour market activation policy. For quite some time now, the country's strong economic performance has gone hand in hand with a large public sector, a regulated and coordinated market system and a generous and comprehensive social security system. These institutional components are interconnected. The institutions of work and welfare are interrelated and mutually reinforce each other; indeed, one is a prerequisite for the other. An analysis of labour market activation policy in the context of the wider political economy of Norwegian society is faced with an interesting question. How is it possible for a market economy to record continuously high rates of growth and yet produce high standard of living for its people when government intervenes so extensively in economic and social affairs? Conventional economic theory predicts that the extensive regulation of the Norwegian economy should produce stagnation and declining standards of living. To further examine this question, six issues will be addressed.

However, it is important at the outset to dismiss one popular explanation of Norway's economic success – Norway is doing so well because of its North Sea oil assets. True, Norway is a special case because it is a significant oil exporting country. However, the presence of oil in itself is not an adequate explanation for Norway's economic success because the other Nordic countries which have adopted the same economic and social model have a similar pattern of development. It is also the case that many oil producing countries have not been very successful at raising the standards of living of their people. Frequently, in the 'petro states', as they are known, oil has crippled economic development and fostered political conflict rather than providing an impetus for sustained economic and social development (Gylfason, 2002; Karl, 1997).

Reforms in the welfare state – the ethos of productivism

Norway, like the other Nordic countries, has a large, dynamic and 'productivist' welfare state. In these countries, economic growth and prosperity have always been at the centre of the political economy (Kautto et al., 2001). In contrast to the liberal notion of 'work *not* welfare', and the conservative 'welfare *through* work', the Nordic countries have always sought to reconcile the two by promoting 'welfare *and* work' (Goodin, 2001). In Norway, since the early 1990s, the focus on work has been characterized by the slogan 'The Work Approach'. At the heart of the Work Approach is the political imperative to enable and to encourage able-bodied people of working age to engage in productive employment. Practically all social policy reform initiatives – in social security and social assistance and in social welfare organization – bear the stamp of the Work Approach.

It is clear, as shown earlier, that the reforms in social security and social assistance are intended to support this approach. As we noted above, social policy reform is characterized by changes in benefit levels and economic incentives, tightened eligibility criteria, behavioural conditions, time limits on benefit duration and measures to enhance the transition from benefit to work. Although reductions in benefit levels are not frequently imposed, tighter restrictions have been introduced and eligibility criteria have been tightened. A frequently applied strategy has been the use of behavioural conditions. Existing conditions have been revived and new ones have been added. Also, time limits have been used rather frequently. For some programmes, time limits have been introduced while for others the duration of benefit has been shortened. Measures to ease transition from benefit to work have also been implemented, especially in the rehabilitation and the sickness programme. Measures designed to make it easier to combine benefits and work have also been introduced.

Although these reforms have all sought to promote the Work Approach, the reform process has been incremental and the main features of the social security system, universalism and generosity have been preserved. Reforms have been initiated by different governments of different political complexion, but they have nevertheless maintained the key features of the Norwegian welfare state while demonstrating a clear commitment to make the welfare state more employment friendly. The reason that is often given is that this policy is needed to preserve the welfare state.

Nevertheless, it may be asked how successful these reforms have been. One obvious assessment criterion is the trend in the employment rate. As shown above, Norway has one of the highest employment rates in world and among women they have continued to rise. However, when measured by the increasing numbers of benefit recipients over the past ten to fifteen years, the picture is gloomier. However, it must be kept in mind that there is a close and causal relationship between the increasing number of benefit recipients and the higher employment rate among women, since women, through paid work, are increasingly earning their own entitlement to social security. An aging working population produces the same trend. When judged by the country's high labour force participation rate, it is possible to conclude that the Work Approach has been a success. However, in a system where entitlement to benefits is related to paid work, it will almost inevitably result in more people claiming benefits. Thus, more people on benefits is also a consequence of the Work Approach, although this is an unintended and undesirable consequence on the policy. In a rights-based system like Norway's, high employment and a high uptake of benefits are two sides of the same coin.

Another issue is what would have happened if the reforms had not been launched. It is an intriguing question whether the Norwegian version of the Nordic model has proven so sustainable and successful because of its inherent more or less permanent qualities, or because it has been reformed to better fit the new challenges posed by economic changes such as globalization. This is a counterfactual question which can not be answered, since no empirical data on this issue exist.

Also, as noted earlier, research evidence on the effectiveness of the labour market activation programmes are mixed. They might improve the employability of certain groups of unemployed people, but they do not do so for all unemployed people and especially not for groups that are more detached from the labour market and who have severe disadvantages. On the other hand, the government's commitment to these policies may have a strong signal effect in that it demonstrates a political will to take measures to promote full employment and, in this way, also expresses the clear expectation that citizens should engage in regular productive employment.

A rigid labour market?

Evidence is accumulating that liberal market economies are not the only ones able to generate high economic growth. Inspired by Esping-Andersen's welfare regime notion, research on 'production regimes' compares differences in political economy and shows how these may lead to comparative advantages (Hall and Gingerich, 2004; Wilensky, 2002). The focus is on how strategic interactions influence economic performance. Firms face coordination problems in many different areas and their success or failure depends on the degree to which they are able to coordinate a number of actors in different economic spheres. In tackling these coordination challenges, firms tend to cluster into two types of production regimes, namely, liberal market economies such as the United States and the United Kingdom and what are described as coordinated market economies such as the Nordic countries. In the former, coordination occurs first and foremost through markets. In the latter, firms coordinate by engaging in strategic interactions with trade unions, financial actors and governments. Empirical research has demonstrated that despite their differences, the two types of production regimes have rather similar outcomes in terms of economic performance (Hall and Gingerich, 2004; Hall and Soskice, 2001).

Coordinated market economies need not have rigid labour markets. Recent figures show that the Norwegian labour market is dynamic. A significant number of employees shift jobs each year, and a high number of new employees enter the labour market. In 2001, 15 per cent of all jobs were filled by new employees compared with the prior year. Moreover, the vast majority of the unemployed enter the labour market quickly. Analyses of employees' movements in the Norwegian labour market show a tendency towards increased mobility (St. meld 9 2006–2007). During the first half of the 1990s, about 20 per cent of Norwegian employees (about 400,000) shifted job each year. During the latter half of the 1990s, the percentage increased to about 25 per cent (Dale-Olsen, 2005). However, international comparisons of job flows show somewhat different results for Norway. One analysis indicates that the job flow is somewhat lower in Norway than in other countries, while another concludes that the job flow in manufacturing is at the same level in Norway as in other OECD countries and not much lower than that in United States (NOU, 2000). These comparisons hardly warrant the use of the word 'rigid' when describing the country's market. Indeed, some economists claim that the Norwegian labour market is more flexible than in most other countries (Isachsen, 2006). To support this view, Isachsen refers to recent organizational changes in public enterprises and also to the dynamics of the private corporations exemplified by the fact that many firms are constantly changing and restructuring, often reducing their work force and even going out of business. A comparative analysis of the stringency of employment regulation in Norway shows that it is on the same level as in Germany and Sweden, but stricter than that in Great Britain and Denmark (NOU, 2000).

The dynamic nature of the Norwegian economy, combined with a universal and generous safety net for those who are unemployed, is an important ingredient of the Norwegian 'flexicurity' arrangement, a term often used to describe the situation in Denmark. A dynamic labour market and a universal and generous unemployment and other social security programmes are in fact mutually dependent and reinforcing. The fact is that the Norwegian labour market is flexible and dynamic and that this is compatible with and supported by a social security system that offers generous and universal protection.

Social capital and social solidarity – the missing link?

Universal social security policies may also contribute to sound economic performance in other ways. Svendsen and Svendsen (2006) have high-lighted the missing link in the economic analysis of why some nations prosper and others do not, namely social capital. By social capital they refer to generalized trust and norms of reciprocity in a society. The authors point out that the Nordic countries, and Denmark in particular, have high rates of social capital. They rely on surveys, known as the 'World Wide Surveys', which covers several decades and more than 80 countries, but the results are corroborated by the European Social Survey which shows almost exactly the same rank order (Halvorsen, personal communication). With regard to horizontal trust, Halvorsen found that the four Nordic countries are among the top 20 countries in Europe. The presence of this high level of social capital, Svendsen and Svendsen argue, is the main reason why the Nordic countries demon-strate some of the highest economic growth rates in the world. Social capital is a productive force inasmuch as it reduces transaction costs, eases collaboration and coordination between economic actors and reduces the free rider problem. In contrast to control, trust is effective *and* cheap. They argue that social capital can explain about 25 per cent per cent of unexplained variance in economic growth when human and physical capital have been taken into account.

There may be different explanations why the Nordic countries have large amounts of social capital, such as culture, history and their homog-enous populations but all are plausible. It will, however, be argued that there is also an institutional source of social capital, the welfare state which emphasizes universality and solidarity. It is likely that a strong link between universalism and social capital can be found. Rothstein (2000) has argued and demonstrated empirically that universalism fos-ters (and also tends to be fostered by) social capital, whereas selective social policies tend to undermine it. In short, Norway's and the other Nordic countries' economic growth over the past ten to fifteen years may, at least in part, be rooted in the universal welfare state which fos-ters social capital and generalized trust which, in turn, is a precondition for smooth and prospering economic activity.

Undermining the work ethic?

As mentioned earlier, adherents of neoliberal economic theory assert that generous welfare programmes like those provided in the Nordic countries tend to undermine work motivation and erode the moral fabric of the society (Lindbeck, 1995). If correct, it is to be expected that work morale and work commitment would be lower in the Nordic countries than in countries with residual welfare systems such as in the United Kingdom and the United States. Examining relevant comparative data, Esser (2005) has studied this question empirically. She has examined four dimensions of work morale: the degree of employment commitment, whether work is valued as a duty towards society or as a free choice, valuations of how people should accept job offers or lose their employment benefit and preferences for early retirement as opposed to continued work. The results are unequivocal and surprising for those with a neoliberal perspective. On all four dimensions, work morale is higher in countries with generous social security benefits, such as Norway and the other Nordic countries. Her main conclusion is 'Findings consistently shows how higher social security benefit levels are broadly associated with stronger work orientations – whether these concern employment commitment, basic work values, or later retirement preferences' (Esser, 2005, p. 40).

A couple of concrete examples may illustrate this finding. On the basis of multi-level analysis, Esser demonstrates how employment commitment among workers in countries with more generous benefits is higher than the commitment in those with less generous benefits. What is perhaps even more important is that people on the margins of the labour market are also positively influenced by institutions characterized by generous social security benefits. She finds that welfare programmes actually exert an independent influence on work orientation. How may these findings be interpreted? Universal and generous welfare regimes may generate high work commitment because everyone – including the middle class – benefits and everyone contributes. There seems to be an analogy with Korpi and Palme's (1998) notion of the 'paradox of redistribution'. When working conditions are favourable, it seems that people are more motivated to make an effort and to be willing to work hard in exchange for comprehensive and universal social rights (Esser, 2005, p. 41). Thus, under the right circumstances, which are present in the Nordic social democratic welfare regimes, it is possible to reconcile work and welfare.

Is equality a productive force?

The current view in mainstream economics is that flexibility in wage setting as well as inequalities in wages and income promotes economic growth. However, the Norwegian case suggests that this might not be true in all settings and at all times. In view of the country's solid record of economic growth and its egalitarian wage and income structure, this poses a problem for the mainstream view. What may account for this situation? In an economy with small inequalities in wages, only a small pay increase in a growing industry or trade may be sufficient to attract highly skilled and competent labour. This means that an economy like Norway's may be as flexible or even more flexible than an economy where wage differentials are larger. In a low inequality economy, it costs less for each company to recruit, motivate and retain valuable and high achieving workers than in a high inequality economy (NOU, 2000).

Moene (2003) argues that one particular coordinating institution, the system of centralized and collective bargaining, is crucial to the understanding of economic growth as well as low income inequality in Norway, thereby reconciling the 'trade off' between efficiency and equality. The core of his argument is that centralized wage setting has promoted modernization and economic growth, because it 'took wage setting out of the hands of the unions representing relatively high paid workers' (p. 18). Central bargaining leads to the same wages in both high productive and low productive sectors (Barth et al., 2003). This results in a compressed wage distribution, but it is also a device for promoting efficiency and economic growth. It allows the most productive, modern and promising sectors to expand, because it becomes more profitable to invest in these new sectors. At the same time, central bargaining prevents sectors with low productivity from paying very low wages and hence they are shut down earlier than they would have been. This logic can be applied to the entire macroeconomy. The institution of centralized collective bargaining promotes efficiency and economic growth and as a side-effect narrows wage inequality.

Further, Moene (2003, p. 4) claims that the social democrats strategically used 'the reduction of inequality among wage earners as a development strategy'. A compressed wage structure generates further support for universal welfare benefits. Moreover, income equality contributes to a steady supply of relatively reasonably priced high qualified labour. Collective bargaining with moderate wage growth and a strong focus on competitiveness has given Norway a competitive and highly qualified work force (Moene, 2003).

This economic way of thinking may be supplemented with other and well-known arguments that social equality fosters social harmony, little conflict and a social climate for collaboration, and a higher quality of life. These arguments are also related to the social capital argument discussed earlier.

The public sector: large but dynamic?

By most measures, the public sector in Norway is large. Does this mean that it is rigid and inefficient and represents a drag on the economy as neoliberal theory contends? The Norwegian experience suggests that this view is questionable. Contrary to neoliberal claims, the public sector has gone through extensive organizational changes over the past 15 years. Politicians, of different motivations and justifications, have initiated these changes. However, the driving force behind the organizational changes to the public sector seems to have been less political control and the deregulation of services. The 1990s were the decade when liberalization and increased competition became catchphrases within the public sector. Since the beginning of the 1990s, the number of public enterprises has been reduced by 31 per cent, while the number of semi-public enterprises has increased by 51 per cent (Trygstad et al., 2006). A number of quasi-market devices have also been introduced in the social services and in the hospital sector (Lian, 2003; Vabø, 2002). Politically, these developments have been justified by a need to make the public sector more competitive, efficient and responsive to technological development and demands from its 'customers'. Many, if not all reforms have been inspired by the 'New Public Management' movement.

A recent report on the consequences of organizational change in four large public sector enterprises has shown that organizational change has led to an increased need for health related social security benefits among former employees (Trygstad et al., 2006). The Norwegian postal service is an example. Here, between 1998 and 2004, more than 35 per cent of employees have been made redundant. Most of this was caused by technological developments. The traditional postal service was changed by the widespread use of electronic services. Estimates suggest that the organizational changes in the Norwegian postal service has led to a 42 per cent increase in sick leave during the reforms, while the use of medical rehabilitation services has increased by as much as 53 per cent (Trygstad et al., 2006). There was also a dramatic increase in applications for disability pensions among former postal workers. Other studies looking at the reorganization and downsizing of public enterprises came basically to the same conclusions (Rege et al., 2005). To sum up, over the past decade, reforms in the public sector have been frequent and comprehensive, and it is hardly appropriate to describe the public sector in Norway as stagnant or rigid.

Whether these reform initiatives have succeeded in bringing about improvements in services and contributed to the well-being of the society, is a more controversial matter (Tranøy, 2007). Another issue which is more pertinent in this context is the unintended consequences of these reforms for former employees and for the employed population in general, especially for the more vulnerable workers in the secondary labour market. This issue will be examined in the next and final section.

Efficiency and productivity come at a price

The above discussion of the Norwegian (and Nordic) experience shows that a comprehensive and generous social security system is compatible with economic growth. There is no necessary trade off between economic efficiency and social welfare. Although criticisms of the social welfare reforms that have been introduced during the past ten to fifteen years have been muted, it is not intended to suggest that there are no problems with this model. Indeed, the Norwegian version of the Nordic economic and social model does have problems that need to be discussed.

As mentioned earlier, around 25 per cent of the population of working age is outside the labour market at any point in time. As indicated in Figure 8.1 the majority of these people receive sickness benefits, rehabilitation benefits and disability pension. Studies show that many who receive social assistance and unemployment benefit also suffer from poor health (Claussen, 1994; van der Wel et al., 2006). This means that non-work in Norway is concentrated among people who are in poor health. This is a well-acknowledged fact. What is less appreciated is that non-employment, receipt of benefit and ill-health are distinctly social issues. Those who are excluded from the labour market and who are in poor health have low socioeconomic status, and come from lower socioeconomic backgrounds (Hansen and Vibe, 2005). Thus, inequalities in health, socioeconomic status and employment are distinct characteristics of Norwegian society. This is a problem for a society with the ambition to be inclusive, and it violates the principles of social fairness and equality of opportunity. The driving force behind this phenomenon is related to the inherent features of Norwegian economic development and especially its high productivity and the rapid pace of economic readjustment in both the private and public sectors. Working life places high demands on human labour and requires a high level education, skills, good physical and mental health, stamina, and ability to adapt swiftly. Not everybody is able to cope with these demands, and people with low status and poor health tend to be most disadvantaged. Since a highly productive economy depends on a highly productive labour force, there is little room for less productive or able workers. On the other hand, this highly productive economy is able to cater for a fairly large number of non-working people.

How should this dilemma be dealt with? What are the options? Not many as far as we can see. In the liberal, market driven model such as in the United States, there are few outsiders, but a large proportion of the insiders are the working poor. At the same time, a significant number are extremely rich due to institutions that are very different from those in Norway. In the foreseeable future, few Norwegians favour the adoption of the American style market liberal model. People in Norway generally agree that although far from perfect, the Norwegian (and Nordic) model is preferable to the market liberal model. Despite the challenges facing Norway, most believe that the system works quite well. Norway still has a very high rate of labour market participation; it is among the richest and most prosperous countries in the Western world, among the most egalitarian, among those with a degree of social capital and among those with the highest quality of life and social well-being for its population.

References

Aakvik, A. (2001). 'Bounding a Matching Estimator: the Case of a Norwegian Training Program', *Oxford Bulletin of Economics and Statistics*, 63, 115–143.

Aakvik, A. (2003). 'Estimating the Employment Effects of Education for Disabled Workers in Norway', *Empirical Economics*, 28, 515–533.

Aakvik, A. and Risa, A. E. (1994). *Success or Selection in Vocational Rehabilitation Programs. Working Papers in Economics*. Report 3. Department of Economics, University of Bergen, Norway.

A-etat (2005). *Rapport om arbeidsmarkedet. Nummer 2*. Oslo: A-etat, Arbeidsdirektoratet.

Atkinson, A. B., Rainwater, L. and Smeeding, T. M. (1995). *Income Distribution in OECD Countries*. OECD Social Policy Studies No. 18. Paris: OECD.

Barnes, M., Heady, C., Middleton, S., Millar, J., Papadoupoulos, F., Room, G. and Tsakloglou, P. (2002). *Poverty and Social Exclusion in Europe*. Cheltenham: Edward Elgar.

Barth, E., Moene, K. O. and Wallerstein, M. (2003). *Likhet under press. Utfordringer for den skandinaviske fordelingsmodellen*. Oslo: Gyldendal akademisk.

Birkelund, G. E. and Petersen, T. (2003). 'Det norske likestillingsparadokset. Kjønn og arbeid i velferdssamfunnet.' In Frønes and Kjølsrød (eds), *Det norske samfunn. Fjerde utgave*. Oslo: Gyldendal norsk forlag.

Børing, P. (2004). *Norsk og annen nordisk forskning om yrkesrettet attføring*. Report 8. Oslo: NIFU Skriftserie.

Claussen, B. (1994). *Deprived of Work and Health? A Two Year Follow up of Long Term Unemployed from Grenland, Norway 1988–90*. Research Report No 1-1994. Oslo: National Institute of Public Health.

Dahl, E. (2003). 'Does "workfare" Work? The Norwegian experience', *International Journal of Social Welfare*, 12, 274–288.

Dahl, E. and Drøpping, J. A. (2001). 'The Norwegian Work Approach in the 1990s: Rhetoric and Reform.' In Neil Gilbert and Rebecca A. Van Voorhis (eds), *Activating the Unemployed. A Comparative Appraisal of Work-Oriented Policies.* New Brunswick: Transaction Publishers.

Dahl, E. and Lorentzen, T. (2005). 'What Works for Whom? An Analysis of Active Labour Market Programmes in Norway', *International Journal of Social Welfare*, 14, 86–98.

Dale-Olsen, H. (2005). 'Etablering og nedlegging av bedrifter, bedrifters størrelse og levetid.' In Torp, H. (ed.), *Nytt arbeidsliv. Medvirkning, inkludering og belønning.* Oslo: Gyldendal Akademisk.

Dale-Olsen, H., Schøne, P. and Røed, M. (2006). *Omfang av arbeidsmarkedstiltak: betyr det noe?* Oslo: Institutt for samfunnsforskning.

Dølvik, J. E. (2007). *The Nordic Regimes of Labour Market Governance: From Crisis to Success-Story?* Fafo-Paper: 7. Oslo: Fafo.

Drøpping, J. A., Hvinden, B. and Vik, K. (1999). 'Activation Policies in the Nordic Countries.' In Kautto, M., Heikkilä, M., Hvinden, B., Marklund, S. and Plough, N. (eds), *Nordic Social Policy, Changing Welfare States*, B. London: Routledge.

Esping-Andersen, G. (1990). *The Three Worlds of Welfare Capitalism.* Oxford: Polity Press.

Esping-Andersen, G. (1999). *Social Foundations of Postindustrial Economies.* Oxford: Oxford University Press.

Esser, I. (2005). *Why Work? Comparative Studies on Welfare Regimes and Individual's Work Orientations.* Doctoral dissertation. Stockholm: Swedish Institute for Social Research.

Fritzell, J. (2001). 'Still Different? Income Distribution in the Nordic Countries in a European Comparison.' In M. Kautto, J. Fritzell, B. Hvinden, J. Kvist and H. Uusitalo (eds), *Nordic Welfare States in the European Context.* London: Routledge.

Goodin, R. E. (2001). 'Work and Welfare: Towards a Post-productivist Welfare Regime', *British Journal of Political Science*, 31, 13–39.

Gough, I., Bradshaw, J., Ditch, J., Eardley, T. and Whiteford, P. (1997). 'Social Assistance in OECD Countries', *Journal of European Social Policy*, 7, 17–43.

Gylfason, T. (2002). 'Moder jord – medspiller eller motspiller?' In A. J. Isachsen (ed.), *Hva gjør oljepengene med oss?* Oslo: Cappelen Akademiske Forlag.

Hall, P. A. and D. W. Gingerich (2004). *Varieties of Capitalism and Institutional Complementarities in the Macroeconomy: An Empirical Analysis*, MPIfG Discussion Paper 04/5. Max Planck Institute for the Study of Societies, Cologne, September, 2004.

Hall, P. A. and Soskice, D. (eds) (2001). *Varieties of Capitalism. the Instiutional Foundations of Comparative Advantage.* Oxford: Oxford University Press.

Hansen, B. H. (2007). Minister of Work and Inclusion, speech 12.02.2007.

Hansen, M. N. and Vibe, U. (2005). 'Behov for sosialhjelp og uføretrygd: individuell ulykke eller sosial arv?', *Søkelys på arbeidsmarkedet*, 22, 149–157.

Hardoy, I., Røed, K. and Zhang, T. (2006). Aetats kvalifiserings- og opplæringstiltak – En empirisk analyse av seleksjon og virkninger. Frischsenteret report 4. Oslo. Frischsenteret.

Hatland, A. (2001). 'Trygd og arbeid.' In Hatland, A., Kuhnle, S. and Romøren, T. I. (eds), *Den norske velferdsstaten*. Oslo: Gyldendal akademisk.

Huber, E. and Stephens, J. D. (2001). *Development and Crisis of the Welfare State. Parties and Policies in Global Markets*. Chicago: The University of Chicago Press.

Hvinden, B., Heikkilä, M. and Kankare, I. (2001). 'Towards Activation? The Changing Relationship between Social Protection and Employment in Western Europe.' In M. Kautto, J. Fritzell, B. Hvinden, J. Kvist, H. Uusitalo (eds), *Nordic Welfare States in the European Context*. London and New York: Routledge.

Isachsen, A. J. (2006). *Verdens rikeste land*. Working paper series 6/06. Oslo: Oslo Business School.

Karl, T. L. (1997). *The Paradox of Plenty: Oil Booms and Petro States*. Berkeley: University of California Press.

Kautto, M., Fritzell, J., Hvinden, B., Kvist, J. and Uusitalo, H. (eds) (2001) *Nordic Welfare States in the European Context*. London and New York: Routledge.

Kolberg, J. E. and Esping-Andersen, G. (1992). 'Welfare States and Employment Regimes.' In J. E. Kolberg (ed.), *Between Work and Social Citizenship*. London: Sharpe Inc.

Korpi, W. and Palme, J. (1998). 'The Paradox of Redistribution and the Strategy of Equality: Welfare State Institutions, Inequality and Poverty in the Western Countries', *American Sociological Review*, 63,661–687.

Lian, O. (2003). *Når helse blir en vare*. Kristiansand: Norwegian Academic Press.

Lindbeck, A. (1995). 'Welfare State Disincentives with Endogenous Habits and Norms', *Scandinavian Journal of Economics*, 97, 477–494.

Lindqvist, R. and Marklund, S. (1995). 'Forced to Work and Liberated from Work – a Historical Perspective on Work and Welfare in Sweden', *Scandinavian Journal of Social Welfare*, 4(4), 224–237.

Lødemel, I. and Johannesen, A. (2005). *Tiltaksforsøket: nytter det? HiO-rapporter nr. 1*. Oslo: Oslo University College.

Lødemel, I. and Trickey, H. (2001) *An Offer You Can't Refuse?* Bristol: The Policy Press.

Lorentzen, T. and Dahl, E. (2005). 'Active Labour Market Programmes in Norway: Are They Helpful for Social Assistance Recipients?' *Journal of European Social Policy*, 15, 27–45.

Moene, K. (2003). *Social Democracy as a Development Strategy*. Memorandum No 35/2003. Oslo: Department of Economics, University of Oslo.

NOU (2000). *En strategi for sysselsetting og verdiskaping*. Oslo: Finansdepartementet, Statens forvaltningstjeneste Informasjonsforvaltning.

OECD (2007). Factbook online. www.sourceoecd.org/factbook. Accessed 24 November 2007.

Øverbye, E. and Hammer, T. (2006). 'Strategier for et inkluderende arbeidsliv.' In Hammer, T. and Øverbye, E. (eds), *Inkluderende arbeidsliv? Erfaringer og strategier*. Oslo: Gyldendal akademisk.

Raaum, O. and Røed, K. (2002). *Do Business Cycle Conditions at the Time of Labour Market Entry Affect Future Unemployment?* Oslo: University of Oslo, Department of Economics.

Raaum, O., Torp, H. and Tzhang, T. (2002a). *Business Cycles and the Impact of Labour Market Programmes*. Report 2002:14. Oslo: University of Oslo, Department of Economics.

Raaum, O. Torp, H. and Tzhang, T. (2002b). *Do Individual Programme Effects Exceed the Costs? Norwegian Evidence on Long Run Effects of Labour Market Training.* Report 2002:15. Oslo: University of Oslo, Department of Economics.

Rege, M., Telle, K. and Votruba, M. (2005). *The Effect of Plant Downsizing on Disability Pension Utilization.* Discussion Papers 435. Oslo: Statistics Norway.

Roed, K. and Raaum, O. (2006). 'Do Labour Market Programmes Speed up the Return to Work?', *Oxford Bulletin of Economics and Statistics*, 68, 541–568.

Rønsen, M. and Skarðhamar, T. (2006). *Virkningen av Arbeids- og velferdsdirektoratets tiltakssatsing blant sosialhjelpsmottakere: en evaluering basert på data fra FD-Trygd.* Oslo: Statistics Norway. Rothstein, B. (2000). 'The Future of the Universal Welfare State: An Institutional Approach.' In Kuhnle, S. (ed.), *Survival of the European Welfare State.* London: Routledge.

Seip, A. L. (1994). *Veiene til velferdsstaten: Norsk sosialpolitikk 1920–75.* Oslo: Gyldendal.

Smeeding, T. M. (2002). 'Globalization, Inequality and the Rich Countries of the G-20: Evidence from the Luxembourg Income Study (LIS)', LIS Working Paper Series No. 320. Luxembourg: LIS.

St.meld. nr. 1 (2005–2006). *Nasjonalbudsjettet 2006.* Oslo: Finansdepartementet.

St.meld. nr. 5 (2006–2007). *Opptjening og uttak av alderspensjon i folketrygden. Kortversjon av st.meld.* Oslo: Arbeids- og inkluderingsdepartementet.

St.meld. nr. 6 (2006–2007). *Om seniorpolitikk. Seniorane - ein viktig ressurs i norsk arbeidsliv.* Oslo: Arbeids- og inkluderingsdepartementet.

St.meld. nr. 9 (2006–2007). *Arbeid, velferd, inkludering.* Oslo: Arbeids- og inkluderingsdepartementet.

Svendsen, G. T. and Svendsen, G. L. H. (2006). *Social kapital: en introduktion.* København: Hans Reitzels Forl.

Tranøy, B. S. (2007). *Markedets makt over sinnene.* Oslo: Aschehoug.

Trygstad, S. C., Lorentzen, T., Løken, E., Moland, L., og Skalle, N. (2006). *Den nye staten: omfang og effekter av omstillingene i staten 1990–2004.* Oslo: Fafo.

UNDP (2003). Human Development reports, http://hdr.undp.org/reports/global/2003/indicator/indic_126_1_1.html. Accessed April 2007.

UNICEF (2005). *Child Poverty in Rich Countries 2005.* Innocenti report no 6. Firenze: UNICEF.

Vabø, M. (2002). *Kvalitetsstyring og kvalitetsstrev. Nye styringsambisjoner i hjemmetjenesten.* NOVA Rapport 18/2002. Oslo: NOVA.

van der Wel, K., Dahl, E., Slagsvold, M., Løyland, B., Naper, S. O. (2006). *Funksjonsevne blant langtidsmottakere av sosialhjelp.* Rapport 2006:29. Oslo: Høgskolen i Oslo.

Wilensky, H. (1992). 'Active Labour Market Policy: Its Contents, Effectiveness, and Odd Relationship to Evaluation Research.' In C. Crouch, A. H. Halsey and A. Heath (eds), *Social Research and Social Reform, Essays in Honour of A. H. Halsey.* Oxford: Clarendon Press.

Wilensky, H. (2002). *Rich Democracies: Political Economy, Public Policy and Performance.* Berkeley: University of California Press.

Zhang, T. (2003). *Identifying Treatment Effects of Active Labour Market Programmes for Norwegian Adults. Manuscript.* Oslo: The Ragnar Frisch Centre for Economic Research.

9
The United Kingdom: The Economic Consequences of Child Poverty

Martin Evans

This chapter looks at the issue of child poverty from two overlapping perspectives: first, its causes and consequences, and second, the justification for and design of programmes that can counter it. The United Kingdom is taken as the core case study because it has undertaken to eliminate child poverty within a generation (by 2020), but this promise can be seen as one element of a wider pan-national concern with extreme poverty and with child poverty. Indeed, child poverty is nearly universally held as a valid justification for state intervention. For this reason, I argue in this chapter for set of commonly held theoretically consistent reasons both for causes of child poverty and justifications for policy intervention. Put simply, this proposes that child poverty is bad for both individuals and hinders economic and social development and that ending child poverty produces both micro and macro socio-economic gains.

What causes child poverty? It is best to think of causes under two headings, child specific and 'other' causes. This is because, while children bring particular costs and constraints to households, there are also non-child-related factors that can cause poverty, and both operate to bring about child poverty.

What are the child specific reasons for poverty? Children are additional mouths to feed and thus add to the needs of the household whose existing resources will be spread across more people, increasing the risk of poverty if resources are constant. We can call these basic costs as the *'costs of needs'*. But children alter the risk profile of the household to new *specific costs*: they are more likely to require services such a healthcare and have significant direct costs of education, for instance. The easiest way to think of the distinction between these and the previous basic needs costs is in the associated policy response involving services which are normally provided outside of the household. There is a wide range of studies that attempt to calculate the 'costs of a child' (Liverpool Victoria Friendly Society, 2006; Middleton et al., 1999), but these studies tend to only identify direct costs and to miss the considerable indirect costs of children on parental earnings and opportunities, so-called *opportunity costs*. These primarily but not exclusively affect the mother through reduced time available for work – both economic activity and housework. But it is important, especially in developing countries, to recognize that there are other household members who can be called upon to care for the child and/or to replace the lost household and market employment of the mother. This means, for instance, that older siblings, themselves children, may be required to do more household chores or may be required themselves to make up the lost maternal income through employment on the arrival of a new baby.

There are also opportunity costs associated with the child itself after a certain age. Child labour is the subject of humanitarian concern across the world but most often occurs in the informal economic sector and in household-level activity (Edmonds 2007). However, in developing countries with clearer economic trade-offs between schooling and employment for children, the lost contribution of children's activity to family incomes can be substantial and poverty is closely aligned with school non-attendance and child labour (ibid.).

Traditionally the economic literature sees these costs as offset in the longer term by children being an *investment* (Becker, 1962). This view says that the costs of meeting their current needs and of the opportunity costs they bring can be offset over time by their future income and contribution. In industrial societies, where household-based production is limited, these investments are seen mostly as social investments – public goods – to ensure that the next generation of workers and taxpayers are productive. There is a long-standing argument that promotes the education of children as a matter of national efficiency – 'involvement in education as it made labour more productive, thus contributing to economic performance' (Barr, 2004, p. 19). In developing countries, where household-based agricultural and informal production are greater, the investment is more appropriately seen as familial and largely within the household or family network, and investment includes the potential to be economic providers for their parents' dotage. Of course, in a view of children as an economic investment it is not just future income generation that may be at stake as some children, most often girls due to dowry, are viewed as a liability.

The consequences of children being current costs and future invest-ment returns mean that issue of child poverty and well-being has to be viewed dynamically. This means that current profiles of need and pov-erty can frustrate a return on investment. It is, therefore, not sufficient to see the underlying drivers of child poverty as solely their particular characteristics (three types of cost and their reconciliation through an investment strategy) because *underlying factors about both the contempo-rary income distribution and the incidence of parenting mean that children are born into economic and social relations that are not of their making.* One major underlying cause of child poverty is thus the contemporary characteristics of parents and the wider socio-economic determinants of inequality as well as the common sets of costs and constraints that children bring. For instance, teenage motherhood is associated with incomplete/interrupted education and thus low skills and poverty, and later motherhood, increasingly the choice in the developed countries, enables women to reduce the lifetime opportunity costs on earnings, with low poverty risk in developed countries. Children living in lone-parent families have high risk of poverty because the opportunity costs on employment are highest without a second parent who can remain constantly economically productive. Parental ill-health, particularly of the main household earner, is the most common cause of long-term poverty in developing countries (Chronic Poverty Research Centre, 2005). Geographical concentrations of child poverty point to macr-oeconomic drivers on production and income generation that affect many parents and their children in those areas.

Finally, one aspect of current circumstances that influences poverty will be social provision – both formal programmes of transfers and serv-ices and also informal family and other provision. Different policy regimes will commit themselves differently to children and will direct resources in different ways (selective or universal approaches, cash transfers and in-kind provision, for instance). This means that countries with similar economic and population characteristics may have very different levels of child poverty, purely because country A puts more into assisting children than country B.

The United Kingdom: poverty and inequality

The United Kingdom consists of densely populated islands with a popu-lation of 62 million off the Atlantic Coast of Europe that in total is slightly smaller than Oregon State. Children aged less than 14 make up 17.5 per cent of the population while a further 15.8 per cent are elderly aged over 65. Population is growing at around 0.3 per cent per annum but the birth rate of 10.71 births/1,000 population is slightly greater than the death rate of 10.13 deaths/1,000 population, and most population growth comes from net immigration at 2.18 migrant(s)/1,000 population. Life expectancy at birth is 76.1 years for men and 81.1 years for women. The United Kingdom is a rich country with GDP per capita of $31,400 in purchasing power parity in 2006 and has had consistent economic growth since the early 1990s, which is currently around 2.5 per cent in real terms per annum. The United Nations Human Development Index (HDI) ranks the United Kingdom 18th in the world (UNDP, 2006).

However, the United Kingdom has high levels of income inequality and poverty for a European country. Figure 9.1 shows the United Kingdom's position in a selection of rich OECD countries in 2000 and 2005.

Time series split by different data sources – Family Expenditure Survey 1979–1992/1993 and then Family Resources Survey.

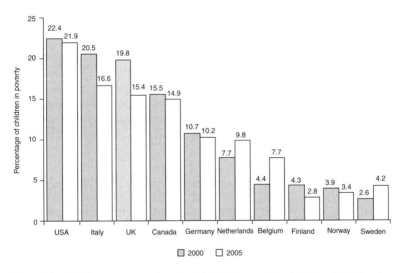

Figure 9.1 Child poverty rates in selected OECD countries 2000 and 2005: using poverty line set at 50 per cent of median equivalized income

Note: Years of surveys differ, and dates 2000 and 2005 relate to UNICEF date of rankings in its Report Cards.

Source: Author's calculations from UNICEF 2000 and 2005.

Poverty in rich countries is usually measured in relative terms. International comparisons show that the United Kingdom has had some of the highest levels of child poverty among the richest countries in recent years. Analysis by UNICEF of incidence and trends in national child poverty rates in rich countries, shown in Figure 9.1, shows that the United Kingdom is among the worst, with 20 per cent of poor children in 2000. While UK child poverty fell during the late 1990s and early 2000s, down to 15 per cent by 2005, this was still three times that of the best European peers, the so-called '*5% club*' (UNICEF, 2000).

Figure 9.2 shows how child poverty rates have changed since 1979 in the United Kingdom. This figure adopts an UK Government adopted poverty target measure (discussed below) of 60 per cent of median income, which is also used by the European Union. But there is some difference between what is useful for international comparison and what is most useful in national policy analysis and debate. Internationally, relative poverty is compared using a standard income definition that does not discount housing costs. United Kingdom transfer programmes include a separate housing allowance to cover 100 per cent of rent liability for those on social assistance, and this distorts incomes at the bottom

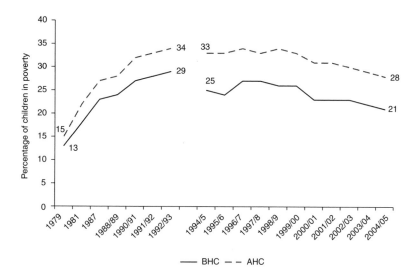

Figure 9.2 Trends in UK child poverty 1979–2004/2005: before and after housing costs measures 60 per cent of median

Notes: Modified OECD scale and Companion AHC scale.

Source: Author's calculations from DWP 2006, Table A3 1.2.

of the distribution and this means that, inter alia, in *national* poverty profiles an alternative 'after housing cost' (AHC) measure is often preferred or used alongside a 'before housing cost' (BHC) measure. After housing cost incomes provide a closer match to both the disposable resources of the poorest and their employment incentives.

Figure 9.2 shows that child poverty soared over the 1980s due to a combination of economic restructuring, demographic change – especially the growth of children in lone-parent families – and constraints on social policy and income maintenance programmes in particular. In the mid-1990s, poverty had fallen but was fairly static at one third (AHC) or one quarter (BHC) of all children. Since 1997, and especially since 1999 with significant changes to fiscal tax and benefit programmes, child poverty has slowly fallen to levels of 28 per cent (AHC) and 21 per cent (BHC) of all children in 2004/2005.

Our discussion in the opening section showed that there were both child-specific risks of poverty and underlying structural factors such as the life course and income distribution. Before looking at programmes that aim to reduce child poverty it is, therefore, wise to understand the underlying structural risks of poverty that are independent of the specific costs of having children. This means comparing the risk of poverty of the whole population to the risks of children and identifying what is shared and distinctive respectively. The underlying risk of poverty for the whole population can be crudely estimated by the difference between the average risk and the various socio-economic and demographic factors that increase risk. Figures 9.3 and 9.4 shows the results for additional lifecourse risk of poverty for children compared to working-age adults and elderly people. Children are 24 per cent more likely overall to be poor than the whole population (BHC) and 33 per cent using an after housing costs measure. This clearly shows the lifecourse effect of housing costs on the probability of poverty – children occur when mortgage payments are in their early years and costs highest for those buying their homes. On the other hand, elderly people have an equal additional probability of poverty using BHC income but a far reduced risk once housing costs are taken into account, minus 14 per cent, as the majority of elderly have no outstanding mortgage. There is also an underlying selection effect as a much higher proportion of children live in rented accommodation than the elderly. Working-age adults (who, therefore, live with no children or elderly) have reduced risk of poverty.

The United Kingdom has low levels of formal unemployment, which is around 5 per cent. However, employment can be seen as a huge factor

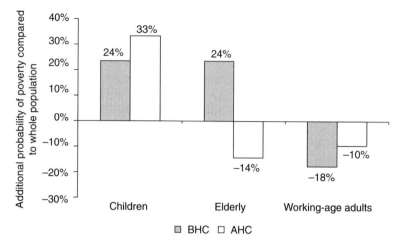

Figure 9.3 Additional risk of poverty for children, elderly and working-age adults compared to whole population, 2004/2005

Source: Author's calculations from DWP 2006.

in the risk of poverty – households where all adults work full time have an 80 per cent reduced risk of poverty, whereas workless households have a 255 per cent increased risk if unemployed and 195 per cent if inactive – ignoring pensioner/retired households. Having children also raises the risks of poverty; a couple with children are 35 per cent and lone parents are 135 per cent more likely to be poor. Ethnicity matters, with black and Asian people more likely to be poor and Pakistani and Bangladeshis having the highest additional risk – 160 per cent more likely to be poor. Disability also increases risk by 25 per cent if adult(s) are disabled and by 40 per cent if children are disabled. Geographic region also influences poverty – with poverty risk highest at the heart of the metropolitan urban core, Inner London, where there is a 70 per cent additional risk of poverty echoing findings across the developed and developing world about the growing incidence and concentrations of poverty in major urban environments.

If we now solely examine children and child poverty, Figure 9.5 shows that many of the same structural reasons remain relevant. The additional risk of child poverty are clearly highest for non-working parents who are 167 per cent more likely to be poor. Lone parents are 75 per cent more likely to be poor than couple parents with a 26 per cent reduced risk overall. The number and age of children matter, although the largest increase in risk is for large families. Disability and non-white ethnicity

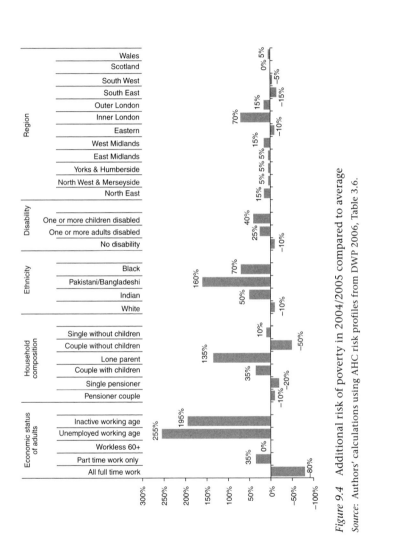

Figure 9.4 Additional risk of poverty in 2004/2005 compared to average

Source: Authors' calculations using AHC risk profiles from DWP 2006, Table 3.6.

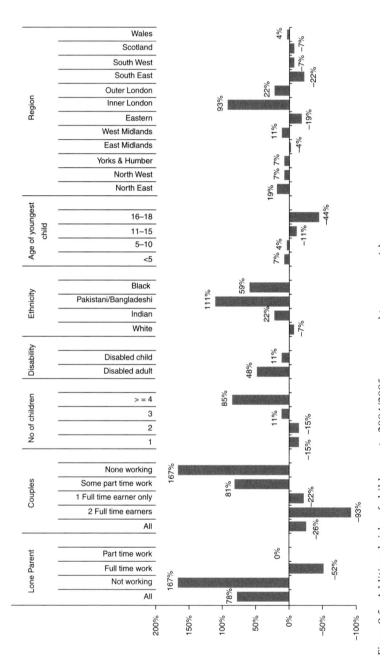

Figure 9.5 Additional risks of child poverty 2004/2005 – compared to average risk

Source: Author's calculations using AHC risk profiles from DWP 2006, Table 3.6.

also raise the risk of poverty. Regional factors also matter, with a 93 per cent increased risk for child poverty in Inner London.

These calculations are only bivariate – and the interdependent nature of poverty risk numbers of non-working lone-parent families living in Inner London create concentrations of child poverty and particular sets of policy constraints. To better understand the nature of poverty and the potential effectiveness of policy responses, the risk groups have to be seen in their relative and absolute population size – are the majority of poor children in high- or low-risk categories?

Figure 9.6 shows the percentage of poor children by their family type and the economic activity of their parents. There is an equal split between those poor with in-work parents and those with out-of-work parents, although the largest single group is in workless lone-parent families (and a further 16 per cent are in workless couple families), one half of child poverty occurs in families where parents work. If all parents work full-time there is very little poverty risk, and only 3 per cent of children are in families where both parents work full time. But less than full-time work (ignoring self-employment) accounts for 21 per cent of child poverty across both types of family and a further 14 per cent is in

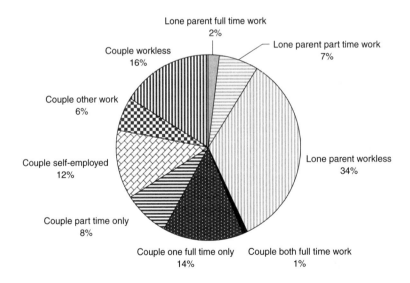

Figure 9.6 Composition of poor children 2004/2005 – by family type and economic activity of parents

Source: Author's calculations from DWP 2006, Table 4.4.

families where only one parent works full-time and the other is not working. It is thus obvious that *the opportunity cost* children – more exactly their constraint on optimal parental full-time working – is the second major cause of poverty after worklessness.

The social security system and the promise to eliminate child poverty

In October 1999, two years after taking power, Prime Minister Tony Blair made a promise to eradicate child poverty 'within a generation'. The promise in outline was couched in terms of moral responsibility to end unequal life chances and the costs and consequences of not doing so in inter-generational poverty and social exclusion. However, one major strength of the UK approach is that it has taken on some of the detailed policy measurement requirements that enable promises, pro- grammes and performance to be consistently squared. In this respect, the United Kingdom can be seen at the forefront of countries which are committed against child poverty in more than rhetoric. By contrast Canada, for instance, made a promise to end child poverty in the early 1990s but set no timetable, benchmarks or targets to achieve it.

By 2006, it is now much clearer about what this UK promise means in terms of measured outcomes. First, the aim of 'elimination' will be to reduce levels of UK child poverty to equal or better those experi- enced by best performing peers in Europe. Looking back at Figure 9.1, this means joining what UNICEF calls the 'five per cent club' and matching Scandinavian and other peers. Second, the measurement issues have been mostly resolved. Measuring poverty is always a tech- nical issue and three measures of poverty will be used together to assess whether the target of elimination has been reached (DWP, 2005b):

- An 'absolute' definition of poverty that takes forward the poverty line from 1998/1999 levels (set as a relative standard) and up-rates this by rising prices. This measure captures how far real living standards have risen for the poorest.
- A 'relative' definition of poverty that bases the poverty line on 60 per cent of contemporary median equivalized income.
- A 'material deprivation' measure that will capture a range of consumption goods, assets and services that indicate material depri- vation and are associated with relative income levels below 70 per cent of contemporary median equivalized household income.

The last of these three measures is still being developed at the time of writing and I limit discussion to the first two.

Finally, the promise to end poverty in a generation was split into a series of temporal targets, to quarter poverty by 2005, to halve poverty rates by 2011 and to finally 'eliminate' by 2020.

These transparent and verifiable targets enable us to look at what is being done currently, what is proposed to be done in the future and to assess how far policy has helped to reduce poverty to date and whether it will enable the target to be met.

Social protection and policy change

The Labour Party manifesto for the election of the Blair Government in 1997 made no mention of combating poverty directly. Indeed, there was an explicit promise not to raise public expenditure for the first two years beyond levels already promised by the outgoing Conservatives. The major promise of a new social policy focus was on improving employment programmes, which in the first instance was based on improving the quality of programmes for young unemployed people aged less than 25. This was the 'New Deal' which was financed from a one-off levy on companies that had benefited from windfalls on privatizations of state-owned utilities in the 1990s. Once in power, 'welfare reform' became a central policy aim but for American readers, this term, imported from the US, is a prime example of British adoption of US rhetoric which hides substantial differences in approach, context and coverage. In the United Kingdom, reform was wide ranging across all state systems of income transfers, which, confusingly, the British call 'Social Security'. This means that reform took in state social insurance pensions (what the United States calls Social Security), means-tested coverage for the elderly and incapacity programmes (SSI) and the comprehensive social assistance safety net including unemployment assistance for all over the age of 18.

The central aim of this process of reform was to promote 'work for those who can, security for those who cannot' (DSS, 1998). This approach prioritized three main areas for reform. First, a widening and deepening of employment activation across all people of working age who claim out-of-work transfers. This led to the setting up of a number of 'New Deals' (employment programmes for particular groups such as lone parents, disabled people, partners and long-term older unemployed alongside the flagship programme for the under 25s) which have since evolved into a wider and less segmented set of employment and activation programmes, the formation of one-stop benefits and employment services and the development of programmes to support low-income employment. Second, recasting of current social assistance for elderly people to more securely protect against poverty and reform of future pensions. Third was a series of changes that both moved provision away from transfers from the Department of Social Security – since renamed Department for Work and Pensions – to the tax system and developed a series of refundable tax credits. These particularly affect families with children and have been the main focus of new resources to combat child poverty.

The United Kingdom has a national centralized system of social transfers of great complexity and coverage. The following description looks at how children are treated and aligns the various programmes to the costs and causes of child poverty outlined in the introductory part of this chapter.

The *basic needs* for children are ensured by specific child transfers and social assistance schemes, which are essentially for their parents. Social assistance provides a basic minimum income for all adults as there are two parallel national comprehensive systems that provide Income Support (IS) for all those aged 18 to 59 who are not unemployed and Jobseekers Allowance (JSA) for those of similar ages who are. Employment is defined as 16 hours a week and anyone working 16 or more hours received alternative in-work transfers. These social assistance programmes represent (together with the pension age equivalent) a long-standing British commitment to a comprehensive income safety net for all those aged 18 and more. But, as previously mentioned, there were two means-tested allowances for housing and local taxation that make up the social assistance safety net and that meets 100 per cent of liability for those who are on IS or JSA.

Child benefit is paid for every child, irrespective of income, in the United Kingdom. It is paid at a higher level for the first child and represents a universal commitment to meeting some of the costs of children across the whole population.

Reform since 1997 has sought to reduce child poverty in three ways. First, improving the level of basic needs provided to children in out-of-work families; second, by 'making work pay' and increasing the generosity and treatment of children in working families; and third, by rolling out improved employment programmes to those out of work, in particular lone parents. For the sake of argument, let us examine them one by one.

Basic needs for out-of-work families

One outcome of post 1997 reform has been to increase the generosity of child transfers. Both child benefit, paid to all, and social assistance rates for children, paid to the poorest, were made more generous in 1997. However in 2003, social assistance rates for children were scrapped and replaced by a single Child Tax Credit that is paid in full to parents who claim social assistance or are on low earnings but tapered for those on middle and higher incomes.

The resulting income transfer package for out-of-work families with children is thus fairly complex and made up of IS/JSA for the parents needs, CTC and child benefit for the children needs and then Housing Benefit and Council Tax Benefit. Additionally, the children will be given benefits in kind through free school meals and milk and vitamins if they are infants.

Figure 9.7 shows such packages for two model families: a lone parent with a single child and a couple with two children. The incomes that result are compared to poverty in both AHC and BHC terms. There are two main conclusions: first, children are poor if their parents rely on social assistance; second, their depth of poverty, the size of their poverty gap, depends on *both* family composition and the definition of poverty used (AHC/BHC). This has significant consequences if we refer

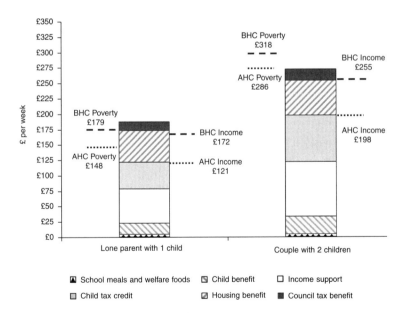

Figure 9.7 Weekly out-of-work income packages for two model families 2005/2006

Source: Author's calculations from DWP 2005a, 2005c.

back to the UK Government's target definition used in respect of ending child poverty. Definitions by BHC, as used in the target, clearly have smaller poverty gaps. Additionally, the size of the poverty gap is lower for single-headed families and for small families than it is for couple-headed and large families. The reason is that the weights given to adults in children income transfers do not match those used to measure poverty – a rather worrying inconsistency but one that puts lone parents nearer to the poverty line and thus easier to carry across the poverty threshold if they enter work.

Basic needs in work

The preferred policy route out of poverty is through employment and promotion of parental employment is at the heart of British anti-poverty programmes for children. Reform of in-work transfers has thus been the most visible and radical element to date of programmes to reduce child poverty. Chancellor Gordon Brown's admiration of US Earned Income Tax Credit (EITC) meant that using the tax system to improve income levels of low-earning parents has been at the forefront of making work pay. In essence, this approach improves incentives to enter work by supplementing earnings mostly for those with lowest earnings who may be faced with small net benefits from taking up a job compared to remaining on social assistance. Additionally, by placing most help on the lowest earners, the poverty impact can be maximized through income targeting.

The existing system of in-work benefits for families with children (called Family Credit) was replaced in 1999 by Working Families Tax Credit and its administration was transferred to the Inland Revenue. Simultaneously, a National Minimum Wage was introduced for the first time in the United Kingdom, and social insurance and income tax thresholds were harmonized. The combined impact was to thus to increase both the micro-economic incentives to work for the low paid and to promote job growth without lowering wages at the bottom of the earnings distribution.

The second set of more radical reforms came into effect in 2003 and coincided with the introduction of Child Tax Credit discussed above. A separate Working Tax Credit was introduced which is payable to all low-paid earners who worked more than 16 hours a week alongside the new Child Tax Credit to working parents. The WTC and CTC when paid together were tapered in turn and not together. However, WTC also helps with 70 per cent of registered childcare costs up to set maxima.

Figure 9.8 shows the income package for the same model of lone parent that we observed out of work in Figure 9.7 and shows poverty lines for a range of weekly hours work at the minimum wage, starting at 16 hours. Compared to income from social assistance, work pays – this lone parent is £40 a week (over 30 per cent) better off when she only works 16 hours a week even after paying her rent. Not only is she better off in work but she also is above the poverty line.

Figure 9.9 shows the same calculations for the model couple with two children previously seen in Figure 9.7. Work still pays but not as strongly as for the lone parent; the family are 15 per cent better off at 16 hours, and the poverty line is not crossed until 58 hours (BHC) or 72 hours (AHC). The reasons for this are the same underlying problems that were seen in social assistance benefits: namely, that the weights for transfers do not match the poverty assumptions.

However, it can be correctly argued that more help has to be given to lone parents who face higher constraints on work. Additionally, as we saw in Figure 9.6, out-of-work lone parents make up the largest single group with poor children, so targeting help to the largest group with the largest constraints does make some sense. But, as we saw from Figure 9.7, lone parents tend to also have smaller poverty gaps out of work and are thus easiest to move across the poverty line – the programme is targeted in part on those who are 'easiest' to move out of

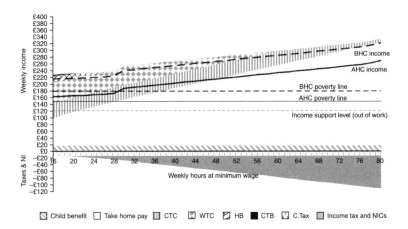

Figure 9.8 Income package and poverty lines for a lone parent working 16 hours a week and more at the National Minimum Wage (2005/2006)

Notes: Levels of rent and council tax adopt DWP assumptions (DWP, 2005a).

Source: Author's calculations from DWP 2005a, 2005c.

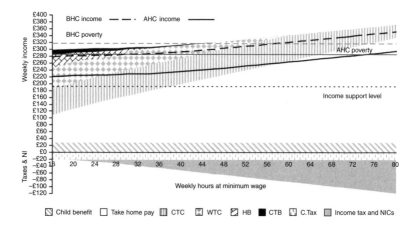

Figure 9.9   Taxes and transfers for a couple with two children with parent(s) working 16 hours a week and more at the National Minimum Wage (2005/2006)

Notes: Levels of rent and council tax adopt DWP assumptions (DWP, 2005a).

Source: Author's calculations from DWP 2005a, 2005c.

poverty, if the underlying logic is restricted to looking at monetary gains and standards alone.

There is one final aspect of work incentives and child poverty that arises from these profiles – this issue of marginal work incentives: to earn more, work more hours or, for couples, for the partner to enter work if there is already one earner. Figures 9.8 and 9.9 clearly show that the income gains from higher earnings, shown by the slope of the income lines, are quite flat. This is because much of the in-work income transfer package tapers out together and interacts with tax and social insurance liability (shown as the grey areas below the zero income line on y-axis). The net effect of earning more can result in keeping very little after paying taxes and rent. The worst case is a 96 per cent marginal rate for those who have HB, CTB, tax credit(s) and who pay income tax and national insurance. Once entitlement to HB and CTB disappear, this falls to 70 per cent combined tax credit reduction and tax liability and this rate continues fairly high up the income distribution and affects a large population of parent earners.

The evidence and argument so far has focused narrowly on income poverty and on basic needs costs and the response from income transfers. Of course, child poverty is multidimensional and reflects a range of formal and informal provision and relationships. By sticking with our simplistic notion of 'costs', however, we can consistently consider areas of service up-take and interventions for children, their costs and differences in their effectiveness that reflect and contribute to child poverty alongside social income transfers.

Education

Primary and secondary education up to the age of 16 is compulsory and free in the United Kingdom. However, even with a universal service with no user charges there are costs and these fall disproportionately on poor families. Average annual costs of school attendance – of uniforms, trips, materials, contributions to school funds and meals at school – paid by parents in 2004 were over £700 (approximately one-tenth of annual income on social assistance for a lone parent) (Brunwin et al., 2004). However, poor children act as protective gatekeepers and do not always pass on requests for cash to their parents – a reflection of how children actively adapt their preferences and behave differently under the constraints of poverty (Ridge, 2003) . However, the effect on income on schooling not only affects costs and participation in wider school-based activities but also affects education outcomes, even when other criteria are held constant

> parental income does matter for the child's education choices. Here the distinction is important between long-run income and current income at a point in time. We have found evidence that both are important for whether a child decides to leave school at 16; whilst long term income is most important, short-term income also matters (Blow et al., 2005, p. 23)

The education policy of the UK government has developed an additional education linked income transfers to poorer children aged 16 and above who choose to continue secondary education, Education Maintenance Allowances. However, the majority of government attention has been focused on school quality, with a more centrally prescribed curriculum, more testing of children and performance ranking of schools and changes in funding to promote improvements in schools in deprived areas. However, school quality and provision and parental choice are still bound together by parental resources – especially reflected in geographical location and the housing market. Inequality in educational outcomes thus is, in part, a reflection of wider income inequalities and the ability to 'purchase' quality of education – even in the state sector. Inequality in the education outcomes of 15 year olds is lower in the Nordic and others countries with low levels of child poverty (OECD, 2000, 2003).

If education outcomes are added to monetary measures of poverty in a composite index of child well-being, the United Kingdom performs comparatively even worse against its rich country peers than when compared on income alone (UNICEF, 2007).

Health

The United Kingdom has a tax-funded National Health System (NHS) which is free at the point of access, but health inequalities remain stubbornly high (Mitchell et al., 2000), and recent epidemiological evidence shows that these inequalities in health remain for children even during the recent period of falling rates of child poverty (Petrou et al., 2006). The difference between poor and non-poor children's use of health services appears to have declined since the mid-1990s as the poorest quintile of children have increased uptake of health spending from 88 per cent to 94 per cent of the overall average (Sefton, 2002). Whether such increased uptake has been sufficient to equalize the slope in the 'social gradient' in health is, however, more in doubt.

The Blair Government has long-standing commitment to reduce health inequalities and set up an independent enquiry that reported in 1998 (Acheson, 1998), which highlighted children's health issues and which led to a series of targets to reduce health inequalities that began in 2001 and led to a cross-cutting Governmental review of health services and their delivery (DOH, 2002). Reductions in infant mortality and overall improvement in early infant health were seen as paramount and led to the setting up of 'Sure Start' – a programme of mother and child centres in very disadvantaged neighbourhoods. Improving access to pre-natal and maternity services for low-income and ethnic minority populations, increasing uptake of breastfeeding, reform of dietary and welfare food services, and promotion of dental education and uptake were highlighted and these initiatives were to be the focus of multidisciplinary family support teams, with local Sure Start programmes being in the forefront of spreading practice across the wider population. However, the distinctive nature of Sure Start as a health and child developmental initiative has eroded over time and child-based provision is increasingly moving towards local pre-school childcare services through Children's Centres (see below).

The most recent evidence on child health inequalities finds reductions in differences in road accident casualties for children, in educational attainment and in housing quality. Infant mortality shows no change between 2001–2003 and 2002–2004, and there were some signs of a widening of inequalities in smoking during pregnancy between the routine and manual group and all mothers between 2000 and 2005 (DOH, 2006).

The opportunity costs of children: childcare and work

The most obvious and important opportunity cost of children relates to maternal employment, a problem which in Britain has partly been approached by in-work tax-credits described previously and partly by the separate development of improved levels of quality childcare services and encouragement of 'family friendly' employment practices. The latter has seen the improvement of both maternity and paternity provision – a statutory minimum maternity leave is now six rather than three months and the aim is to move to a year. Maternity leave in the first year of infancy is not just a matter of parental income and opportunity costs but also one of improved developmental outcomes for the children. Studies clearly show that maternal leave is associated with better maternal and child health and maternal employment, with poorer cognitive development and behavioural problems for some children (for an overview see Waldfogel, 2006). Parents now have the additional right to ask for part-time or other flexible working practices – however, the high association of part-time female work with low pay makes this right a mixed blessing in terms of disposable income for many who are not in high status employment.

In the years prior to 1997, there had been some attempts to increase pre-school provision through income maintenance programmes using vouchers and through a limited additional element to in-work benefits. However, the biggest impact was from primary schools by changing their rules on access and opening more places to younger children (and collaring voucher and subsidy income). Of course, school provision remains the largest single source of childcare and extensions of hours of schooling and opening up nursery and other pre-primary provision make the largest impact on the opportunity costs of maternal employment. In 1998, the Blair Government set up the first ever National Childcare Strategy but left most improvements to the combination of local initiatives, a commitment to earlier part-time entry into education for three to four year olds and the demand-led subsidies that were part of in-work Tax Credits. Progress was patchy across municipal boundaries with greater deficiencies for more needy children and much of new provision not surviving when start-up funding ended (Skinner, 2006).

One of the major problems for up-take is that low-income mothers, in particular out-of-work lone parents returning to employment, the key group for child poverty reduction, were risk adverse and tended to choose informal childcare from relatives or friends – at low or little cost but that did not attract subsidy or support. Given the clear evidence on the need for good quality childcare for pre-school children in order to prevent behavioural and other problems (Waldfogel, 2006) this, and the fact that there was also a mixture in quality of more formal provision, is potentially crucial for child outcomes. The costs of childcare (outside of the school system and informal care) is also very high and meant that middle to high-earning parents tended to dominate supply and demand.

The response was The Government's Ten Year Strategy for Childcare in late 2004. This proposes Children's Centres in every community – a more generalized and less developmentally focused provision that previously envisaged in Sure Start and a parallel continued expansion of school provision – both for pre-primary 'early years' schooling and provide school-based care from 8 a.m. to 6 p.m. five days a week and extend provision from 33 to 38 weeks in the year. Quality will be improved through better training and supervision of childcare workers. Affordability will remain mostly a matter of improvements to income transfers – Working Tax Credits – to meet increased charges.

Social security and economic aspects of child poverty

This final part of the chapter addresses three questions: First, what do the UK's programmes to eliminate child poverty tell us about effectively combating child poverty? Second, how do these lessons fit into wider concerns about micro-economic and macro-economic economic concerns and thus economic growth? Third, what do the theoretical causes and justifications for social programmes to prevent child poverty suggest about the future of social protection, child poverty and economic growth?

Lessons from UK child poverty programmes

UK programmes concentrate on a combination of increased generosity of income transfers to children and improvements in child-related services, in particular education and pre-school provision. There has been a mixture of targeting approaches, which together have been termed as 'selective universalism', and they proceed by not only targeting the poorest individual children and poorest neighbourhoods but also additionally serving all children for some aspects and reducing income transfers at or above average income.

The policy approach of improving the generosity of income transfers can be accused of poor targeting because cash benefits are likely to be spent on things that do not benefit children best. However, this is not borne out in the United Kingdom where it has been shown that the increased resources given to parents through higher benefits and tax-credits have been largely spent on children's needs (Gregg et al., 2005). This is a crucial finding in both turning around growing differences in consumption in poor and non-poor families found previously in the United Kingdom (Gregg et al., 1999) and in confounding critics of income transfers who hypothesized that transfers would increase paren-tal consumption on alcohol and tobacco, for instance, and thus be det-rimental to child well-being.

The improved generosity of child transfers has had a direct effect on material hardship and absolute measures of poverty. The number of families with children reporting material hardship in both workless and in-work families has fallen (Lyons et al., 2006), and real incomes of the poorest families with children have grown over time (DWP, 2006).

Reductions in relative poverty have been more difficult to achieve as median income has risen ahead of prices in the United Kingdom. Even so, relative child poverty measures have fallen by 23 per cent (BHC) and 17 per cent (AHC) between 1998/1999 and 2004/2005. These are impres-sive reductions but unfortunately not sufficient to meet the intermedi-ate target of reducing child poverty by a quarter set for 2005. Figure 9.10 shows over a shorter time-frame how the numbers and composition of relative child poverty has changed since 2000/2001. The largest numeric changes have been in the reduction of non-working lone parents. However, countering this has been the rising but lower overall numbers of poor working lone parents. Overall, one half of reduced poverty has been through fewer workless lone parents. These results complement and confirm the labour market effects of the policy changes that have made work pay especially for lone parents (Brewer et al., 2005; Gregg and Harkness, 2003).

These successes have to be set alongside some mitigating effects of the transfers programmes. The high marginal tax rates that result from the combination of means-tested tapers and income taxation, explained in the previous section, have had an effect in reducing employment entry from potential second earners (predominantly women) in couples with children and have resulted in some lone parents reducing their hours of work.

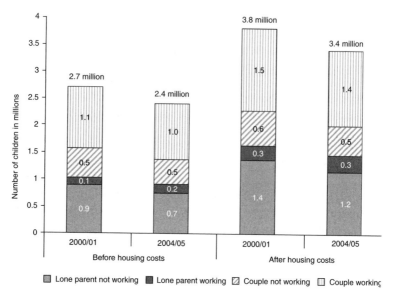

Figure 9.10   Number of children in relative poverty (below 60 per cent of median) in 2000/2001 and 2004/2005

Source: Authors' calculations from DWP 2006 and previous version.

Additionally, given the medium to long-term nature of the UK's child poverty target, it is also important to assess how far the current package of transfers and services will continue to deliver reductions in child poverty. It is clear that continued improvements in parental employment will raise the numbers of working parents, but the general agreement is that substantial constraints on parental employment will remain unless there is a greater investment in childcare. At the moment, the policy balance between specific and basic costs is not matched by sufficient resources to reduce the opportunity costs of employment (Gregg et al., 2006). More crucially, when the current in-work income support packages are projected into the future, they do not sustain their anti-poverty impact (Evans, 2006; Evans and Scarborough, 2006) particularly for relative poverty. The relative poverty line will rise roughly in line with earnings, but the in-work income package of Tax Credits and Child Benefits lag behind. Somewhat bizarrely, given the emphasis of ending child poverty through parental employment, the absolute poverty target based on increasing real income above poverty income levels in 1998/1999 will be met by social assistance package rising faster than prices (Evans, 2006). Child poverty in non-employed families will basically be eliminated on one absolute target measure but in-work poverty will worsen against the other relative target.

What greater commitment would be necessary to meet the target of ending relative child poverty by 2020? The answer is greater government spending. Hirsch (2006b) has demonstrated that a further £4 billion a year (0.3 per cent of GDP) is needed to halve child poverty by 2010 but that the cost increases for elimination by 2020 – and a further 1.6 per cent of GDP will be needed to meet the child poverty promise.

Child poverty, social policy and economic development

In this chapter, so far, we have considered the causes of child poverty, its incidence in the United Kingdom and the programmes that have been put in place to eliminate it in the country. Lessons from these programmes suggest that a mixture of income transfers and services targeted on families with children, some of which are additionally targeted on poor children, can make significant impacts. But these findings miss out any discussion of the wider impacts on child poverty and related social policy on economic and social development, the core concern of this book, and it is to these that I now turn.

The crucial and unavoidable fact about children is that they are the future productive population of a country. These future consequences can thus put a break on economic development both in terms of basic productivity and returns from skilled labour and in fiscal revenues. National efficiency can be achieved through 'involvement in education as it made labour more productive, thus contributing to economic performance' (Barr, 2004, p. 19). This is true for both developing and advanced economies as economic growth thus depends in part on human capital, productivity and social development of citizens. Child poverty thus undermines the crucial human investment that underpins any economy. It is, perhaps, easiest to illustrate this by discussing the consequences of child poverty. These can be both short-term and immediate on the children of today but also long-term on the adults as they represent the next generation. The consequences can also be immediate and individual to the persons concerned and have wider social and economic outcomes.

Even if we solely consider a 'minimal' view of needs based solely on short-term consequences, adequate nutrition and health during childhood has direct effect on individual well-being and ill children affect parental economic activity. Even minimal definitions of needs have social consequences leading to increased use of health services and can have second-order effects on school provision, protective care and spending to deal with behavioural problems. Where these second-order costs do not call on socially provided public services, as in many poorer developing countries, they will be taken on by informal care – by family in the main, with all the associated opportunity costs on their economic and productive activity.

But the consequences of child poverty are also long-term. Evidence from developing countries (Harper, 2004) and from US and British birth cohort studies (Duncan and Brooks-Gunn, 1994; Gregg et al., 1999) clearly show that child poverty has a lifetime consequence of having higher chance of adult poverty. The consequences of not completing primary education have been estimated in Latin America as lowering entry level earnings by 50 per cent (Harper and Marcus, 2000) while Gregg and Machin have shown the link between child poverty and later earnings capacity in the United Kingdom, where there is universal primary education (Gregg and Machin, 2000). Health is a crucial factor. International evidence shows that the link between child poverty and child morbidity and mortality, the so-called 'social gradient' in health, is strong (Marmot and Wilkinson, 1999). This is true across developing and industrialized countries. The recent European Health Report confirmed that 'The evidence clearly demonstrates that social factors account for the bulk of health disparities, and people from socially disadvantaged groups get sicker and die sooner than people in more privileged social positions' (WHO, 2005, p. 46).

Overall, it is estimated that one billion children worldwide will have grown up with impaired mental development by 2020 (Harper, 2004). Individuals who were poor as children have greater incidence of educational, employment and psychological disadvantage. Their view of the consequences of child poverty on individuals are summarized by UNICEF as follows:

> there is a close correlation between growing up in poverty and the likelihood of educational under-achievement, poor health, teenage pregnancy, substance abuse, criminal and anti-social behaviour, low pay, unemployment and long-term welfare dependence. It is acknowledged that such problems may arise from circumstances that are associated with, but not necessarily caused by, low income (for instance, low levels of parental education or parenting skills); nonetheless, child poverty appears to be a consistent and catalytic element in the mix of circumstance that perpetuates such problems from one generation to the next. (UNICEF, 2005, p. 6)

Some of the adults who grew up poor and who have low earnings are likely to transmit poverty to their children; although, it is dangerous to be over-deterministic about this inter-generational transmission of poverty, and UK evidence points to a 12 per cent likelihood of poor children being a poor adult (Blanden and Gibbons, 2006). It is thus important to remember that there is both an 88 per cent chance of a poor child not being a poor adult in Britain and that other contemporary factors determine a far larger set of reasons for poverty of adults and thus of parents and children.

The longer term social consequences of child poverty are wider than merely deprivation leading to health and education consequences within individuals, families or households over time. Looking at the United Kingdom, Hirsch sees the social impacts as increased public expenditure on health, crime and other areas, reduced economic performance due to losses in productivity from skilled workforce with the resulting loss in income and in tax take (Hirsch, 2006a).

What role does social policy for children have in economic development? The core problem for policy is that if it wants to combat child poverty it has to respond on short-term needs; it has to meet the contemporary cost problems associated with children and assist in investment in them, but the majority of any economic gain from this will be in the future. Help with contemporary costs means that children can usually only be targeted through their parents – adults, especially for those needs that are best responded to in the household – by meeting the basic and specific costs of children. Cash and in-kind transfers to assist with these needs bring with them the potential to influence adult behaviour as well as child well-being. Contributing to household income can lead to poor incentives for additional economic activity, and the so called *income substitution* effects are well known in the economic literature.

Transfers for children may also affect fertility behaviour: a particular problem where families with many children are more likely to be poor. An alternative and sometimes preferred approach (for reasons of both fiscal constraint and ideology) is to provide services for children – primarily healthcare and education at subsidized or no cost. These can be designed to be pro-poor through charging policies and thus justified as equalizing *opportunity* without interfering with parental incentives.

The combination of recent economic and financial crises and the adoption of child poverty programmes across a number of developing countries provides some clear evidence of the effectiveness of transfers and services to children (Das, Do and Özler, 2005; Shady and Arujo, 2006;

Skoufias and di Maro, 2006). Harrison in her overview of globalization and poverty points to the important contribution that scholarship programmes and conditional transfers made to maintaining human capital in times of financial crises across the developing world (Harrison, 2006). There is a newly emerging consensus on the appropriateness of social security for children.

However, if we return to the issue of costs and causes of child poverty outlined previously, an approach that relies entirely on income transfers or food aid tries to neutralize only one area of cost – the *specific costs* – and does little to address the underlying importance of both basic need costs and of opportunity costs that will still affect take-up. Taking education as an example, a child can neither walk to free schooling with no shoes nor concentrate if hungry. Furthermore, education is rarely 'free' in practice with 'informal charges' common in developing countries alongside costs of materials. The time the child spends at school is lost to the household in informal or formal employment. Transfers and services also help the poorest to adapt to the pressures of schooling and employment for children (Edmonds, 2007).

There are important trade-offs to be considered by policymakers across the world – in both developing and industrialized countries. If we turn once more to consider the United Kingdom, in its attempt to match the lowest European incidence of child poverty and the '5 per cent club' of Nordic Europe, the United Kingdom is employing a very different model of anti-poverty support that focuses on means-tested transfers to both supplement income and help towards childcare charges. The Nordic countries have approached these trade-offs differently, and their low child poverty rates reflect publicly funded childcare services at minimal charge and maternity and parental leave that is generous in both duration and income terms. The opportunity costs of children are lower because the costs of childhood are far more socialized and risks to income and consumption in having children are less. This means that even if the United Kingdom converges with these countries when measuring incomes, it is not clear whether living standards will converge similarly, because Nordic countries' services and subsidies to provision will not be matched but replaced by what the United Kingdom counts as family income, which will be whittled away by high childcare and other costs.

It is not clear whether these tradeoffs are being consistently approached in developing countries either. If we think carefully about a set of programmes that protect rights to education and prohibit child labour, then these can be seen to impose additional opportunity costs that can least be met by poor families, and these programmes sit awkwardly alongside the aim to end child poverty when poor families are not able to participate in education in a cost neutral way. This suggests that transfers in addition to schooling are required to enable the poor to participate equally.

Indeed, the choice between investing in opportunity and in supporting today's consumption needs and income inequalities is too often posited as mutually exclusive when in fact it is a trade-off that is difficult to reconcile conclusively. Is it *ever* really possible to solely equalize opportunities without addressing underlying differences in resources? Today's parental and social inequalities affect children's lifetime opportunities and solely equalizing opportunities for children without tackling underlying wider inequality leaves many of the causes of poverty and inequality of opportunity untouched. Of course, current ideology and political marketing mean that programmes that use the label of 'opportunity' are viewed more favourably than ones couched in terms of redistribution. But by placing rhetorical emphasis on programmes that address opportunity and which are thus seen as "investments" while focusing negative rhetoric on programmes of passive transfers, policy makers have signed up to an unachievable trade-off in which tomorrow's equalized opportunity is always prejudiced by today's inequality. Opportunity and inequality are thus chasing themselves down an endless hall of mirrors rather than squaring up face to face.

Facing squarely up to child poverty is something that the United Kingdom has done and nothing should deter admiration of the United Kingdom's promise to eliminate child poverty. It has set an international example of how to put a promise into place, set benchmarks and be transparent in its policy aims and measurement. Indeed, this approach has stimulated interest and similar programmes in New Zealand and admiration among progressive policy analysts in the United states. The bottom line is that since 1997 reduced child poverty in the United Kingdom has flowed from political commitment to redirect resources to ending it.

However, a final coda is appropriate at this point, because recent evidence also highlights the limitations of seeing children just in purely quantitative terms – as investments, risks to consumption levels etc. – and this approach has underpinned this chapter in order to best capture the economic arguments. The new UNICEF multiple indicator index of children's well-being across rich countries has worsened the United Kingdom's ranking than previous use of income alone. The United Kingdom is now ranked lowest when child health and safety, education, family and peer relationships, behaviour and risks and subjective well-being are taken into account alongside material well-being (UNICEF, 2007). However, this does not exactly overturn all of the previous discussion as, even when the basic costs and needs of children have mostly been assured, it is still those countries where more socialized child interventions are prominent that promote child well-being best. It is no coincidence that Nordic states fare best in this new league – they have both squared up to child poverty and reconciled the opportunity and inequality dilemma more squarely.

References

Acheson D. (1998). Independent Inquiry into Inequalities in Health Report. London: The Stationery Office.

Barr N. (2004). *The Economics of the Welfare State: fourth edition*, Oxford: Oxford University Press.

Becker G. (1962). 'Investment in Human Capital: A Theoretical Analysis', *The Journal of Political Economy*, 70, 9–49.

Blandon J. and Gibbons S. (2006). The Persistence of Poverty across Generations: A View from Two British Cohorts. Bristol: The Policy Press.

Brewer M., Duncan A., Shephard A. and Suárez M.-J. (2005). Did Working Families' Tax Credit work? The final evaluation of the impact of in-work support on parents' labour supply and take-up behaviour in the UK, London: H.M Revenue and Customs.

Blow L., Goodman A., Walker I. and Windmeijer F. (2005). Parental Background and Child Outcomes: How Much Does Money Matter and What Else Matters? Research Report RR660, London: Department for Education and Skills.

Brunwin T., Clemens S., Deakin G. and Mortimer E. (2005). *The Cost of Schooling*, Research Report RR588. London: Department for Education and Skills.

Chronic Poverty Research Centre (2005). *Chronic Poverty Report 2004–05*. Manchester: CPRC, University of Manchester.

Das J., Do Q.-T. and Özler B. (2005). 'Reassessing Conditional Cash Transfer Programs', *World Bank Research Observer*, 20(1), 57–80.

Department of Health (DOH) (2002). Tackling Health Inequalities: 2002 Cross-Cutting Review. London: DOH.

Department of Social Security (1998). A New Contract For Welfare: New Ambitions For Our Country, Cm 3805, London: The Stationery Office.

Department for Work and Pensions (2005a). Tax Benefit Model Tables: April 2005, London: Department for Work and Pensions.

Department for Work and Pensions (2005b). Measuring Child Poverty, London: DWP.

Department for Work and Pensions (2005c). Households Below Average Income: 1994/95-2004/05, London: Department for Work and Pensions.

Department of Work and Pensions (DWP) (2006). Households Below Average Income 1994/5–2004/5. London: DWP.

Duncan D. J. and Brooks-Gunn J. (eds) (1994). *The Consequences of Growing Up Poor*. New York: Russell Sage Foundation.

Edmunds E. (2007). *Child Labor*, NBER Working Paper 12926. Cambridge, MA: NBER.

Evans M. (2006). 'Target Practice: Ambition and Ambiguity in the Aim to End Child Poverty', *Poverty*, 124, Summer 2006, 11–14.

Evans M. and Scarborough J. (2006). *Can Current Policy End Child Poverty by 2020?* York: Joseph Rowntree Foundation.

Gregg P., Harkness S. and Machin S. (1999). *Child Development and Family Income*. York: Joseph Rowntree Foundation.

Gregg P., Harkness S. and Macmillan L. (2006). *Welfare to Work Policies and Child Poverty*. York: Joseph Rowntree Foundation.

Gregg P. and Machin S. (2000). 'The Relationship between Childhood Experiences, Subsequent Educational Attainment and Adult Labour Market Performance.' In K. Vleminckx and T. Smeeding (eds), *Child Well-Being, Child Poverty and Child Policy in Modern Nations*. Bristol: The Policy Press.

Gregg P., Waldfogel J. and Washbrook E. (2005). *Expenditure Patterns Post Weflare-Reform in the UK: Are Low Income Families Catching up? Casepaper 99*, London: Centre for Analysis of Social Exclusion, London School of Economics.

Gregg P. and Harkness, S. (2003). 'Welfare Reform and the Employment of Lone Parents', in Dickens R., Gregg P. and Wadsworth J., *The Labour Market under New Labour*, Oxford: Oxford University Press.

Harper C. (2004). *Breaking Poverty Cycles – The Importance of Action in Childhood*, CHIP Policy Briefing 8. London: Childhood Poverty Policy and Research Centre.

Harper C. and Marcus R. (2000). 'Mortgaging Africa's Future: The Long-term Costs of Child Poverty', *Society for International Development*, 43(1), 65–72. London: Sage.

Harrison A. (2006). *Globalization And Poverty*, NBER Working Paper 12347. Cambridge, MA: National Bureau of Economic Research.

Hirsch D. (2006a). The Cost of Not Ending Child Poverty: How We Can Think about It, How It Might Be Measured, and Some Evidence. York: Joseph Rowntree Foundation.

Hirsch D. (2006b). What Will It Take to End Child Poverty? Firing on All Cylinders. York: Joseph Rowntree Foundation.

Liverpool Victoria Friendly Society (2006). *Annual Child Cost Survey 2005*. Bournemouth: LVFS.

Lyons N., Barnes M. and Sweiry D. (2006). Families with Children in Britain: Findings from the Family and Children Survey 2004, DWP Research Report 340. Leeds: Corporate Document Services.

Marmot M. and Wilkinson R. (1999). *Social Determinants of Health*. Oxford: Oxford University Press.

Middleton S., Ashworth K. and Braithwaite R. (1999). *Small Fortunes*. York: Joseph Rowntree Foundation.

Mitchell R., Shaw M. and Dorling D. (2000). *Inequalities in Life and Death: What If Britain Were More Equal?* Bristol: The Policy Press.

OECD (2000). Knowledge and Skills for Life: First Results from PISA 2000. Paris: OECD.

OECD (2003). Learning for Tomorrow's World First Results from PISA 2003. Paris: OECD.

Petrou S., Kupek E., Hockley C. and Goldacre M. (2006). 'Social Class Inequalities in Childhood Mortality and Morbidity in an English Population', *Paediatric and Perinatal Epidemiology*, 20(1), 14–23.

Ridge T. (2003). *Childhood Poverty and Social Exclusion: From a Child's Perspective*, Bristol: Policy Press.

Schady N. and Araujo M. C. (2006). *Cash Transfers, School Enrollment and Child Work: Evidence from a Randomixed Experiment in Ecuador*, Impact Evalauation Series no 3 World Bank Policy Research Working Paper 3930. Washington DC: The World Bank.

Sefton, T. (2002). *Recent Changes in the Distribution of the Social Wage*, CASE paper 62, London: Centre for Analysis of Social Exclusion, London School of Economics.

Skinner C. (2006). *How Can Childcare Help to End Child Poverty?* York: Joseph Rowntree Foundation.

Skoufias E. and di Maro V. (2006). *Conditional Cash Transfers, Adult Work Incentives and Poverty*, Impact Evalauation Series no 5 World Bank Policy Research Working Paper 3973. Washington DC: The World Bank.

UNDP (2006). *Human Development Report 2006*. New York: United Nations Development Programme.

UNICEF (2000). *Child Poverty in Rich Countries, 2000*, Innocenti Report Card No 1, Florence: UNICEF Innocenti Research Centre.

UNICEF (2005).*Child Poverty in Rich Countries, 2005*, Innocenti Report Card No 6. Florence: UNICEF Innocenti Research Centre.

UNICEF (2007). An Overview of Child Well-Being in Rich Countries, Innocenti Report Card No 7. Florence: UNICEF Innocenti Research Centre.

Waldfogel J. (2006). *What Children Need*. Cambridge, MA and London: Harvard University Press.

WHO (2005). *The European Health Report 2005*. Copenhagen: WHO European Regional Office.

10
Singapore: Social Investment, the State and Social Security

James Lee and S. Vasoo

Robert Wade's (1990) study of South Korea, Taiwan and Japan in the late 1980s resulted in a better understanding of East Asian developmentalism as the 'governed' or 'guided' market and further invigorated the study of the 'developmental state' since Johnson's (1982) formative study of economic development in Japan. Despite the fact that the diversity of the developmental experiences in East Asia defies easy generalization, one pivotal element is the centrality of the role of the state in fostering economic growth and development. Developmental theorists have pointed to two linked and yet quite independent issues: first, the capacity of government, or what Evans (2006) termed 'bureaucratic capacity' to respond to changing circumstances both within and outside the national economy; second, the degree to which institutional arrangements are capable of being fully integrated, or simply put, whether state institutions are capable of synergizing with social institutions in such a way as to foster growth.

A developmental state with strong state capacity could stifle such synergy while one with low state capacity could foster chaos, either way failing to attain developmental objectives. This chapter will focus on the second element – institutional arrangements that aim to facilitate integration. In particular, the unique case of the integration between social investment and social welfare will be examined. This is the case of the Central Provident Fund and the public housing system in Singapore. This example is unique in two respects. First, the social security system of Singapore is fully integrated with the housing system resulting in a first-level integration within the welfare system. Second, the welfare system is integrated with the economic system largely through capital formation, housing investment, mass housing consumption, using asset appreciation as an incentive to maintain a second-level integration and also boosting the economy and employment through an expanding construction sector.

This chapter examines the nature of these institutional arrangements and demonstrates through a case study how Singapore's housing system contributes towards understanding the feasibility of socio-economic integration (Vasoo and Lee, 2001). The chapter begins with a brief description of Singapore's economy and its social security system. It then examines Singapore's economic development with reference to housing and social security by focusing on the two levels of integration mentioned earlier. The chapter concludes with a discussion on a number of issues and challenges facing Singapore arising from these institutional arrangements.

Singapore: basic facts and the social security system

In the middle of the twentieth century, Singapore was a small tropical city with high humidity, plenty of marshland and a population of about one million people, mostly of Chinese descent. However, by 1980, the country emerged as one of the new economic powers of East Asia with a per capita GDP of US$6,865 and a population of 2.4 million (see Table 10.1). In 2005, Singapore had a per capita GDP of US$44,738 (ranked 5th in the 2006–2007 *Global Competitiveness Index*) and a population of 3.54 million. Since the early 1960s, public housing has been developed specifically to advance social and economic development. What are the factors responsible for this dramatic change since Singapore became an independent country in 1965?

One explanation is that Singapore has the right combination of leadership, vision, development strategy and high quality labour. Henry Kissinger emphasized the role of leadership. In the Foreword to Lee Kuan Yew's memoir *From Third World to First*, he states 'As the main British naval base in the Far East, Singapore had neither the prospect nor aspiration for nationhood...but history shows that normally prudent, ordinary calculations can be overturned by extraordinary personalities' (Lee, 2000, p. x). However, despite its importance, leadership is only one factor and vision and strategy, or more accurately, the institutional arrangements that combine them need to be considered.

For Singapore, the beginning of one such institution was purely accidental. When introduced by the British colonial government in the 1950s, the social security retirement system was never meant to be run as it is today. The Central Provident Fund (CPF) began as a self-funding

Table 10.1 Key macroeconomic indicators on Singapore 1960–2005

	1960	1970	1980	1990	1999	2001	2003	2004	2005
Population (thousands)	1646	2075	2414	3016	3894	3325	3438	3484	3544
GDP (at 2000 price)	6710.8	16057.5	37631.7	76996.4	145229.8	156006.3	167549.3	182301.1	194371.3
GDP growth rate	–	13.7	9.7	9.2	7.2	-2.4	3.1	8.8	6.6
GDP per capita	1306	2789	10405	21915	35371	37014	38434	42833	44738
Gross fixed capital formation (at 1990 price)	–	6.9bn	19.2bn	32.7bn	68.5bn	–	40.3bn (2000 price)	44.4 (2000 price)bn	44.4bn (2000 price)
Inflation rate	0.3	0.4	8.5	3.4	0.4	1.0	0.5	1.7	0.5
Total labour (thousands)	471.9	650.9	1115.3	1537.0	1911.6	2330.5	2312.3	2341.9	2594.1
Unemploy–ment rate	–	–	–	–	2.8	2.7	4.0	3.4	3.1
Annual growth in ext trade %	–	–	–	12.4	6.2	-7.3	20.5	21.0	9.4
Govt. debts	–	–	–	51.4bn	125.8bn	148.9bn	169.3bn	186.6bn	200.0bn

Note: Values here are in Singapore dollars millions (S$mn) and billions (bn).

Source: Author's computations based on statistics Singapore (various years). http://www.singstat.gov.sg/papers/economy.html#other%20econ

savings scheme or a save-as-you-earn (SAYE) system rather than a pay-as-you-go (PAYG) system. The self-funding model was similar to provident funds created by the British for their colonies for good political reasons. This model ensured that British funds would not be drained to meet the colony's social security needs. The Singaporean provident fund turned out to be a valuable bequest when the People's Action Party (PAP) government took over in 1965. From the beginning, the CPF scheme was designed to provide retirement pensions. Despite pressures from workers who wanted to be able to withdraw their savings should they fall ill or become unemployed, the government stood firm insisting that savings could only be withdrawn upon retirement. However, the rule was subsequently liberalized in the late 1960s when a home ownership scheme was introduced to allow people to finance the purchase of public housing with their CPF savings.

Since then, the provident fund has been slowly adapting to the changing needs of an increasingly affluent population. Singaporeans can now use their provident fund accumulations for various purposes, including retirement, health care, meeting the costs of higher education and even investments. However, the most salient features of the scheme have remained intact since its creation in 1955. It is compulsory for all employees and is non-redistributive. The Central Provident Fund has three separate accounts. First, the Ordinary Account, which is used for retirement, buying a home, buying insurance, investment and education. Second, the Medisave Account, which can be used to pay hospital bills and approved medical insurance; and third, the Special Account, which is reserved for old-age contingencies.

It can be seen from Table 10.2 that the employers' contribution had stabilized at 13 per cent since 2003, but recently it was increased to 14.5 per cent. In July 2007, the total contribution rate was 34.5 per cent, with 14.5 per cent coming from the employer and 20 per cent from the employee.[1] The recent increase of 1.5 per cent in the employers' contribution represents a favourable assessment of the country's future economic performance and is seen as an afforded contribution designed to protect workers' future. The percentage contribution rate also changes with age. Elderly people contribute only 12.5 per cent after the age of 55 years and 7 per cent after 60 years regardless of their income level. Monthly contributions (in Singapore dollars) are subject to a maximum of $600 for the employer and $1,200 for the employee, based on a salary ceiling of $6,000 a month. Although contributions to the Ordinary Account are not mandatory for the self-employed, many do contribute in order to enjoy the tax break and the benefit of setting

Table 10.2 CPF contribution rate (per cent)

Year	Employer	Employee	Medisave	Total
1955	5	5	–	10
1968	6.5	6.5	–	13
1970	8	8	–	16
1972	14	10	–	24
1973	15	11	–	26
1974	15	15		30
1977	15.5	15.5	–	31
1978	16.5	16.5	–	33
1979	20.5	16.5	–	37
1982	22	23	–	45
1984	25	25	6	50
1985	25	25	6	50
1986	10	25	6	35
1989	15	23	6	38
1992	18	22	6	40
1995	20	20	6	40
1997	20	20	6	40
1999	10	20	6	30
2000	14	20	8	34
2002	16	20	6–8.5	36
2003	13	20	6–8.5	33
2004	13	20	6–8.5	33
2005	13	20	6–8.5	33
2006	13	20	6–8.5	33

Source: Author's computations based on Singapore Annual Reports various years and Singapore CPF Annual Report various years.

aside funds for old age. However, self-employed people are required to contribute 6 per cent of their annual net trade income to their Medisave Accounts on a monthly basis.

Each member's savings account earns a market-linked interest rate, which is based on the 12-month fixed deposit and month-end savings rates of four major local banks. The rate is revised every three months. The programme guarantees members a minimum interest rate of 2.5 per cent. Savings in the Ordinary and Special Accounts earn an additional 1.5 per cent above the normal rate of interest, because they are used for retirement and longer-term savings purposes. Earned interest is tax free.

It is of course possible to challenge the fundamental organizing philosophy of the Central Provident Fund and conclude that Singapore is merely operating a large paternalistic saving bank with rules and restrictions on withdrawal and consumption, and that it is nothing like a traditional social security scheme that embodies the advantages of pooled risk and social justice. From the perspective of neoliberal economics, it might even be argued that the Singaporean arrangement is detrimental to the general welfare of the population, because consumption is orchestrated by the state and hence thwarts individual choice and self-determination in the disposition of wealth. However, these questions need to be answered on the basis of empirical evidence and, in this regard, several economic studies by economists provide some useful insights which are discussed in the next section.

Social security and economic development in Singapore

For many economists, grappling with the relationship between social security and economic development has been a difficult one. Social security has been a major component of Western welfare states since Chancellor Bismarck launched the first state-run social insurance programme in Germany in the late nineteenth century. However, the question of whether social security is compatible with economic growth only emerged in the past three decades when the global economy became more volatile and inter-connected. Is social security expenditure harmful to economic growth? How compatible are social security expenditures and economic development? In the early 1960s, very few economists were interested in the compatibility issue conceptually or theoretically. Full employment, rising real wages and state pensions, augmented by adequate child benefit, were assumed to be able to eliminate poverty. Social security was regarded as a technical topic best left largely to those specializing in social policy. Since then, the situation has changed as welfare state performance has been extensively studied by economists. Research on unemployment insurance, invalidity benefits, the funding of pensions and other economic aspects of social security have been studied by both macroeconomists and microeconomists and many are quite divided over the issue of whether social and economic policy are compatible.

Martin Feldstein (1974, 1976) was one of the earliest opponents of the incompatibility thesis. He examined two types of social security spending – retirement pensions and unemployment insurance – and concluded that both had adverse effects on economic development. He argued that the 'social security programme in United States consumed approximately half of the personal savings, implying that it substantially reduced the stock of capital and the level of national income' (Feldstein, 1974, p. 22). He also suggested that 'unemployment insurance encourages temporary layoffs and that a reform of it could substantially lower the permanent rate of unemployment' (Feldstein 1976, p. 956). In his more recent work, Feldstein (2005) claimed that many social security programmes appear to be redistributive but that, in fact, most social security benefits go to middle- and higher-income households.

While Feldstein focused on the non-saving effects of social security, other economists focused on the problems of the pay-as-you-go social security system. Ehrlick and Zhong (1998) suggested that social security would soon face financial collapse as a result of a slow down in labour productivity and a continuously aging population. Thus, the general disposition of contemporary debates on social security is towards privatization and the individualization of social security accounts. However, one of the weaknesses of the incompatibility approach is that most studies are based on regression analyses, meaning that cultural and institutional variables are either assumed to be constant or are otherwise taken for granted. Accordingly, findings based on time series data run the danger of yielding relatively static and crude results.

Proponents of the incompatibility thesis make varied arguments. While some are clear that there is a trade off between economic growth and social welfare, others tend to suggest that the problem is really associated with the suitability or workability of institutional arrangements and of integrating seemingly unrelated policy domains. On the other hand, some economists believe that there is no fundamental contradiction between social security and economic development. In the words of a pro-compatibility economist, Anthony Atkinson (1999, p. 4), 'it is now widely realized that social and economic policy are inextricably intertwined. It makes no sense to discuss economic and social policy in isolation. To a considerable extent, the present problems of the welfare state are the result of economic failures.' Even anti-compatibility economist like Martin Feldstein agrees that there are two legitimate economic reasons for providing social insurance: the first is the presence of asymmetric information that weakens the functioning of private insurance, and hence explaining why the state needs to assume some responsibility of provisions; and the second is 'the inability of the government to distinguish between those who are poor in old age because of bad luck or a lack of foresight from those who are intentionally "gaming" the system by not saving' (Feldstein, 2005, p. 7).

A gap in social policy analysis: social investment and social development

Outside the realm of economics, social policy analysts are also interested in studying the impact of social security expenditures on the economy. Primarily, their focus has been on its structure, coverage, strategies and methods of financing (Dixon, 1999). They assume that social security expenditure is essentially concerned with consumption and that its investment effect is negligible. Midgley (1994, 1995, 1997, 1999) was one of the first to suggest that social expenditures could and should be viewed as part of society's investment portfolio and should not, therefore, be considered as consumption. He believed that the neglect of the investment impact of social expenditures is partly the result of a strong ethical tradition in British social policy in the post-Second World War era when the welfare state was premised on the ideal that the government should distribute welfare resources collectively irrespective of its impact on economic development. Nonetheless, this does not mean that the main proponents of redistributive social policy were dismissive of social policy's impact on the broader economy. For example, Richard Titmuss's (1962) study of British income redistribution statistics insisted that the social, political and economic dimensions were interrelated.

The study of social policy took a turn in the 1970s when the oil crisis triggered a sea change in the world economy. From a post-war social consensus about welfare expansion, social policy development was hijacked by economic recessions and took on a different trajectory. Stability began to evaporate in the 1970s and 1980s as governments sought to rationalize welfare through privatization. Market liberalism and neoconservative political practices soon became important aspects of government action. Towards the end of the twentieth century, Western scholars had shifted their focus from the study of welfare-state expansion to analyzing its regress. The study of European welfare-state retrenchment has now become a growth industry (Korpi, 2003).

Almost parallel with this development, was a strand of social policy studies that sought to review the role of social investment in social policymaking. The idea that social expenditures, when properly integrated with the economy, bring positive impact to growth slowly gathered momentum in the 1990s. Social expenditures here refer to a broad spectrum of social policies, including public housing, education and health. How various social policy domains interact with each other, and how they collectively affect macroeconomic development thus forms new focus of policy studies. Originating in the field of development studies in the 1960s and the 1970s, social investment was seen as a concerted effort by the governments of the developing countries to concentrate limited human and capital resources on economic development. Midgley's work, which was mentioned earlier, highlights 'the need to integrate economic and social policy because social expenditures in the form of social investment do not detract from but contribute positively to economic development' (Midgley and Tang, 2001, p. 246). From this perspective, social development is selective rather than universal, inclusive rather than exclusive in that it emphasizes social interventions that transcend remedial and maintenance-oriented approaches by implementing programmes that draw previously marginalized people into the mainstream of the economy. 'In a strict sense, social development cannot take place without economic development and economic development is meaningless if it fails to bring about significant improvements in the well-being of the population as a whole' (Midgley, 1997, p. 181).

The developmental approach in social welfare thus challenges the basic neoliberal argument that social programmes are harmful to growth. In addition, the United Nation Research Institute for Social Development (UNRISD) has also revived in recent years its interest in the contribution of social policy to economic and social development. In a recent paper, Mkandawire (2001), Director of UNRISD, argues that social policies can be used to enhance social capacities for economic development. In addition, there is also a revival of interest in growth economics and the emergence of the so-called 'new growth theories' which recognize that social development contains crucial instruments for economic development. These ideas will be explored with reference to Singapore and, particularly, its housing and social security policies.

First-level integration: integrating housing and social security

Singapore's public housing programme was launched in the 1960s, and it has now grown to become one of the largest of its kind in the world today. Many Western observers believe that the Singapore's achievement in the field of housing has been spectacular, but others have questioned the desirability and sustainability of such high level of state involvement (Chua, 2003; Yeung, 2003). In Singapore, public housing generally refers to the dominant state-subsidized home ownership sector. The state produces and distributes 86 per cent of the housing stock mainly in the form of for-sale residential flats, perhaps the largest share by any modern government. It provides one of the most sophisticated housing ladders in East Asia in terms of housing choice and quality. The Singapore housing system has effectively achieved a monopolistic position, to the extent that private housing constitutes only a very small percentage of the housing market (10 per cent), largely confined to top-end housing for the very rich. Singaporeans have two lifetime opportunities to purchase government-built flats, and this right is confined to nationals only. In the early 1980s, people nearing retirement capitalized on house-price inflation and used their gains to buy in the private housing market, thus fuelling speculative activities, something that former Prime Minister Lee Kuan Yew (2000) regretted in his memoir. He noted that as property prices rose, everybody wanted to make a profit on the sale of their homes and then upgrade to the biggest home they could afford. Instead of the government choking off demand by charging a levy to reduce windfall profits, it accommodated the citizenry by increasing the availability of new homes. Unfortunately, this decision aggravated the real estate bubble and made it more painful when the currency crisis struck in 1997.

However, from a broader perspective, a second chance to purchase a government flat stimulates the development of an active resale market, thus providing much needed impetus to the economy. This was achieved by fusing two ingenuous institutions: namely, the Housing Development Board (HDB) and the Central Provident Fund (CPF). The HDB, which commenced the public home ownership programme in 1964, has since become one of the largest public developers in the world. The board was already in place prior to independence. The provident fund was initiated during the colonial period in 1955, and it aimed to provide some form of retirement benefits but incurring little financial risks for the government. In the beginning, the contribution rate was kept at a low 5 per cent for workers and a matching 5 per cent from employers. However, in 1984 the contribution rate reached its peak of 25 per cent totalling 50 per cent of the payroll. The rate has since gone down and has stabilized at 13 per cent for employers and 20 per cent for employees (Table 10.2). However, for new residents to Singapore, the contribution rate is maintained at 5 per cent for the first two years' of residence to allow them to adjust to the job market. Originally, the major part of the accumulated savings could only be withdrawn at the age of 55 for retirement purposes. In 1968–1981, however, provident fund rules were modified to allow savings to be withdrawn earlier for a down payment on a home, stamp duties and other related costs.

At first, Singaporeans did not show much enthusiasm for home ownership. This was largely because few could afford to purchase private homes. However, when the government changed the legislation in 1968 to allow members to use their provident fund savings as a down-payment for housing, the sales of Housing Board flats increased significantly. In 1981, the rules were further relaxed to allow withdrawals to be used to finance mortgage repayment for private housing. As was mentioned earlier, the rules for the use of CPF savings have since been augmented further to allow for the creation of healthcare (Medisave) and education (Edusave) accounts. The diversification of the use of CPF savings is intended not only to reduce reliance on the state to meet old-age retirement and healthcare needs but also to boost investment. From Table 10.2, it can be seen that the rate of contribution has been used as a leverage mechanism to regulate investment and consumption. From 1997 to 1999, the contribution rate was cut from 40 per cent to 30 per cent, largely to boost consumption after the East Asian financial crisis. Using Keynesian ideas, the government's policy reflects the view that economic contraction requires a boost in consumption and that savings should not be encouraged.

In operational terms, the government provides development loans and annual grants to finance the Housing Development Board. This funding comes largely from the Central Provident Fund. This takes the form of government bonds at a fixed interest rate, thus explaining why Singapore has debt servicing even during a time of positive economic growth (see Table 10.1). The circuit of capital is completed by the Central Provident Fund providing loan repayments to the Housing Development Board on behalf of public housing buyers. The essence of this phase of the circuit of capital is the integration of the individual saving function with the collective housing investment function, thus enabling the possibility of mass mobilization in effective consumption which is an essential condition for growth. Housing here fulfilled two important roles: the mass satisfaction of both spatial needs and investment needs (DisPasquale and Wheaton, 1996). The Housing Development Board mortgage interest rate is pegged at 0.1 per cent above the Central Provident Fund interest rate, which is generally about 2 per cent below the market mortgage interest rate provided by commercial banks. The advantage of the first circuit is that it overcomes the problem of market failure in terms of low-income housing finance which is encountered by most countries.

Second-level integration: capital formation and growth

The second circuit of capital concerns a more complex interaction of the housing sector with the wider economy. However, what is demonstrated here is at best a partial view of the effects of housing investment in the second circuit of capital. First, housing investment forms an important part of fixed capital formation. For the period 1976–1997, an average of 9 per cent of Singapore's GDP was devoted to housing construction each year, while comparative figures for the United States and the United Kingdom were less than 4 per cent (Phang, 2001). In 1965–1998, the construction sector grew at a rate of 9.4 per cent, exceeding the average GDP growth of 8.8 per cent. Of the roughly one million housing units that were built, 82 per cent are attributable to public sector developers. The domination of public housing construction means that government housing policy has a direct impact on the creation of employment for construction workers and hence its direct effects on income and social well-being. According to the Economic Survey of Singapore 2006 (MTI, 2007), the construction sector continued to grow by 4.7 per cent in the final quarter of 2006, slightly lower than the 5.8 per cent rate of growth in the previous quarter. Although the construction sector suffered during the 1999–2004 period as a result of the East Asian financial crisis, it has rebounded in the past two years as a result of the continued recovery of the Singapore economy.

Second, the link between housing and social security also has a direct effect on the development of the housing loan market. For a long time, the Housing Development Board did not only provide concessionary housing interest rates for eligible Singapore citizens but also provided 'market rate' loans to those who were not eligible for low interest loans, thus playing the role of a commercial bank. During the peak of the Board's mortgage business, it took up 66 per cent of the market share (Phang, 2001, p. 451). Including the 10 per cent market share of the then Post Office Savings Bank – Credit POSB, the government practically monopolized three quarters of the mortgage market since 1986. It should be noted that the bank is a subsidiary of the Development Bank of Singapore (DBS).

The extension of Central Provident Fund for private housing finance has also led to rapid growth of housing loans from commercial banks. These increased from 6 per cent in 1975 to 37 per cent in 1995. As was mentioned earlier, the Post Office Saving Bank – Credit POSB, has also played a major role in providing housing loans. Other commercial banks have also participated in granting loans to buyers of public housing flats.

The involvement of commercial lenders has been on the increase since the turn of the new century as the government progressively shifts to a policy of liberalization in equity markets. In 2003, the government decided that the Housing Development Board should stop providing market rate loans, and housing loans should more appropriately be provided by commercial banks. In the words of Mr Mah Bow Tan, Minister for National Development, 'with such change, now the HDB can better fulfil its core responsibility, which is to provide basic affordable housing to the majority of Singaporeans. As a general rule, HDB should consider allowing the private sector to take over those functions which extend beyond its core responsibility' (Mah, 2005). However, this move by the government only serves to confirm and expand the role of the housing sector in the development of the country's financial market. This is why I have coined the phrase, second circuit of capital, which seeks to integrate the Central Provident Fund and the Housing Development Board system with larger economy. Through the Central Provident Fund's loan payments on behalf of buyers, financial institutions and commercial banks are able to strengthen their credit portfolio and, in turn, provide loans to private housing buyers. At the same time, private developers also benefit indirectly from the increased credit facilities provided by commercial banks. Given the intimate relationship between the Central Provident Fund and the financial sector, any interest rate change or contribution rate change would have an impact on the stability of the mortgage market. In other words, the government is perfectly capable of using policy instruments to either stabilize or destabilize the financial market. This, to some extent, explains why housing prices in Singapore are always comparatively more stable when compared to other Asian housing markets such as that of Hong Kong or Taiwan.

Issues and challenges

The two levels of economic integration described above assume that the economic environment is relative stable. However, once economic fluctuations are taken into account, the CPF and HDB configuration will be subject to dynamic challenges which require policy intervention. For example, since 2003, in order to boost a rather lacklustre property sector, the HDB has extended credit to low-income families and it has also capped the mortgage loan ceiling at 90 per cent. Second, also starting from 2003, owners of HDB flats who have occupied them for 15 years or more were permitted to sublet their flats irrespective of whether the flats were bought directly from the HDB or from the resale market. The objective of this policy is to provide homeowners greater flexibility to monetize their asset and to provide income for their retirement.[2] Homeowners in financial difficulty will then be able to generate some income from their flats to meet their retirement needs.

This policy will also stimulate the private rental market and provide more affordable housing to those who are unable to purchase a home. Third, by relaxing the closed HDB and CPF housing finance circuit, it is anticipated that more commercial lenders will be engaged in home financing in the long run. This development will eventually change the HDB's role both as the builder and financer of public housing. All these policy adaptations suggest that the Singaporean model is not aiming to establish a static equilibrium but one that is dynamic and flexible. The integration of social policy and economic policy requires dynamic adaptations. Institutional arrangements must be able to adjust to suit a continuously changing socio-political situation.

Another challenge for public housing is its role in the *social integration* of the country's various ethnic groups, namely the Chinese, Malay, Indian and Eurasian people. Obviously, attempts at economic and social policy integration would fail if the country is faced with frequent disintegrating ethic conflicts. The government recognizes that social integration is a precondition for economic and social prosperity. Singapore's housing policy enhances social integration by requiring that different ethnic groups live and interact with one another. This policy also aims at integrating different income groups. However, the government also recognizes that it is insufficient to just require different ethnic groups to live in physical proximity to one another. Accordingly, education and various community programmes have been organized so that different ethnic groups interact in many different settings and learn to appreciate cultural diversity. Efforts to prevent racial discrimination through legislative prohibitions have also been introduced. The government takes pride in asserting that Singapore is a multiracial society, and its future development is dependent on the maintenance of racial harmony and social cohesion. All of these measures prevent social fractures that impede economic development.

It has been argued that CPF is useful as an asset building mechanism, but when so much of the individual's resources have been invested in housing, the danger is that Singaporeans will have less cash at their disposal during old age. Singaporeans have become 'asset rich, but cash poor'. To improve this situation, the government now promotes what is known as the step down replacement scheme or a reverse mortgage scheme that allows citizens to realize their asset value during old age.

Stored housing wealth with stable appreciation can produce a life-long income stream and hence a reduction of dependency on state elderly welfare. However, the greatest worry of the Singaporean government is another international financial crisis. If the state fails to sustain a stable level of house prices and a steady rate of growth, the present social equilibrium would be seriously disrupted. Although the government is able to manage internal disturbances such as fluctuations in demand and supply through its control of the market and other economic policies, the greatest challenge lies in exogenous economic factors which are beyond its control.

In a globalizing world, no country can be totally independent of the effects of international economic disturbances. However, since the Singaporean system promotes integration and consensus, it is capable of absorbing economic vibrations through wage-cuts, labour market adjustments and careful monitoring of the CPF contribution rates during economic crisis. The tripartite relationship forged among the state, entrepreneurs and labour has made it possible to reach a consensus in formulating and implementing policies that achieve both economic and social development objectives.

Singapore is an interesting but unique case of East Asian developmentalism. Unlike the other East Asian tiger economies, it uniquely integrates housing and social security and, as was shown earlier, the integration of economic and social policy is seen through the two levels of capital circuits operating under conditions of dynamic equilibrium, with policy adaptations being made over a sufficiently long time scale. However, no attempt will be made here to generalize the Singaporean example and to ask whether it is one that other countries can emulate. The question of whether certain institutional arrangements might work on other societies is not only dependent on the integration process but also on cultural, political and other forces. People not familiar with Singapore are often amazed at the efficiency and effectiveness of government and the level of consensus which few other regimes enjoy in terms of policy formulation and implementation. But, obviously, there are unique political, social and cultural forces at work. In terms of bureaucratic capacity, the government of Singapore has been able to mobilize political support, foster national cohesiveness in the face of ethnic diversity and promote bureaucratic efficiency. It has also been able to exercise a laboratory like level of control. This has permitted it to experiment with public policy changes. Another aspect is the fact that Singapore is small by international standards. This makes governance much easier, and it also permits the government to mobilize the population and exercise social control. Obviously, the levels of integration discussed earlier are facilitated by size of the economy and by state effectiveness and must be understood within this context.

Nevertheless, three generalizations can be drawn from the Singaporean case. First, the integration of economic and social policy is possible when governance creates favourable institutional arrangements. This requires dynamic and creative leadership and, as such, the role of state matters a great deal if developmentalist goals are to be achieved. Second, social security configuration must move beyond its traditionally narrow focus to link with other social policy domains if it is to promote economic development. The inter-sector integration of social policies and programmes is thus a new and vital area for policy development and also for social policy research, particularly in the development context. Third, developmentalism in Singapore has been transformed in the past three decades from one which was based on a highly state-subsidized system to one promoting a tripartite system with some similarities to the European corporatist model requiring worker organizations such as the unions, the employers and the state to coordinate for optimal social provisions. The question here is whether the success of the Singaporean system points to the possibility of a global trend in social policymaking based on integration and corporatism as opposed to one based on fragmentation and liberalism which has characterized much of the social security policy so far.

Notes

1. http://mycpf.cpf.gov.sg/Members/Gen-Info/Con-Rates/ContriRa.htm, 19/06/2007
2. HDB Website: http://www.hdb.gov.sg/fi10/fi10296p.nsf/PressReleases/373FB 45C96555B1F4825708300208BF1?OpenDocument, 21/6/2007

Bibliography

Atkinson, A. B. (1999). *The Economic Consequences of Rolling Back the Welfare State.* Cambridge, MA: MIT Press.

Chua B. H. (1997). *Political Legitimacy and Housing: Stakeholding in Singapore.* London: Routledge.

Chua, B. H. (2003). 'Maintaining Housing Values under Conditions of Universal Home Ownership', *Housing Studies,* 18 (5), 765–780.

CPF Story (2006). Central Provident Board: Singapore.

DisPasquale, D. and Wheaton, W. (1996). *Urban Economics and Real Estate Markets.* New York: Prentice Hall.

Dixon, J. (1999). *Social Security in Global Perspective.* Westport, CT: Praeger.

Doling, J. (1997). *Comparative Housing Policy.* London: Macmillan.

Elrlick, I. and Zhong, J.G. (1998). 'Social Security and the Real Economy: An Inquiry into Some Neglected Issues', *AEA Papers and Proceedings,* May 1998, 151–158.

Evans, P. (1995). *Embedded Autonomy: States and Industrial transformation.* Princeton, NJ: Princeton University Press.

Evans, P. (2006). 'What Will the 21st Century Developmental State Look Like? Implications of Contemporary Developmental Theory for the State's Role', Paper presented at the Conference on *The Changing Role of the Government in Hong Kong,* Department of Sociology, Chinese University of Hong Kong.

Feldstein, M. B. (1974). 'Social Security, Induced Retirement and Aggregate Capital Accumulation', *Journal of Political Economy* 83 (4), 447–475.

Feldstein, M. B. (1976). 'Temporary Layoff in the Theory of Unemployment', *Journal of Political Economy,* 84 (5), 937–957.

Feldstein, M. B. (2005). 'Rethinking Social Insurance', *American Economic Review,* 95 (1), 1–24.

Johnson, C. (1982). *MITI and the Japanese Miracle: The Growth of Industrial Policy* (1925–1975). Stanford: Stanford University Press.

Korpi, W. (2003). 'Welfare State Regress in Western Europe: Politics, Institutions, Globalization and Europeanization', *Annual Review of Sociology,* 29 (4), 589–609.

Lee Kuan Yew (2000). *From Third World to First: The Singapore Story, 1965–2000.* New York: Harper and Collins.

Low, L. and Aw, T. C. (1997). *Housing a Healthy, Educated and Wealthy Nation Through the CPF.* Singapore: Institute of Policy Studies.

Mah (2005). Speech by Minister of National Development Mr. Mah Bow Tan at the Ministry of Manpower on 19 July 2005. Available from website http://www.mom.gov.sg/publish/momportal/en/press_room/mom_speeches/2005/20050719-speechbymrmahbowtanministerfornationaldevelopment-minist.html, on 27 December 2007.

Midgley, J. (1994). Defining Social Development; historical trends and conceptual formulations, *Social Development Issues,* 16 (3), 3–19.

Midgley, J. (1995). *Social Development: The Developmental Perspective in Social Welfare.* London: Sage.

Midgley, J. (1997). *Social Welfare in Global Context.* London: Sage.

Midgley, J. (1999). 'Growth, Redistribution and Welfare: Towards Social Investment', *Social Service Review,* 77 (1), 3–21.

Midgley, J. and Tang, K. L. (2001). 'Social Policy, Economic Growth and Developmental Welfare', *International Journal of Social Welfare,* 10 (4), 244–252.

Mkandawire, T. (2001). Social Policy in a Development Context. Social Policy and Development Paper No. 7, June 2001.

MTI (2007). *Economic Survey of Singapore 2006.* Singapore: Ministry of Trade and Industries. Available from website: http://app.mti.gov.sg/data/article/7062/doc/ESS_2006Ann_FullReport.pdf

Phang, S. Y. (2001). 'Housing Policy, Wealth Formation and the Singapore Economy', *Housing Studies,* 16(4), 443–459.

Quigley, J. (2001). 'Real Estate and the Asian Crisis', 10(2), 129–161.

Titmuss, R. M. (1962). *Income Distribution and Social Change.* London: Allen & Unwin.

Vasoo, S. and Lee, J. (2001). 'Singapore: Social Development, Housing and the Central Provident Fund', *International Journal of Social Welfare,* 10 (4), 276–283.

Vasoo, S. and Lee, J. (2006). 'Promoting Social Development Through Integration of the Central Provident Fund and Public Housing Schemes in Singapore', *Social Development Issues,* 28 (2), 71–83.

Wade, R. (1990). *Governing the Market: Economic Theory and the Role of the Government in East Asian Industrialization.* Princeton, NJ: Princeton University Press.

Yeung, H. (2003). 'Managing Economic (In)security in Global Economy: Institutional Capacity and Singapore's Development State'. http://course.nus. edu.sg/course/geoywc/henryht. Accessed 17 February, 2007.

11
India: Inclusive Development through the Extension of Social Security

Wouter van Ginneken[1]

India's spectacular economic achievements over the past decade have contributed to a strong decline in poverty, but the number of people living in poverty is still very high. A total of 370 million people – or about one-third of India's population – live under the basic poverty line (less than 1 US$ [make consistent]per person per day, in 1993 purchasing power). A total of 855 million – or about two-thirds of the Indian population – cope with less than 2 US$ (ILO, 2006a). Moreover, employment in the formal economy has hardly grown. On the other hand, employment in the informal economy is rising, regrouping currently about 93 per cent of the labour force. The 7 per cent of all workers who are employed in the formal economy are the civil servants as well as most employees in medium and large enterprises. A small part of workers in the informal economy are also covered by social security schemes, such as welfare or micro-insurance schemes, with the result that only some 10 per cent of the Indian population enjoys some level of social protection.

Social security for all Indians is one of the dreams that lie at the foundation of Indian society (van Ginneken, 1998). Article 38 of the Constitution requires the state to promote the welfare of the people by securing and protecting, as effectively as it may, a social order in which justice – social, economic and political – shall inform all the institutions of national life. Article 41 requires the state to make effective provision for securing the right to public assistance in case of unemployment, old age, sickness, disablement and other cases of undeserved want. Articles 42 and 47 require the state respectively to make provisions for maternity relief and to regard the improvement of public health as among its primary duties. Though not expressly stated, these constitute the major elements of social security in the Constitution. Social justice is said to be the signature tune of the Indian Constitution and is one of the major objectives of the five-year plans.

This dream has to – and can – be realized. Extending social security is a necessary condition for achieving broad-based and inclusive development. Access to basic social services, such as health care and education, play a crucial part in processes towards inclusion and empowerment (van Ginneken, 2006). They provide people, and in particular the poor and the vulnerable, with the capabilities to fully participate in economic, social, cultural and political life (Sen, 1999). Kannan (2007) also argues that an enlarged concept of social security is necessary to addresses the twin problems of deficiency – through Basic Social Security (BSS) – and of adversity – through Contingent Social Security (CSS). Contingent social security deals with adversity and with particular vulnerable situations or contingencies, such as old age, injury, and sickness, for example. Basic social security is often envisaged for citizens, while CSS is generally provided (and co-financed) by workers. Basic social security and contingent social security are complementary, and achievements in contingent social security can hardly be obtained without first meeting the need for basic social security.

Kannan also shows that the experience of the rich countries in developing their Welfare States and social security systems in general has relevance for developing countries. In fact, the state had a strong role in developing basic social security even before full-scale industrialization. States of (low-income) developing countries are, therefore, also in a position to address the whole range of issues relating to basic social security . The social dynamics – in the form of tripartism, civil society organizations and liberation movements – also play a role in this process. The difference is, however, that the current expectations of people in developing countries are perhaps much higher than they were among people in Europe in an earlier era. This has to do with the process of globalization of communication and the worldwide transmission of ideas and images. Incidentally, these processes have also led to the conceptualization of global policies to deal with the social dimension of globalization, such as the notion of a global social floor.

In the first section this chapter will review India's main social security programmes and assess the efforts that have so far been undertaken to extend social security coverage. It will then focus on access to health care and show the important link with the productivity of employment. The third section will attempt an initial assessment of the National Rural Employment Guarantee (NREG) scheme – a novel social security instrument that was launched in 2005 by the present Indian government.

The chapter will be closed with some concluding remarks on key issues and future direction.

India: basic facts and social security

With the world's twelfth largest economy by official exchange rates and the fourth largest in purchasing power, India has made rapid economic progress in the past decade. Although the country's standard of living is projected to rise sharply in the next half century, it currently battles high levels of poverty, illiteracy, persistent malnutrition and environmental degradation.

At the time of India's independence in 1947, its literacy rate was 12.2 per cent. Since then, it has increased to 64.8 per cent (53.7 per cent for females and 75.3 per cent of males). The state of Kerala has the highest literacy rate (91 per cent), Bihar has the lowest (47 per cent). The national gender ratio is 944 females per 1,000 males. India's median age is 25 years; its annual population growth rate is 1.4 per cent, and there are 22 births per 1,000 people per year.

With an estimated population of 1.1 billion, India is the world's second most populous country. Almost 70 per cent of Indians live in rural areas, although in recent decades migration to larger cities has led to a dramatic increase in the country's urban population. India's largest urban agglomerations are Mumbai (in the state of Maharashtra), Delhi, Kolkata (formerly Calcutta, in West Bengal), Chennai (formerly Madras, in Tamil Nadu), Bangalore (in Karnataka), Hyderabad (in Andhra Pradesh) and Ahmedabad (in Gujarat). Within the next 30–40 years, India is projected to overtake China as the world's most populous country.

The Indian Constitution recognizes 23 official languages. Hindi and English are used by the Union Government of India for official purposes, wherein Hindi has a de jure priority. Tamil and Sanskrit were designated 'classical languages' by the Indian government in 2004 and 2005. The number of dialects in India is as high as 1,652.

About 80 per cent of the country's population are Hindus. The next-largest religious group are Muslims, who make up less than 14 per cent; due to India's large size, this is among the world's largest Muslim populations. Other religious groups constitute the remaining six per cent, including Christians, Sikhs, Buddhists, Jains, Jews, Zoroastrians and Bahá'ís. Persons belonging to the so-called 'scheduled castes' constitute 16 per cent of the population and tribals about 8 per cent.

India is the largest democracy in the world. The Constitution defines India as a sovereign, socialist, secular, democratic republic. India has a federal form of government and has three branches of governance: the Legislature, Executive and Judiciary. The Constitution designates the Lower House of Parliament (Lok Sabha) as the legislative branch to oversee the operation of the government.

India is a union of 28 states and seven federally governed union territories. The Constitution uses the so-called Seventh Schedule to delimit the subjects under three categories, namely the union list, the state list and the concurrent list. The central government has the powers to enact laws on subjects under the union list, while the state governments have the powers to enact laws on subjects under the state list. Both the central as well as the state governments can enact laws on subjects under the concurrent list. However, the laws enacted by the central government under the concurrent list override the laws enacted by the state government when a conflict arises between those laws.

For most of its democratic history, the federal Government of India has been led by the Indian National Congress (INC). State politics have been dominated by several national parties including the INC, the Bharatiya Janata Party (BJP), the Communist Party of India (CPI) and various regional parties. After a long period of mainly INC-dominated federal governments, the BJP in 1998 formed the National Democratic Alliance (NDA) with several regional parties and became the first non-Congress government to complete a full five-year term. In the 2004 elections, the INC won the largest number of seats in the Lok Sabha and formed a government with a coalition called the United Progressive Alliance, supported by various left-leaning parties and members opposed to the BJP.

For most of its post-independence history, India adhered to a quasi-socialist approach with strict government control over private sector participation, foreign trade and foreign direct investment. However, since 1991, India has gradually opened up its markets through economic reforms and reduced government controls on foreign trade and investment. Foreign exchange reserves have risen from US$5.8 billion in March 1991 to US$177 billion in January 2007, while federal and state budget deficits have reduced. Privatization of publicly owned companies and the opening of certain sectors to private and foreign participation has continued amid political debate.

The Indian economy has grown steadily over the past two decades; however, its growth has been uneven when comparing different social groups, economic groups, geographic regions and rural and urban areas. India has a labour force of about 510 million, 60 per cent of which is employed in agriculture and related industries. Major agricultural crops include rice, wheat, oilseed, cotton, jute, tea, sugarcane and potatoes. The agricultural sector accounts for 28 per cent of GDP while the service and industrial sectors make up 54 and 18 per cent respectively. Major industries include automobiles, cement, chemicals, consumer electronics, food processing, machinery, mining, petroleum, pharmaceuticals, steel, transportation equipment and textiles.

Formal social security schemes

There is a large variety of social security schemes in India. The most well-known are the formal programmes, covering mainly health care and pensions (ILO, 2006a). But over the years, new programmes have emerged that are more attuned to the needs and contributory capacity of workers and persons outside the formal economy, such as the welfare funds, special packages provided by public and private insurance companies, as well as micro-insurance schemes.

Launched in 1948, the Employees' State Insurance Scheme (ESIS) not only provides free medical care but also cash benefits towards loss of wage due to sickness, maternity protection, permanent or temporary disablement, survivors' benefits and funeral expenditure. It is a compulsory social security system targeting employees of non-seasonal power using factories with 10 or more employees and non-power using factories employing 20 or more. The maximum monthly wage limit is Rs. 7,500 (1US$ = 40 Rs.). Employers and employees contribute respectively 4.75 and 1.75 per cent of the wage bill. Employees State Insurance Corporation (ESIC) currently covers some 7.1 million workers, but it has been plagued by high desertion rates as many workers prefer to enrol in other schemes providing better benefits. Its present network of health care facilities is generally found understaffed, ill-equipped and underused. In August 2005, ESIC launched a new programme providing new unemployment benefits to the former employees covered by its other activities. Legal barriers still prevent ESIC to extend its benefits to informal economy workers, and the poor quality of the services provided through its own network of health care facilities does not make it attractive enough.

Created in 1952, the Employee's Provident Fund (EPF) caters to the needs of establishments with 20 or more workers. To this day this compulsory scheme provides both old-pension benefits and a provident fund together with some disability benefits to some 39 million workers. The scheme does not benefit from any kind of government subsidy. In

January 2004, EPF launched on a pilot basis in 50 districts the 'Unorganized Sector Workers' Social Security Scheme' which combined an accident insurance, old-age pension and the benefits provided under the Universal Health Insurance Scheme. The scheme targeted all informal economy workers with an income lower than Rs. 6,500. The monthly premium to be paid was Rs. 50 for the age group of 18 to 36 and Rs. 100 for the age group of 36 to 50, with a matching contribution from the employer and a contribution from the government set at 1.16 per cent of the monthly wage. Due to its very high price (Rs. 100 to 200 per month), the scheme failed to attract informal economy workers. At the end of its first year, only 3,500 workers had enrolled.

Introduced in 1954 as a contributory plan, the Central Government Health Scheme (CGHS) provides comprehensive medical care to central government employees (both in service and retired) and their families to replace the cumbersome and expensive system of reimbursement. The contribution by the employees is, however, nominal (maximum of Rs. 50 per month). The total number of beneficiaries is estimated today at 4 million.

The government also provides state-owned and state-managed health care facilities to most of the state-owned departments such as railways, defence, police, mining and education services. These departments have set up their own system of dispensaries, hospitals and personnel, and the services are provided free of charge.

Efforts to extend social security

The large majority of the non-covered and poor workers in India are employed in the informal economy, which includes both urban- and rural-based activities. The fundamental reason for exclusion from statutory contributory social security coverage is that many workers outside the formal economy are unable or unwilling to contribute a relatively high percentage of their incomes to financing social security benefits that do not meet their priority needs (van Ginneken, 1999). In general, they prioritize more immediate needs, such as health and education in particular, because budget restrictions and poor public management have often reduced or eliminated access to free health care and primary education. In addition, they may not be familiar with, and/or distrust, the way statutory social security schemes are managed. Other factors affecting the extension process are a general lack of awareness among the excluded groups or perhaps even reluctance where the scheme is perceived either to be inefficient or not in their best interests (van Ginneken, 2004). Some people (both employers and workers) feel overwhelmed by the bureaucratic obligations associated with registration under the formal social security scheme or may fear that entry into the 'public system' will have other unwelcome implications. As a result, various groups of workers outside the formal sector have set up schemes that better meet their priority needs and contributory capacity.

Labour Welfare Funds have been a unique Indian institution to extend social security to workers in the informal economy. They were invented in the state of Kerala in 1950s–1960s, and they now cover a large variety of workers in different occupations and sectors. Recent efforts in Kerala have attempted to merge a number of welfare schemes into a larger and comprehensive state-wide scheme. In the 1970s and early 1980s the Central Government (Ministry of Labour) set up welfare funds for particular groups of workers, such as bidi (cigarette-rolling) workers and construction labourers, financed by ear-marked taxes (the so-called 'cess') on production. In 1996 a national enabling legislation was passed to set up such schemes for construction workers at the state level. Another similar legislation for agricultural workers was up for adoption by parliament in 2007.

In general, welfare schemes provide a large variety of benefits, such as for maternity, disability and old age, as well as facilities, such as access to health care, support for children's education and low-interest housing loans. However, in many cases the attribution of benefits is not based on clear eligibility rules (see, for example, Krishnamurty and Nair, 2003). In general, welfare funds in the future will have to operate on a much more uniform basis. The funds should offer fewer facilities and benefits, some in return for specific contributions from workers – and employers, if identifiable (ILO, 2000a). Although not all operational, the number of welfare funds is steadily increasing (ten new welfare funds created in the past five years) and amounts now to a total of 62 schemes distributed among 14 states (ILO, 2006a).

Over the past few years, micro-insurance schemes have also proliferated all across India (van Ginneken, 2007) with most initiatives choosing to tie up with insurance companies. This development was reinforced by the Indian Insurance Regulations which oblige insurance companies to transact a certain proportion of their business in the 'rural and social sectors'. Representing the bottom segment of self-reliant micro-finance entities, women Self Help Groups (SHG) have multiplied in recent years while proving to be increasingly successful in tying up with various financial institutions allowing them to access additional external resources. Some 2.1 million SHGs have already entered into these new partnership arrangements with many having added new health insurance services to their classical financial services such as savings and loans (ILO, 2006b). The regular savings organized through these community-based organizations may be used to maintain insurance contributions or to finance other forms of protection.

In 2004, 60 micro-insurance schemes covered 5.2 million people (ILO, 2004), while in 2006, 71 schemes were estimated to cover more than 6.8 million people. The majority of these schemes cover health insurance, and the so-called Yeshasvini scheme is one of most recent and successful examples. In 2003, its first year of operation (ILO, 2006c), it covered about 1.6 million rural peasants and farmers in rural Karnataka. For a premium payment of Rs. 60 (1 US$ = 40 Rs.) per year, participants are covered for all surgical interventions and for related outpatient services at a network of private hospitals. At the end of the first year of operations in June 2004, about 9,000 surgeries had been performed, and about 36,000 patients had received outpatient consulting services. In its second year of operation, the scheme covered an increased number of people (2.2 million). The scheme was replicated and extended to other parts of Karnataka as well as to other states such as Gujarat.

Since 2004 the central government has been very active in setting up social security schemes for workers in the informal economy. The first is the Universal Health Insurance Scheme (UHIS) scheme. It provides (1) up to Rs. 30,000 for hospitalization expenses, (2) Rs. 50 per day for up to 15 days to make up for loss of income during hospitalization, and (3) Rs. 25,000 in the event of death of income earners due to accident. It is financed by (1) Rs. 1 per day for individual members and Rs. 1.5 and Rs. 2 for households up to five and seven members respectively and (2) a subsidy of Rs. 100–400 per year for Below Poverty Line (BPL) households of different size. While it was initially designed to cover only members of particular groups, such as cooperative societies, beedi (cigarette rolling) workers and handloom workers, it has subsequently been revised to include any individual or household as well. The UHIS scheme was expected to cover 10 million in its first year, but in reality it reached only 417,000 households or 1.16 million individuals. Since then it has hardly increased coverage for a variety of reasons, such as the assumption that BPL households could or would contribute to the scheme, as well as the inadequate supply of health services at the local level. Moreover, in 2006 the central government decided to restrict the scheme to only BPL households thereby effectively barring the non-poor households who had been the main contributors to the scheme before.

In 2004 the central government also set up the National Social Security Scheme for Unorganized Workers, which provides a pension of Rs. 500 per month on retirement or disability. It also includes the two UHIS hospitalization benefits as well as a much higher coverage (Rs 125,000) in case of death or disability. The scheme was meant to be piloted in 50 selected districts, but it did not get off the ground. The draft Unorganized Sector Workers' Social Security Bill, 2006, improves on the 2004 scheme in various respects: (1) it broadens the eligibility to APL (up to Rs. 6,500 per month) households; (2) the government fully subsidizes the contributions for BPL households (Rs. 3 per day); and (3) it provides a subsidy of Rs. 1 per day to all APL households and an additional Rs. 1 per day subsidy to income earners who have no or no identifiable employer. The bill was put before parliament in August 2007. When this bill falls into place, there is a legal binding on all states to implement it and ensure that the workers are covered under the scheme (ILO, 2006d).

A number of important issues need to be resolved for this bill to achieve its aim of universal coverage. India's public health care infrastructure, particularly in rural areas, is underdeveloped (see the next section on health, productivity and growth) so that meaningful health insurance benefits cannot be provided. The eligibility cut-off point of Rs. 6,500 per month prevents important solidarity financing in particular, since insurance companies are targeting commercial health insurance and pension policies on households with an income beyond Rs. 6,500 per month. Finally, the pension benefits to be provided by the proposed 2006 scheme are likely to compete with other government financed pension schemes, and in particular with the means-tested N(ational) S(ocial) A(ssistance) P(rogramme), which currently covers more than 5 million elderly people.

Health, productivity and growth

In a recent overview article, Baeza and Packard (2007) observe that general tax financing is the most equitable way of providing access to health care. It prevents poor and vulnerable people suffering the financial consequences of health care costs, and it reduces the effects of ill health. Social health insurance is usually most equitable in a situation where a large part of the population is covered, so that high-income earners can subsidize access to health care for the low-income population. Many developed and some middle-income country societies have already moved to such systems. The problem for many low- to middle-income countries, including India, is that no fiscal space is (made) available for public health expenditure and that there are a host of governance problems that prevent the effective delivery of public health care services. On the other hand, there is a lot of evidence that effective access to health care has a significant, if not decisive, impact on the productivity of employment as well as on social and economic development, particularly in low- to middle-income countries.

Financing and organizing access to health care

The majority of Indians are still in poor health, particularly in low-income and poor households. There is high maternal and child mortality; there is the dual burden of communicable and non-communicable diseases, and there are new diseases, such as HIV/AIDS, and the re-emergence of some diseases, such as TB and malaria. Even though there were some improvements in antenatal care between 1998/1999 and 2002/2003, many dimensions of service provision worsened during that period (World Bank, 2006). For example, the number of children delivered in public institutions went down and so did the prevalence of children with full immunization for childhood diseases.

Although India has a constitutional commitment to universal provision of health care, the ratio of government (including formal social security) to total expenditure in health is only 21 per cent – half the public spending ratio of ideologically 'free market' countries such as the United States (45 per cent) and Chile (44 per cent). If one takes expenditures as a measure, India has one of the health systems in the world where out-of-pocket expenditure is highest even in comparison with other countries at the same level of economic development. This high private spending in India is not the result of an announced public policy to reduce services but rather a coping strategy to deal with the failure of the public sector to actually provide promised services adequately.

It therefore came at no surprise that the new Indian government launched in 2005 the National Rural Health Mission (NRHM) programme. It focuses on primary health care services in states with the lowest health outcome statistics such as in the north and the centre. The thrust of the Mission is on establishing a community owned, decentralized health delivery systems with simultaneous action on a wide range of determinants of health such as water, sanitation, education, nutrition and social and gender equality. One of the new elements of the programme is the Accredited Social Health Activist (ASHA) scheme – that is, the appointment of a woman who is to take care of all the health problems in a village so as to make sure that basic health care is brought closer to the vulnerable groups in each village. According to Taneja

(2005), the proposal to strengthen institutions of primary health care and Community Health Centres as functional Rural Hospitals along with introduction of Indian Public Health Standards and accountability of public health institutions to the public is likely to revolutionize the status of health care in rural India.

For the time being this has not yet happened, but progress has been made. The presence of more than 200,000 ASHAs in the states with poor health indicators has laid the foundation for village level health care. In total, 600,000 ASHAs are needed. For the time being, only the state of Madhya Pradesh seems to have finalized the state and district level action plans for implementation. Most importantly, none of the states have yet signed the memoranda of understanding with the central government to integrate all the health programmes under the NRHM (ILO, 2006d). This also means that public expenditure on health is presently still not higher than 1 per cent of GDP, while the NRHM's aim is to raise it to at least 2–3 per cent by 2012.

Under these circumstances, complementary efforts to promote community-based and other health insurance schemes, as discussed in the previous section on India: basic facts and social security, remain an important part of an overall policy to extend health care coverage.

Poverty, health, productivity and growth

Inadequate access to health care, which is often the destiny of the poor, is one of the key obstacles to employment productivity and economic growth in India. Gupta and Trivedi (2004), for example, quote a variety of sources showing that in India the poor are hardest hit by the lack of health care coverage, so that they have much higher levels of mortality, malnutrition and fertility than the rich. In addition, a study by the World Bank (2001) shows that a much higher percentage of the poor in India do not seek care compared to the rich.

This lack of access to health care has serious consequences for employment productivity and stable-income levels and is most apparent at the micro-level (van Ginneken, 2005). Ill health affects employment capacity and income levels, whereas high medical bills can reduce household savings or plunge people into permanent poverty (OECD, 2003). The WHO estimates that, worldwide, every year about 100 million people are vulnerable to falling into destitution as a result of unaffordable health care. The latter situation has been described as the medical poverty trap in which poverty and ill health reinforce each other in vicious circles. These are often maintained in the long run as successive generations become trapped in chronic poverty (ILO, 2003).

Illness leads to important direct economic costs such as financial and time costs. But the indirect economic costs are probably as important. Illness can lead to the sale of livestock and other assets as well as to a reduction in labour supply. These economic costs result in the reduction of productive capacities, credit worthiness, and opportunity to hire out or hire in labour. The non-economic costs, such as low leisure time, exclusion from social activities and the risk of being handicapped or of death, are also substantial.

Many studies on the macro-links between public health expenditure and economic growth have also found a strong positive relationship. Low-income countries have a high disease burden and deficient health services (Wagstaff, 2002), or, alternatively, countries with the highest burden of disease have low economic growth, are stagnating or regressing (Sachs et al., 2004). According to a recent review undertaken by Mares (2007), even moderate spending on health care can lead to significant reductions in infectious diseases and malnutrition particularly in early stages of economic development.

Employment guarantee and local development

India has extensive experience with employment-intensive programmes, some of which provide some sort of employment guarantee. Historically most well-known is the Maharashtra Employment Guarantee Scheme introduced in 1972/1973, which in its peak year 1979–1980 created 205 million workdays. This was followed by two national schemes, that is, the Jawahar Rojgar Yojana (JRY) scheme launched in 1989, the result of a merger between the National Rural Employment Programme and the Rural Landless Employment Guarantee Programme, and the Employment Assurance Scheme launched in 1993/1994 and broadly modeled on the Maharashtra scheme. According to Mohan (2004), these employment guarantee schemes generated 1.2 billion workdays during 1994–1995 and 1995–1996 periods but then tapered off to 750-odd million during the rest of the 1990s.

The NREGA programme

India's present United Progressive Alliance government enacted the National Rural Employment Guarantee Act (NREGA) on 25 August 2005. The NREGA provides a legal guarantee of 100 days of employment in each financial year for every rural household whose adult members are willing to do unskilled manual work at the statutory agricultural minimum wage in their state. The NREGA is designed as a safety net to reduce migration by rural poor households in the lean agricultural season. The NREGA focuses on water conservation, land development and drought proofing to be undertaken in the context of an overall watershed development plan.

The social security aspect of this guarantee is strengthened by the provision of an unemployment allowance of half the minimum wage per day to be paid to workers with a job card and who are not provided with work within 15 days after they have sent in their application (ILO, 2000b). This allowance is to be financed by the state governments and can be seen as an incentive for them to come up with sufficient number of viable employment projects. The central government generally finances 90 per cent of the project cost with a minimum of 60 per cent devoted to the wage bill and a maximum of 40 per cent devoted to material and some specific overhead costs.

The social protection aspect of the guarantee is also strengthened by a number of dispositions with regard to working conditions, health care and social benefits. The Ministry of Rural Development which is responsible for the implementation of the NREG Act has now regulated that facilities for safe drinking water and a first-aid box with adequate material for emergency treatment for minor injuries and other health hazards connected with the work should be available at each project site. Moreover, workers should benefit from regular periods of rest and a place in the shade should be available for children so that they can be attended to while their parents are at work. A recent report commissioned by the Supreme Court shows that these facilities are often not provided (Sood, 2006). In case of work accident, the person is entitled to free medical treatment from the state government. In case of hospitalization, the injured person will also be entitled to a daily allowance that shall be not less than 50 per cent of the wage applicable. If a registered labourer dies or becomes permanently disabled due to an accident at the work site, an ex-gratia payment of Rs. 25,000 will be paid to the legal heir or to the disabled person. Incidentally, this payment is the same as provided under the UHIS scheme described earlier in this chapter. In fact, it would be logical to cover all participants of NREGA under this social security scheme.

Impact on local development

A study by Murgai and Ravallion (2005) estimated the fiscal cost of nationwide NREGA implementation at 1.7 per cent of GDP per year. That would reduce the lean season rural poverty rate from 37 per cent to around 23 per cent or to around 30 per cent on a yearly basis. Nation-wide implementation would principally benefit the poorest quintile accounting for 29 per cent of all participants and whose consumption levels would rise by 51 per cent. In comparison, the richest quintile would account for only 10 per cent of participants, and their consumption gain would be 7 per cent. The bulk of the expected participants would be casual labourers.

At the beginning of 2006, the scheme was launched in 200 of India's poorest districts. At the beginning of 2007 the Union Government announced the addition of another 130 districts for the financial year 2007–2008. It is planned to be extended to all the 600 districts in the country by 2011. According to the most recent statistics of the Ministry of Rural Development, which still need to be cross-checked, in the 2006–2007 fiscal year about 0.9 billion workdays of employment were created for more than 20 million rural households, which means an average of about 45 workdays. According to Mohan (2004), 5.7 billion of workdays are needed for reaching full employment in India. Out of this, 2.7 billion are needed to take care of the poorest of the poor, who are mostly casual wage earners in rural India.

The advantage of an employment guarantee scheme in comparison with social assistance is that it is self-targeting. Only persons willing to work for the minimum wage will come forward to participate in the scheme, and many costly and cumbersome administrative arrangements can be avoided that characterize the targeting mechanisms of social assistance benefits. Employment guarantee and social assistance schemes have in common that wages and cash benefits have a significant impact on the local economy and on family welfare. However, employment guarantee schemes not only incur wage costs but also material, supervision and other overhead costs, so that their effectiveness critically depends on the economic assets that they produce.

A significant improvement of NREGA over previous programmes is the strengthened role for the panchayats (village councils) in the design, implementation and monitoring of projects. The infrastructure created by NREGA projects, such as feeder roads, land reclamation, minor dams, wells and irrigation systems and sewerages have a strong economic impact on the local economy even though that cannot be easily quantified. Some of this infrastructure, such as village water supply and feeder roads, benefit the population as a whole, whereas other forms of infrastructure, such as irrigation and soil conservation, tend to benefit specific user groups. The NREGA programme does not finance the maintenance of the newly created infrastructure, and these costs will, therefore, have to be foreseen in local or state budgets.

For NREGA to be successful (Nanavaty and Pandya, 2004), it will have to take a holistic approach to the livelihood creation of the rural poor and develop the mindset of a businessman in them. Even though the work provided under NREGA is unskilled, most rural workers are (self-) employed and have skills by which they earn their livelihoods. In the design and implementation of NREGA projects, it is therefore necessary to be mindful of, and develop links with, the micro-enterprises of the rural poor and with agencies engaged in financial assistance, market facilitation as well as in education and training.

Conclusion: key issues and future direction

Since 2005 the Indian government has launched an impressive array of measures to extend social security, in particular, to the rural poor. This article has briefly reviewed some of them, such as the National Social Security Scheme for Unorganized Workers, the Unorganised Labour and Agricultural Workers (Welfare) Bill, the National Rural Health Mission and the National Rural Employment Guarantee scheme. Progress towards universal primary education is also a key component of what we called earlier Basic Social Security (BSS). All these programmes are crucial for achieving inclusive development; in other words, they are a process in which every Indian can participate in economic, social, cultural and political life.

There are various favourable factors for these schemes to achieve their objectives and for inclusive development to take place. With buoyant economic growth and tax revenues, governments at all levels are able to finance these programmes. There is a general up-beat mood which accompanies this process. Moreover, the fast development of Internet and other communications make it in principle possible to participate in and benefit from inclusive development.

But for the process of inclusive development to be sustainable more will be needed. The first observation is that there are too many schemes that have evolved over the past ten years. Each scheme means more administrative cost and, therefore, fewer benefits that can flow to the intended recipients. Based on our analysis, the priority first of all is the provision of better health care facilities, particularly in rural areas. As we have shown, this will have a key impact on the productivity of workers in the informal economy and on sustainable economic growth in general. Our second priority would be the NREGA scheme under two conditions: first, that viable economic assets can be created at the local level; second, that the provision of unskilled employment links up with training for self-employment in agricultural and non-agricultural occupations so that the generation of employment becomes a sustainable process.

Second, with regard to the vast array of social security schemes, it is necessary to better design the linkages between them as well as with other programmes and to avoid overlapping of administrations and benefits. It is therefore important to look at the cross-links between the various programmes. It would be logical, for example, to extend the newly adopted National Social Security Scheme for Unorganized Workers (NSSSUW) to all NREGA participants. With regard to the health component of the NSS scheme, it is necessary to improve access to health care facilities under the NRHM scheme before meaningful health insurance benefits can be provided. There is also a great need to streamline the various proposals on social security and think through their overlaps, benefit structure and administration. For example, the existing and proposed welfare funds are overlapping with the proposal on the NSSSUW scheme. In addition, the old-age pension benefits under the means-tested National Social Assistance Programme are in direct competition with the virtually universal old-age benefits proposed under the NSSSUW.

In general, there also seems to be a problem with programmes initiated by the central government under the so-called 'concurrent list' that state governments cannot or do not (want to) follow up. One example of this is the fact that state governments – so far at least – have apparently not followed up on the unemployment allowance benefits under the NREGA scheme.

Another general key issue is the question of implementation and accountability. As mentioned earlier, it is essential for India's growing economy to improve the delivery of core public services such as health care, education, power, water and social security. A recent World Bank report (2006) concludes that it is essential for people to be empowered to demand better public services through reforms that create more effective systems of public sector accountability. India has achieved a democratic system from top to bottom, but in many cases there are too few countervailing powers against those who are in authority leading to harassment and corruption particularly towards the poor. With increased education and communication, these countervailing powers are getting stronger at all levels. A very good recent development is the Right to Information Act that came into force in 2005 and provides that any person may request information from a 'public authority' which is required to reply expeditiously or within 30 days. There is also a strong need for citizens, and in particular the poor, to be better organized, so that their interests are taken into account. For some of the proposed social security schemes, such as the NSSSUW, to be successful, it is necessary to involve genuine civil society organizations that constitute the backbone of, for example, some micro-insurance schemes.

In general, the challenge for social security is to contribute to employment creation and economic growth. We have noted that access to health care plays a fundamental role in productivity and economic growth and that especially the poor lack and need this access. Also more indirectly, the presence of adequate social security and social protection fosters social cohesion and social peace which are pre-requisites for long-term economic growth.

Note

1. Many thanks to Sarosh Ghandy for his most useful comments.

References

Baeza, C. and Packard, T. (2007). 'Extending The Risk Pool for Health in Developing Countries: The Challenges of Moving to General Tax Funding', *International Social Security Review*, 60(2–3), 83–97.

Gupta, I. and Trivedi, M. (2004). *Social Health Insurance Redefined: Health for All through Coverage for All*. Delhi: Institute of Economic Growth.

ILO (2000a). *India: Social Protection for the Unorganized Sector*. Geneva: Report financed by the UNDP under Technical Support Services 1 (ILO/UNDP/India/R.36).

ILO (2000b). *World Labour Report 2000. Income Security and Social Protection in a Changing World*. Geneva. Chapter 7.

ILO (2003). *Report of the Director-General: Working out of poverty*. International Labour Conference, 91st Session, Geneva.

ILO (2004). *India: An inventory of microinsurance schemes*. Geneva: STEP.

ILO (2006a). 'Extension of Social Protection: Overview of the Present Situation', in India: Answering the Health Insurance Needs of the Poor: Building up Tools for Awareness, Education and Participation – Workshop Report (New Delhi, May 29–31).

ILO (2006b). *India: Microsavings and health*. New Delhi.

ILO (2006c). *Karnataka: Yeshavini co-operative farmers' health scheme*. New Delhi, Subregional Office for South Asia, Social Protection Working Papers.

ILO (2006d). Showing the Way Forward: India's Redistribution Experience in Extending Social Protection to All. New Delhi, Subregional Office for South Asia, Social Protection Working Papers.

Kannan, K. (2007). 'Social Security in a Globalizing World', *International Social Security Review*, 60(2–3), 19–37.

Krisnamurty, V. and Nair, R. P. (2003). *The Welfare Fund for Construction Workers in Tamil-Nadu*. Geneva: ILO. Extension of Social Security. ESS-Paper No. 18.

Mares, I. (2007). 'The Economic Consequences of the Welfare State', *International Social Security Review*, 60(2–3), 65–81.

Mohan, N. (2004). 'Guaranteeing Work in India's Countryside', *The Financial Express*, Mumbai, Indian Express Newspapers. December, 23.

Murgai, R. and Ravallion, M. (2005). 'Employment Guarantee in Rural India: What Would It Cost and How Much Would It Reduce Poverty?', *Economic and Political Weekly*, July 30, 3450–3455.

Nanavaty, R. and Pandya, D. (2004). National Rural Employment Guarantee Programme. SEWA's perception and implications. A perspective note. Ahmedabad, Self Employed Women's Association.

OECD. (2003). *The DAC Guidelines. Poverty and health*. Paris: OECD and WHO.

Sachs, J. D., McArthur, J. W., Schmidt-Traub, G., Kruk, M, Bahadur, F., Faye, M. and McCord, G. (2004). 'Ending Africa's Poverty Trap', in *Brookings Papers on Economic Activity*. Volume 1, Washington DC.

Sen, A. (1999). *Development as Freedom*. Oxford: Oxford University Press.

Sood, T. (2006). 'NREGA: Challenges in Implementation', *InfoChange Features*. (http://www.infochangeindia.org/features380.jsp). Accessed on 31 December 2007.

Taneja, D. K. (2005). 'National Rural Health Mission', *Indian Journal of Public Health*, 49(3), 152–155.

van Ginneken, W. (ed.) (1998). *Social Security for All Indians*. Delhi: Oxford University Press.

van Ginneken, W. (ed.) (1999). *Social Security for the Excluded Majority: Case Studies on Developing Countries*. Geneva: ILO.

van Ginneken, W. (2004). 'Social Protection for the Informal Sector in India', in Agarwala, R., Kumar, N. and Riboud, M. (eds) *Reforms, Labour Markets and Social Security in India*. New Delhi: Oxford University Press, pp. 186–197.

van Ginneken, W. (2005). *Managing Risk and Minimizing Vulnerability: The Role of Social Protection in Pro-Poor Growth*. Paper produced for the DAC-POVNET Task Team on Risk, Vulnerability and Pro-Poor Growth. Geneva. ILO.

van Ginneken, W. (2006). 'Conclusions' *Social Protection and Inclusion: Experiences and Policy Issues*. Geneva: STEP/Portugal, pp. 217–231.

van Ginneken, W. (2007). 'Extending Social Security Coverage: Concepts, Global Trends and Policy Issues', *International Social Security Review*, 60, (2–3), 39–57.

Wagstaff, A. (2002). 'Poverty And Health Sector Inequalities', *Bulletin of the World Health Organization*, 80(2), 97–105.

World Bank. (2001). *India– Raising the Sights: Better Health Systems for India's Poor*. Washington D.C.

World Bank. (2006). *India: Inclusive Growth and Service Delivery: Building on India's Success*. Development Policy Review. Washington D.C. Report No. 34580-IN.

Index